British

Georg Germaine
Burgoyne
Henry Clinton
Howe
So. creek & cherokee
Arch Campbell in GA
Provost up from FL
James Wright
CORNWALLIS

Occupied America

EARLY AMERICAN STUDIES

Series editors
Daniel K. Richter, Kathleen M. Brown,
Max Cavitch, and David Waldstreicher

Exploring neglected aspects of our colonial,
revolutionary, and early national history and culture,
Early American Studies reinterprets familiar themes
and events in fresh ways. Interdisciplinary in character,
and with a special emphasis on the period from about
1600 to 1850, the series is published in partnership with
the McNeil Center for Early American Studies.

A complete list of books in the series
is available from the publisher.

OCCUPIED AMERICA

British Military Rule and
the Experience of Revolution

DONALD F. JOHNSON

PENN

UNIVERSITY OF PENNSYLVANIA PRESS

PHILADELPHIA

Published by
University of Pennsylvania Press
Philadelphia, Pennsylvania 19104-4112
www.upenn.edu/pennpress

Printed in the United States of America
on acid-free paper

10 9 8 7 6 5 4 3 2 1

Library of Congress Cataloging-in-Publication Data

Names: Johnson, Donald F., author.
Title: Occupied America: British military rule and the experience of revolution /
  Donald F. Johnson.
Other titles: Early American studies.
Description: Philadelphia: University of Pennsylvania Press, [2020] | Series: Early
  American studies | Includes bibliographical references and index.
Identifiers: LCCN 2020015395 | ISBN 9780812252545 (hardcover)
Subjects: LCSH: Military occupation. | United States—History—Revolution,
  1775–1783. | United States—History—Revolution, 1775–1783—British forces.
Classification: LCC E208 .J64 2020 | DDC 973.3/41—dc23
LC record available at https://lccn.loc.gov/2020015395

For Sara, Susan, Syd, and Gale

CONTENTS

Introduction. The Experience of Occupation   1

Chapter 1. Revolutionary Occupations   16

Chapter 2. Collaborator Regimes   55

Chapter 3. Within the Lines   80

Chapter 4. Starving amid Plenty   112

Chapter 5. Ambiguous Allegiances   138

Chapter 6. Making Peace   162

Epilogue. Forgetting Occupation   191

Notes   207

Index   245

Acknowledgments   252

The Experience of Occupation

ordinary

The (quotidian) experiences of military occupation and the transformations
they wrought were central to the failure of British authority in North
America. The American Revolution transformed deeply held beliefs in radical ways. The results of this upheaval are well known: by 1783, a group of
anti-tax revolutionaries had defeated the most powerful empire in the
world and established an independent republic. But despite two centuries
of historical study, the experience of revolution for ordinary Americans
remains frustratingly unclear.[1] Rejection of imperial authority did not take
place only, or even primarily, in the abstract realm of political philosophy.
Nor did change happen solely based on social conditions or military campaigns. Rather, it occurred for most people in the course of their everyday
lives, in intensely personal and highly contingent ways, especially when
confronted with the most visceral aspects of the Revolutionary War. Most
women and men living in what became the United States did not switch
their loyalties in an instant but did so gradually, as their lived experiences
of enduring war altered their attitudes toward British rule. Nowhere is this
everyday process of political change more evident than in the port cities the
British Army occupied during the war.

We are not accustomed to thinking of the American Revolution in
terms of intense and prolonged personal struggles. In 1815, an aging John
Adams influenced centuries of popular memory when he reflected that the
American War of Independence "was no part of the revolution; it was only
an effect and consequence of it." For the second president, "the revolution
was in the minds of the people"; rejection of British authority had already
occurred "before a drop of blood was shed at Lexington."[2] Although
Adams's words have shaped numerous historical interpretations, many of
his contemporaries would have balked at the idea that the war played no

role in shaping their politics. William Tillinghast—a physician living in occupied Newport, Rhode Island—had a profoundly different experience of the American Revolution; one that reflects how the wartime experience of occupation, more than radical political arguments during the imperial crisis, caused many to abandon their faith in royal rule.

Tillinghast, who had trained with the physician Benjamin Rush in Philadelphia before the war, remained politically neutral and continued his medical practice when British forces occupied his native Newport in late 1776. A devout Quaker, he likely supported an early address delivered by many of the city's most prominent Friends congratulating General Sir Henry Clinton on his bloodless conquest of Aquidneck Island, praising Clinton's "distinguished lenity" to the local population and professing their hopes that the general would "restor[e] peace and Tranquility to this (at present) distressed Country."[3] As a man of learning, Tillinghast likely socialized with the British military and their loyalist allies as well. In late 1777, he was elected librarian of the Redwood Library, which during the occupation was frequented by a wide array of royal officers and their loyalist allies— although, in the words of one British observer, its books were "not very well-chosen, & worse preserved." Tillinghast and his wife also had their first two children under occupation, and as evidenced by his account book, the doctor conducted a thriving practice among Newport's military population as well as its civilians.[4]

Indeed, the soldiers and sailors of the occupying force may well have boosted an otherwise lackluster endeavor. In his medical treatments, Tillinghast came into close daily contact with the British Army, which certainly enriched him. The physician's account book, which spans nearly the entire three-year occupation, describes many encounters with members of the British military, from camp followers to the British officer corps. One of the first patients listed in the book is a soldier's wife the doctor visited and charged three shillings for a course of pills to cure a heat rash. In April of 1777, Tillinghast prescribed General Hugh Earl Percy—Newport's then-commander—a dose of purgatory pills and followed up a week later to make sure that his directions were followed. In May, he treated a "Mr. Barns" of the royal artillery for venereal disease—a feat he repeated in June when he cured the gonorrhea of a sailor aboard a British transport. Over the next two years, treating such ailments would become one of his most common services, as dozens of entries in his account book attest. Tillinghast also regularly visited the British hospitals, receiving compensation for treating the wounds that his Majesty's soldiers had suffered in battle against his countrymen. Such work was vital to his practice, as the British Army paid in cash, whereas civilians often did not. One civilian patient he visited paid him with "a breast & neck of Pork," while another used a pair of stockings and a piece of beef to recompense the doctor's services. Others seemingly never paid, or their bills were still outstanding upon his death in 1785. Tillinghast's business, thus, likely depended on the British military for its solvency.[5]

In addition to attending the soldiers themselves, Tillinghast's practice also put him in the midst of frequent liaisons between the British military and the local population. One of his patients was Sally Leake, whom one British officer noted operated "a house of Pleasure" in Newport during the occupation. Likely, many of the women that Tillinghast saw were forced to engage in prostitution or other, more informal relationships with British soldiers to survive. Tellingly, civilian women outnumber civilian men in his account book, indicating that these encounters often led to the same venereal diseases that the physician treated in military personnel. Some of these affairs had more long-lasting consequences. In June of 1778, Tillinghast delivered a child for Sally Allan at her grandfather's house in Middletown, a few miles from Newport. The doctor identified Allan as the "girl" of one Mr. Griffin, purser to HMS *Kingfisher*, which was then stationed in Newport. Whether or not the affair between Griffin and Allan was consensual, the delivery's location at Allan's grandparents' house rather than Griffin's quarters, as well as the transitory nature of the entry, suggests that it did not last long beyond the *Kingfisher*'s posting, likely leaving Allan and her family with a fatherless child to care for. While the details he recorded for most patients were more fleeting, in his day-to-day work Tillinghast must have seen his fill of the seedy underbelly of British military culture.[6]

Beyond soldiers, sailors, and their sexual partners, Tillinghast's practice also gave him unique insight into the myriad traumas inflicted on city residents by British military rule. In addition to the horrors he must have witnessed at the British military hospitals he visited, the doctor also paid regular visits to Coasters Island, where a smallpox hospital had been set up and where American prisoners of war faced isolation to contain the disease. Tillinghast also visited at least one—and likely more—of the prison ships in Newport Harbor, on which both rebel soldiers and civilians suspected of revolutionary sympathies were exposed to harsh weather, starvation rations, and frequent illnesses. The families of those interned suffered more;

as one witness recalled, "Great Numbers of Inhabitants who are now imprison'd have Left their families in great Distress" and "Upon Application to the [British] General For Relief [they] are Treated with Contempt and Turn'd out." Tillinghast had a personal stake in the treatment of those in the smallpox hospital and on the prison ships. In the summer of 1777, his kinsman, Charles Tillinghast, died in the smallpox hospital, and in October another relative, Joseph Tillinghast, was interned aboard the *Lord Sandwich* prison hulk for refusing to sign an oath of loyalty to the Crown. It also could not have been lost on the pious Quaker that one of the military hospitals he frequented was located in Newport's Society of Friends Meeting House, with injured German mercenaries displacing the Friends' congregation. Moved by the plight of his patients, his family, and his coreligionists, by the end of Newport's occupation Tillinghast had abandoned his allegiance to the British cause and seemed ready to embrace revolutionary rule. When several dozen transports arrived in October 1779 to carry the British force back to New York City, Tillinghast named them "the Blessed Fleet of empty ships," a striking descriptor in an otherwise unemotional account book. Over the course of a three-year occupation whose countless ordeals he had seen closer than most, the doctor had gone from a position of neutrality or even tacit support for the British at their landing to sighing relief at their departure.[7]

Disillusioned by military occupation in Rhode Island, Tillinghast's wartime experience belies Adams's assertion that rejection of British authority was all but completed by the outbreak of war in 1775. For the physician, and for thousands of Americans, the experience of the war—and of military occupation in particular—was crucial to the transformations wrought by the American Revolution. Frustrations, privations, threats, and humiliations at the hands of the British military caused people like Tillinghast to question and ultimately discard their allegiance to the only form of government most had ever known. This process was intimate and varied greatly from person to person. The aggregate effect, however, is clear enough. By the end of the war, for a variety of reasons, most people who lived under British military rule had renounced their loyalty to the king, and British authority had unraveled. In this way, occupation played a critical role in deciding the outcome of the American Revolution.

Between 1775 and 1783, every large North American city—Boston, New York, Newport, Philadelphia, Savannah, and Charleston—fell under British military rule for some period. As centers of population and commerce, these cities should have been bastions from which the British could restore order and inspire loyalty to the Crown. Revolutionary authorities recognized as much, and moved to secure them as they established new governments in late 1775 and early 1776. Neither were imperial officials ignorant of the importance of cities. In each one, British officers and prominent American civilians collaborated to craft municipal governments intended to entice Americans to pledge their allegiance to the Crown. Under these administrations, military rule provided avenues for many people, especially women and the enslaved, but also free men and even British soldiers, to transform their lives for the better. These enticing new opportunities came with dire risks, as the military also ushered in repression and violence, and many people found themselves newly vulnerable to harassment, robbery, assault, rape, and even murder. Still, the hope of bettering their lives tempted thousands to embrace restored British rule.

Although the official policies of military occupation defined the nature of these new, precarious, opportunity-rich societies, civilians and soldiers contributed equally to their creation. Soldiers imposed a distinct military culture on each port town, which many civilians eagerly joined. From the socializing of elite officers to the earthier customs of ordinary soldiers, British military culture played out in the theaters, dance halls, gambling dens, and illicit grogshops that popped up wherever the army encamped. It was in this milieu that military personnel and civilians arranged political alliances, made business deals, and discussed all manner of topics. In the process, local residents incorporated British soldiers into the rhythms of their everyday lives. They accepted officers into their voluntary societies, charitable organizations, and churches. They invited them to their tea parties and soirees. They rented rooms and houses to military personnel and their families. They hired off-duty soldiers to work on ships and in workshops. In each city they occupied, British soldiers courted and married local women, worked alongside local artisans and contractors, and drank and relaxed with locals of all social and ethnic backgrounds. While this growing familiarity brought the army and the local population together in new and intimate ways, it also highlighted the differences between them and, when cracks appeared, served to cleave urban populations from their loyalty to the Crown.

Despite its promise, military occupation failed to bring about a restoration of the British Empire in America. By the end of the war, the experience of occupation had weakened imperial authority to its breaking point.

Armies that in some places outnumbered the civilian population by more than half created severe food and fuel shortages. These deprivations forced even the most loyal subjects to turn to smuggling, begging, and other illicit means to feed and shelter themselves. To facilitate these activities, and to navigate the treacherous political waters of the revolutionary period, those living in occupied cities also learned by necessity to obfuscate their loyalties. They took advantage of the British military's periodic offers of generosity to those who declared themselves loyal while maintaining ties to the rebel camp as well. The need to preserve allegiances on both sides steadily undermined the legitimacy of British governance as occupations persisted for months and years. In city after city, by the time the army withdrew, most residents, even many who had supported the Crown at the onset of the conflict, no longer saw restored royal rule as a viable option. Their belief in self-governance was forged through the intimate experience of military rule.

After the war, those who endured occupation reinterpreted their experiences to align with new, postwar realities. For these survivors, this process was a matter of necessity. Their wartime actions left many vulnerable to prosecution by revolutionary authorities, and many less fortunate found themselves imprisoned or forced into exile after the conflict's end. Early historians and public figures, many of whom had firsthand experience with occupation, came to these survivors' aid, creating a new public memory of the American Revolution in which all but the worst of those who had embraced British military rule could be forgiven and integrated into republican society. Forgotten were individual experiences of accommodation and compromise under harsh conditions; in their place, early national leaders crafted a founding mythology in which heroic patriots resisted and fought against villainous British soldiers and misguided loyalists. This new narrative proved so successful that even now much of the complexity of occupation experience during the Revolutionary War has disappeared from our collective memory.

Occupied America recovers that lost history, revealing how the lived experience of military occupation shaped the outcome of the Revolutionary War. Using accounts of those who lived under military rule in the six American cities occupied by the British Army, this book demonstrates how, over the course of the eight-year conflict, military occupations slowly frayed and eventually severed the bonds of imperial authority. Although the experience of occupation differed from place to place and person to person, common themes persisted from Boston to Savannah and from the poorest wretch to the wealthiest member of the colonial elite. Despite the goals of British commanders for reconciliation and peace, military occupation served to muddy allegiances, fracture what economic ties remained between the colonies and their former mother country, and alienate civilians both inside and outside of the zones controlled by the British military. Yet occupied cities also provided spaces for individuals on both sides to make their own personal peace at the end of the conflict; they served as bargaining chips for both the republic and the empire in the formal peace process, and as rhetorical symbols of resistance in the face of oppression for those who sought to build a new national culture. The intimate experiences of those living under British occupation thus had a profound effect on both the American Revolution and the new world that it produced.

These experiences find little resonance in most conceptions of the American Revolution. Until recently, most historians have located political change in the years prior to or just after the Revolutionary War, discounting the effect of the war itself in changing attitudes toward the British Empire. Rather than treating the vagaries of war as an integral part of the revolutionary experience, these histories—following Adams's lead—tend to deal with "the American Revolution" and "the War for Independence" as disparate events.[8] Although this approach is commonplace for the American Revolution, it is unusual in studies of revolutions elsewhere in the world. Few historians would treat the French or Russian Revolutions without including the long civil wars they spawned and the radical changes that occurred during those conflicts. By taking the Revolutionary War seriously as a vehicle for political change, we deepen our understanding of how the experiences of ordinary people shaped the radical transformations wrought by the American Revolution.

The pages that follow bring to bear questions, techniques, and concepts honed in the studies of occupations elsewhere to the experience of the American Revolution. Histories of other times and places reveal that the transformative experiences born of occupation are a distinctive feature common to many revolutionary upheavals. For example, during the English Civil Wars of the 1640s, highly contingent, localized social conditions shaped ordinary people's politics. Studies have demonstrated that political identities during that period were of a malleable, pragmatic character, one which was based in local community contexts and shaped by surprisingly mundane considerations. In many cases, these considerations—protecting families, securing food and shelter, and preventing destruction of property

—caused ordinary English people to switch sides multiple times or even take a hostile attitude toward both sides during the war.[9] In an Atlantic context, a recent study of the British occupation of Havana, Cuba, during the Seven Years' War reflects many of the same themes but also demonstrates how commercial and interimperial contacts shaped peoples' allegiances in surprising ways—in many cases causing once-loyal Spaniards to cooperate with the British occupation force. In addition, Britain and Spain both disrupted Cuba's racial hierarchy, alternately offering freedom in exchange for service and renewed enslavement as punishment for resistance in much the same way that Britain and the American revolutionaries would twenty years later.[10] Studies of the French Revolution bear these trends out even more, as historians have demonstrated that allegiances changed a great deal based on geography and individual experience, and—perhaps most importantly—that they depended on everyday hardships, experiences with revolutionary and counterrevolutionary violence, and radical challenges to racial, gender, class, and religious hierarchies. These processes, which occurred in the course of everyday life, changed the politics of millions of ordinary French people in very real and visceral ways, which in turn shaped the course of events, from the deposition of Louis XVI to the terror to the military coup of Napoleon Bonaparte.[11]

Iterations of these same themes occur in occupation experiences beyond the eighteenth century. Literature on the occupation of the South in the aftermath of the American Civil War and of occupied territories during World War II, for example, are well populated with examples of how military violence, conflicting notions of race and class structures, and contingencies of place and circumstance combined to shape the course of important events. In each of these situations, ordinary people had to carefully negotiate their allegiances to multiple sides in order to ensure their survival, in a careful triangulation that had dire consequences if one guessed wrong.[12] All of these phenomena—localized, quotidian concerns; challenges to the existing social order; contingent allegiances; and, above all, the experience of wartime violence and deprivation—were also present in the American Revolution, shaping the course of the event and the coming of American independence.

Scholars have only recently begun to seriously consider how similar dynamics of allegiance, violence, and everyday experience molded the course of the American Revolution, and their work has yet to be fully incorporated into popular understandings of the event. This book builds on a _series_

spate of new studies of the revolution that examine the intricacies of how ordinary Americans chose and switched sides over the eight-year war. Over the past generation, scholars of loyalism have incorporated both contingency and change over time in histories of loyalty formation on local and regional levels.[13] Works on conflict zones and "no-man's-lands" have also challenged the stability of concepts of patriotism and loyalism in the face of social pressure and wartime conditions, most recently leading to a new analytical category of neutral or "disaffected" Americans who favored neither side strongly, and who indeed feature prominently in the history of occupation.[14] Histories of Native American groups and enslaved people during the war have added further nuance to the concept of loyalty by explicating how those two groups overwhelmingly sided with the Crown for a variety of political and economic reasons.[15] Despite all of this new research, however, we still do not fully understand how everyday experiences shaped the larger political and social changes wrought by the war. Examining British occupation both fleshes out the ambiguities and contradictions of the revolutionary experience and reveals the critical role that ordinary people played in determining the outcome of the conflict.

Occupied America also contributes to a new wave of histories that both recover the violence of the American Revolution and examine its effect on the contours of the event. In the last several years, historians have begun to take a tack first suggested by John Shy in the 1970s, demonstrating that violence had a transformative effect on the revolution—transforming what had been understood to be a relatively conventional war for national independence into a chaotic and asymmetrical revolutionary struggle. In these new narratives, we find that armed conflict begat seemingly endless cycles of revenge killings on the frontiers, the destruction of Native American communities throughout North America, the deaths of tens of thousands of enslaved and free blacks, and the mistreatment of prisoners of war on all sides. Historians have begun to argue convincingly that this bloodshed radicalized, intensified, and changed the stakes of the revolutionary project just as much as political developments and the social changes that occurred alongside the butchery. The story of urban occupations fits into this new, violent turn in studies of the American Revolution, demonstrating how intimate experiences of military conquest and martial rule changed the nature of imperial authority—and people's responses to it—over the course of the war.[16]

Although it does not feature in most narratives, military occupation and the experience of the revolution in cities have not totally escaped the notice of American historians, and this study owes a great deal to works which have allowed us to understand urban life in revolutionary America. A long tradition of urban social history has demonstrated port towns' essential role in the course of the revolution, analyzing politics in the social context of municipal development. Still, most stop short of the war years, instead focusing on the period of imperial crisis between 1763 and 1775.[17] Several works have analyzed the events of military rule in each city occupied by the British, revealing important social, political, and cultural aspects of each specific context.[18] Most recently, explorations of occupied Philadelphia and Charleston use military rule as a canvas to depict the fungibility and interconnectedness of political authority, allegiance, and social relationships under wartime conditions.[19] As a comparative study, *Occupied America* synthesizes many of these contributions, using the rich backdrop they provide to focus on the lived experience of occupation across the temporal and geographic breadth of the entire Revolutionary War.

Because of the volume of ink spilled on the American Revolution over the past two centuries, and because of the paucity of surviving records from a chaotic, unstable period, many of the sources used to explore the revolutionary occupations will be recognizable to students of the era. The stories of individuals like the enslaved South Carolina carpenter Boston King, the Philadelphia diarist Elizabeth Drinker, the restored Georgia governor Sir James Wright, and the New York jurist William Smith Jr. have been told by other scholars—often at great length.[20] But, drawn together, these narratives and other, lesser-known ones shed new light on the commonalities of experience across their respective cities. Still, some familiar figures, such as the political economist Tench Coxe and the reluctant loyalist Joseph Galloway, play unexpected roles when examined in the context of military rule.[21] And other, more obscure people, such as customs collector Andrew Elliot of New York and colonial attorney general James Simpson of South Carolina, assume new significance when considered for their roles in conceiving and administering occupation governments.[22] These well-known narratives, combined with lesser-known archival evidence—drawn from contemporary newspapers, the writings of civilians and soldiers in occupied cities, official military records, and other sources depicting life on the ground under military rule—give as full an accounting as possible of the experience of occupation for people of diverse ethnicities, social backgrounds, and nationalities. In so doing, they demonstrate that the experience of military occupation played a decisive role in the course and outcomes of the American Revolution.

Military rule marked urban life during the Revolutionary War from its earliest days until its close. In Boston, the presence of British forces to enforce trade regulations became a full-fledged occupation with the appointment of General Thomas Gage as military governor of Massachusetts in 1774, displacing the colony's civil government. After Boston's evacuation in March 1776, New York City became British headquarters for the remainder of the war; its citizens lived under army authority from September 1776 until November 1783. In the winter of 1776, imperial forces garrisoned Newport, Rhode Island, to secure its valuable harbor, protect the Royal Navy's route to New York, and combat rebel privateers operating out of New England. The British Army occupied Philadelphia during the winter of 1777 and the spring of 1778, as part of a wider campaign to retake the middle colonies and break the will of the Continental Congress, and then withdrew after France's entry into the war forced the Crown to deploy troops elsewhere. In late 1779, British commanders focused their efforts on the southern colonies. They abandoned the garrison at Newport and invested troops in Savannah, Georgia, and, in the summer of 1780, Charleston, South Carolina, both of which remained under military rule until late 1782. One by one, occupied cities became strongholds from which the British government attempted to restore imperial rule to the rest of the colonies and also served as refugee camps for those fleeing violence or persecution in the revolutionary-held countryside.

These six cities—Boston, New York, Newport, Philadelphia, Savannah, and Charleston—comprised the most prominent towns in colonial British North America, yet contained less than 1 percent of its population.[23] And although cities were experiencing rapid growth on the eve of the revolution—they increased in population by 35 percent in the fifteen years from 1760 to 1775—most Americans lived in small towns, in rural communities, or on isolated farms and plantations.[24] These places also experienced military rule. At various points, the British Army controlled vast territories of the hinterland in the thirteen rebelling colonies. During the northern and mid-Atlantic campaigns of 1776–1778, British forces took control of large swaths of New Jersey, all of Staten and Long Islands, parts of upstate New York, slivers of Maryland, and areas of southeastern Pennsylvania and Delaware. King George III's army also launched occasional incursions into coastal Connecticut, Massachusetts, and Rhode Island, exerting control beyond formally occupied territories. During the southern campaigns of 1778–1781, the king's troops at one point controlled virtually the entire states of Georgia and South Carolina, as well as outposts in North Carolina and Virginia. No colony was left untouched by British military occupation. Urban occupation was by no means the only, or even the dominant, experience of military rule during the revolution.[25]

Still, the experience of occupation in cities was crucial to the outcome of the conflict, because of the important roles port towns played in the British Atlantic world and the intensity and frequency of the civilian-military interaction in urban areas. People living in cities experienced occupation on a much more intimate and regular basis than their neighbors in the countryside. In rural communities, a civilian could go for weeks or even months without seeing a single British soldier, whereas in port towns, locals often interacted with the occupying force multiple times a day. The small size of colonial cities made these interactions ever more personal and ever more political. The crowded houses, commandeered public buildings, and busy streets of occupied ports fostered friendships, rivalries, flirtations, and business relationships between civilians and soldiers—all of which became freighted with political meaning. Selling produce to the army or renting rooms to soldiers could be both acts of economic survival and potential signals to one's neighbors of loyalty to the king, while failing to attend a ball hosted by British officers because of another obligation could just as easily be construed as a sign of revolutionary sympathy. Because urban occupations played out in tight spaces with limited casts, cities provide the perfect laboratories to understand how the dynamics of military rule changed individual allegiances over the course of the revolution.

Beyond the intensity of the occupation experience in urban areas, cities played a role in British American society that made them more important than their small population sizes might indicate. Eighteenth-century British ports served as the nodes of a commercial empire, transmitting goods, people, and ideas across oceans. Lumber and fish from New England were funneled through Boston and Newport to supply sugar plantations in the West Indies, as were rice and indigo from Charleston and Savannah. Agricultural produce from the mid-Atlantic came through Philadelphia and New York for sale across Europe. In exchange, each port city became a depot for European manufactures, as urban merchants imported farm equipment, building materials, textiles, and luxuries from the workshops of

Europe. Some urbanites dealt not only in imported goods but in people. The slave trade existed in each city, but especially in Charleston and Savannah, where enslaved men and women constituted a majority of the population, and where slave ships arrived regularly to sell their human cargo to plantation owners from the surrounding countryside. Philadelphia and New York were hubs for the arrival of hundreds of thousands of German and Scotch-Irish farm laborers, often under terms of indenture. The vast majority of these migrants stayed in the city only a few weeks, quickly moving on to more sparsely settled areas of the colonial frontiers. Still, even though they had relatively few permanent residents, port cities had an outsize position as centers for the distribution of both goods and people throughout the British Empire. By disrupting these economic relationships, the experience of military occupation of these towns influenced the lives of the majority of British subjects in America who were not themselves city dwellers.[26]

Port cities in British North America were also established centers of political and legal authority. As administrative hubs of their colonies, each city hosted not only a permanent coterie of royal officials but also, at various times of the year, legal courts and colonial assemblies. When these bodies met, the populations of these provincial capitals could swell by hundreds of people with business before the government or the courts. Beyond lawmaking and justice-seeking, cities were also prime places for power-jockeying, as different factions used the loyalty of city dwellers to put pressure on colonial governments or to express dissatisfaction with their policies. By the 1770s, each major city had developed its own distinct form of street politics in which everyday people—artisans, laborers, apprentices, sailors, and others on the margins—organized and involved themselves in the business of governing both the municipality and the surrounding province. While street politics varied, from the chaotic waterfront of Boston's rioting sailors to the peaceful and civic-minded voluntary associations of late eighteenth-century Philadelphia, through their political actions urbanites had an outsize role in how power was exercised in late colonial America. In the sense that city dwellers were used to being courted for political allegiance, British occupation would continue a long-standing tradition.[27]

Each of the six cities occupied by the British Army during the American Revolution had its own particular economy, politics, and culture, and to ignore their differences would be a mistake. Even though all were connected in the commercial Atlantic, urban economies differed drastically in the American colonies—the mid-Atlantic cities of Philadelphia and New York largely focused inland, connecting incoming migrants to the vast and rich rural areas surrounding them and providing a place to sell their produce to the rest of the world; the southern capitals of Charleston and Savannah resembled their counterparts in the British Caribbean as centers for both the importation of enslaved labor and the export of products produced by that labor; and the New England cities of Boston and Newport were diversified commercial ports whose merchants, sailors, and ships' captains carried people and goods across the entire British Empire. Each city's politics differed vastly as well. In Boston and Newport, wealthy merchants ruled with the support of sailors and laborers, while in New York and Philadelphia merchants and artisans competed with landed gentry for control over city and colony politics. Rural farmers in the surrounding hinterlands pressured the elites in all of the northern seaports, especially Boston and Philadelphia, where the countryside became far more radical than the cities in the opening stages of the imperial crisis. In Charleston and Savannah, wealthy plantation owners—many of whom did not even reside in the capitals full-time—dominated society in both town and country. Demographically, Boston retained much of the culture and ethnic stock of its seventeenth-century Puritan founders, while Newport, New York, and Philadelphia were ethnically and religiously diverse. Enslaved Africans outnumbered Europeans in both Charleston and Savannah, but whereas the former was home to opulent mansions maintained by wealthy South Carolina planters and a sizable middle class of artisans and merchants, the latter maintained a more rough-and-tumble character befitting its relatively recent founding—only forty-two years before the revolution—and its role as a center for Native American diplomacy in the Southeast. These local differences shaped the nature of military rule just as much as strategic objectives and army policy.[28]

Still, similar elements of military occupation persisted from city to city, and the pages that follow seek to draw out these common threads. All of the occupations came on the heels of earlier, armed repression of dissent by revolutionary groups that assumed power in 1775 and 1776. In every occupied port, military officers and civilian officials collaborated to create functioning regimes. These administrations evolved as the war went on, with later occupation governments learning from the successes and failures of those already in existence. Over the course of occupation, elements of each town's population saw opportunities for social advancement as well as disastrous risks. To varying degrees, each port city experienced both plenty and scarcity, with influxes of cheap luxuries but soaring prices for food, fuel, and housing. These conditions forced inhabitants to turn to illicit and often desperate means to ensure their survival. In the process, residents of each city developed flexible loyalties that helped them navigate the tumultuous social, economic, and political climate of military rule. At the end of occupation, inhabitants of each city cannily negotiated their own wartime settlements, using connections with those in rebel-held areas to achieve personal peace settlements, as elite diplomats agreed to a deal in Paris. Finally, early historians in the postwar era created a new narrative of the revolution in which the complexities of occupation everywhere had very little importance.

Despite its near erasure from our collective memory, the experience of occupation during the Revolutionary War played a crucial role in the outcome of the American Revolution as a political and social event. An examination of the everyday lives of those living under military rule reveals that the failure of British imperial authority in America did not come with the drafting of the Declaration of Independence or the Continental Army's victory at Yorktown; rather, the failure occurred gradually in the course of the ordinary lives of ordinary people. As occupations wore on, those living under military rule alternately accommodated, collaborated with, took advantage of, and subverted the structures of royal authority during their day-to-day lives. As they did so, royal authority's grip on their allegiance weakened to the point where, by the end of the war, and for a majority of city dwellers, it no longer even existed.

CHAPTER 1

Revolutionary Occupations

Before British troops arrived in North American towns, revolutionary authorities from Massachusetts to Georgia had already asserted military force to coerce locals to support the insurgent cause. Most of these actions took place between the summers of 1775 and 1776, and they influenced both the nature of later British occupation and its results. In each city, revolutionary violence divided neighbors and created exiles, a development the royal army would use to its advantage by cultivating the loyalty of disenfranchised loyalists and displaced imperial officials. In the short term, these schisms made the process of British military rule easier; however, in the long run, these persistent tensions prevented the restored colonial regimes from ever completely uniting city dwellers behind the royal standard.

For a year after the outbreak of violence at Lexington and Concord, local committees, councils, and congresses seized the reins of power and displaced former colonial officials and their supporters.[1] As insurgents in communities across British North America overthrew their former rulers, they invariably seized the port cities, which had been the political and economic capitals of most of the colonies, and which became power centers for the new regimes. Taking possession of provincial records, controlling government buildings, and possessing the trappings of royal rule—all of which resided in the provincial capitals—proved essential to establishing the legitimacy of the new state regimes.[2] The coups in which revolutionaries seized power could be both subtle and overt, but they were rarely couched in the terms of formal occupation. Still, all involved the use of military force to suppress dissent and ensure control over the populations of these vital political and commercial centers, even as the revolutionaries sought to legitimize their new governments by directing attention away from the violence that undergirded them. The effect was unmistakable. When British troops arrived in each of the six cities during the war, they found a political landscape marred by violence and coercion.

The process of establishing control at the local level was intensely personal. At seven o'clock in the morning on a late January day in 1776, Henry Preston of Savannah received a sharp knock on his door. Preston, the Clerk of the Crown for His Majesty's Province of Georgia, opened it to find his neighbor, Adam Trick, sent by Savannah's revolutionary Committee of Safety to retrieve the keys to Savannah's courthouse for the use of Georgia's insurgent Provincial Congress. Preston refused, citing his oath of allegiance to the royal government and his duty to safeguard the records of the colony. Later in the morning, three more men arrived at Preston's house, again demanding the keys to the courthouse and, now, the clerk's office within it. Upon Preston's adamant refusal to betray his oath to the king, the men became irate, searching the first floor of his house and threatening, according to Preston's later account, to call forth "a file of Muskiteers [sic]" to "take me into Confinement." Nonetheless, Preston refused to hand over his keys.

A few hours later, Trick knocked once more, this time to summon Preston to the courthouse. Upon arriving at the courthouse, the royal clerk found the doors broken open and the building guarded by armed men. When he entered the building, a committee member approached the frightened bureaucrat, explaining that "they had sent for [him] as a privat[e] Gentleman" to organize the records found in the clerk's office, which the insurgents had also burglarized. This proposition Preston agreed to, viewing it his duty "to see them as much taken care of as I possibly could," even as the revolutionaries appropriated the provincial records. As he directed the emptying out of his own office, he recalled that the revolutionaries "behaved very politely, & gave me every paper & other matter I asked for that either belonged to my self or P. P. [Preston's wife]." Still, it must have been a bizarre experience to index and explain to the usurpers how to organize the land deeds, legislative records, and official letters that had, until that morning, been his sacred responsibility. After he packed the records into trunks for safekeeping, the Committee of Safety sent the now-deposed clerk home. Still, perhaps sensing the official's alienation, a neighbor returned later that night warning him "not to go without the limits of the town" without permission from the new revolutionary authorities.[3] After a day spent in abject humiliation and terror, Preston still had to live among those who had both dispossessed him of his livelihood and forced him to abrogate his sacred duty to his sovereign.

On the streets of port cities, the struggle for authority took place within close-knit communities. As revolutionaries seized power, they often had to reckon with supporters of the old regime whom they had known all of their lives. Preston certainly recognized the members and associates of the committee who came to his house, and he likely knew the militiamen guarding the courthouse as well. Revolutionary committees and councils also often kept those they suspected of loyalism under close supervision and often even imprisoned or exiled them to prevent potential challenges to the new regimes. As revolutionaries seized the trappings of power and persecuted rivals, though, they did so among neighbors, family members, and old friends, many of whom did not share their fervor. With the exception of Boston, occupied by the British Army from 1768 to 1770 and then again in 1774, in each port city from Newport to Savannah, revolutionary authorities asserted power with the type of odd, intimate violence reflected in Henry Preston's experience.

Formal British military occupation thus came on the heels of an unspoken yet unmistakable occupation of port cities by insurgents, one that was contested in many places until the day the British arrived. When imperial troops decamped later, the structure of their military rule built upon already existing tensions within towns that were already at least partially under martial law. In nearly every context, British commanders relied on people like Henry Preston—former officials and prominent loyalists disenfranchised by the revolutionary regimes—to provide information and, in some cases, help to govern the cities' populations. With officers usually preferring to devote their attention to strategic and logistical concerns, civilians took advantage of their willful ignorance of local politics to seek vengeance on revolutionaries and to settle scores from earlier insults. While commanders and loyalist officials in their service sought to rally urban populations behind the king, factionalism caused by years of revolutionary strife and violence persisted just beneath the surface.

As occupations wore on, Americans living in occupied ports experienced these divisions in their day-to-day lives, even as British and loyalist authorities sought to unite urbanites behind the royal standard. As military officials took advantage of preexisting conflicts to assert their authority and maintain governing structures, everyday interactions between the royal army and local populations increasingly became fraught with conflict. Largely because these officials did not know how deep tensions ran, earlier struggles reemerged, and authorities proved either powerless to stop them or did not care to, so long as their rule was secure. As a result, ordinary citizens were left to their own devices, unable to rely on the royally sanctioned government to resolve what should have been routine issues and, as conditions deteriorated, to survive on a day-to-day basis.

The city of Boston had perhaps the longest and most contested history of armed conflict among the major North American ports. By the time Massachusetts militiamen and British soldiers first clashed twenty miles outside of the city in April 1775, imperial troops and gangs of protesters had been vying for authority for seven long and often bloody years. Boston's waterfront—always a rowdy scene where tradesmen, laborers, and sailors drank, swore, and participated in a rough-and-tumble mob politics—grew out of control during the riots following the passage of the Stamp Act in 1765. These armed clashes pitted protesters against customs officials and their supporters. In their midst, prominent merchants like John Hancock and Samuel Adams, members of an organized protest group known as the Sons of Liberty, rallied the waterfront crowds to loot the house of Lieutenant Governor Thomas Hutchinson and intimidate the city's royally appointed stamp inspector into renouncing his post. While such violence subsided after the act's repeal in 1766—in large part due to street violence not only in Boston but also in port cities as far south as the West Indies—it flared up again after the passage of a new set of duties in 1767, culminating a riot in June 1768 with the seizure of Hancock's merchant sloop *Liberty* for customs violations. After a crowd failed to prevent the *Liberty*'s impoundment by the Royal Navy, a mob of several thousand rampaged through the city, assaulting customs officials and other representatives of the Crown, until one o'clock in the morning.[4]

This violence led to the imposition of direct military rule for the first time during the imperial crisis. In response to the *Liberty* riots, Massachusetts's royal governor, Francis Bernard, requested the presence of British troops to keep order in Boston. In mid-September 1768, two regiments from Halifax, Nova Scotia, encamped on Boston Common. For the next two years, these soldiers lived among the city's populace, guarding key government buildings and protecting royal officials. Still, the investiture of troops did not stop the contest for authority in the city. Even with the army in place, gangs supporting the protest movement continued to intimidate traders who sided with the government and customs officials who followed their duty too scrupulously. The two sides clashed perhaps most vividly in March 1770 when a detachment of British troops opened fire on a group of civilians armed with clubs and rocks in front of the royal customs house—an event that quickly became notorious throughout the colonies thanks to engravings distributed by the insurgent silversmith Paul Revere. Three years later, the conflict remained in full flush as the Sons of Liberty organized the destruction of 342 chests of tea to protest the newly passed Tea Act. In response, the British Parliament passed a series of laws known as the Coercive Acts to punish the city and intimidate would-be rebels in other colonies. These laws closed the port of Boston to all trade, changed laws in the colonies to make it easier to forcibly quell protests in America, and, significantly, rescinded civil government in Massachusetts Bay.[5]

Even after the revocation of civilian authority, the contest for authority continued for nearly a year. In May 1774, six months after the destruction of the tea and three months after the passage of the Coercive Acts, General Thomas Gage arrived in Boston to take up the military governorship of Massachusetts Bay. The capital, a city of approximately sixteen thousand people, now played host to four thousand British soldiers, along with several hundred military families who travelled with the army. Even with British troops quartered on Boston Common and their families living among the population, insurgents continued to mobilize street gangs and sailors. In the face of this resistance, Gage proved reluctant to turn to naked military force as a means of government, preferring to work with Boston's town council and the city's loyalist elite in his attempts to maintain order. Upon taking office, Gage attempted to summon the colony's executive council as a civil governor, but many councilors declined to serve under the general, fearing reprisals from the extralegal committees and councils that ruled the streets. As loyalist official Peter Oliver recalled, the Massachusetts Assembly itself "locked their Selves into their Apartment, to pass some seditious Resolves," forcing Gage to dissolve their meeting. As a result, "the people began now to arm with Powder and Ball, and to discipline their militia," and Gage made similar preparations among his troops. Although tensions persisted, however, the new governor continued to pursue his duties as both civil governor and military commander.[6]

Full-fledged military rule still did not take firm shape until after the outbreak of violence at Lexington and Concord in April 1775. Between that clash and the Battle of Bunker Hill in June, what had been a punitive yet restrained occupation by British troops transformed into a formal military government. As nearly twenty thousand colonial militiamen from across New England shouldered their muskets and marched on the city of Boston,

Gage fortified the town's defenses, drafting citizens and using his heavily outnumbered force to construct redoubts and siege barriers across Boston Neck, tightly controlling movement in an out of the city with checkpoints and armed guards. In late May, more officers and men arrived, including renowned Generals William Howe, Henry Clinton, and John Burgoyne, along with seven hundred more troops. On June 10, Gage received reinforcements from Canada, bringing his forces to nearly six thousand British soldiers and marines. On June 12, conceding the obvious, he declared martial law, marking the official imposition of a military rule that had existed for at least two months prior. This move, and not the 1768 imposition of troops or the 1774 abolition of Massachusetts's civil government, marked the beginning of the occupation of the city as well as the British war effort against the rebels. From June 12, 1775, undisguised military force would be employed to coerce citizens to submit to authority on both sides.[7]

Meanwhile, insurgent New England militias made swift preparations for armed conflict, forming siege lines around Boston—establishing guard posts and digging trenches around the town—and fortifying nearby islands and towns to deprive the British Army of supplies from the countryside. As soldiers continued to arrive, bolstering the colonial force to nearly sixteen thousand by June 1775, the siege lines proved a formidable sight from within the city. Although not as well trained as the king's forces, the provincial militias effectively defended their positions against British foraging expeditions to nearby islands and contemplated storming the city, although lack of cannon prevented a direct assault.[8] Still, the New Englanders bottled Gage's forces inside the town of Boston and, by preventing their resupply from the countryside, sat ready to starve them out of the city.

The British Army's actions during the siege of Boston presaged many of the strategies deployed by future commanders in other occupied zones, as well as some of the problems that would continue to plague British efforts. As the siege developed outside the lines of the city, General Gage took several measures to secure his authority within the town and on the siege lines. An early priority was purging the city of potential insurgents within. To do so, he negotiated with the leaders of Massachusetts's Committee of Safety to allow those who wished to leave occupied Boston to go out of the military lines of the city with their belongings intact, provided they gave up their arms, in exchange for insurgent forces' allowing loyalists in the countryside to enter the city. In the weeks after the battles of Lexington and Concord, the British Army seized more than 2,300 muskets and

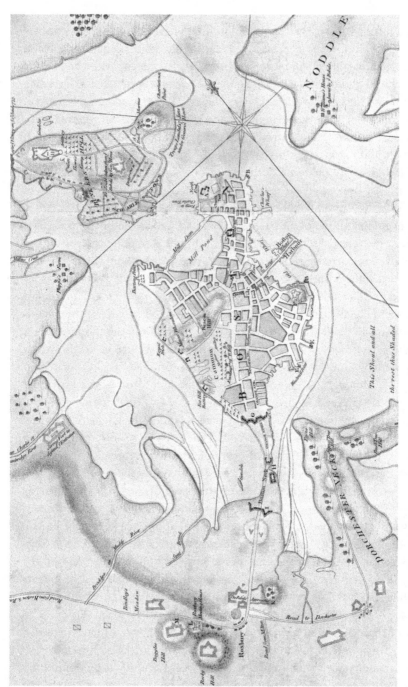

Figure 1. *A Plan of Boston, and its Environs[,] shewing the true Situation of His Majesty's Army. And also those of the Rebels. Drawn by an Engineer at Boston, Octr. 1775.* Courtesy William L. Clements Library.

pistols, along with nearly a thousand bayonets and other weapons of war from the city's townspeople. Ultimately, however, Gage reneged on his promise to allow townspeople to leave with their property, instead forcing them to leave their belongings behind to succor the army and discourage the provincial militia from a full-on assault. Still, over the next two months nearly nine thousand people left the city, leaving the once-vibrant port with a population of just over five thousand civilian residents, who were themselves outnumbered by the British soldiers residing alongside them. Gage had turned Boston from a port city under military governorship into a garrison town.[9]

This transformation traumatized citizens of the city, as the partisan violence that had afflicted Boston for eight years devolved into open war. Peter Oliver recalled that the insurrectionist militia were "constantly urging the Inhabitants to quit the Town, & threatening to destroy it." He credited these threats with driving away many residents, lamenting that by early June "the Town was reduced to a perfect Skeleton."[10] Those who sided against the king, or remained neutral, felt the trauma of occupation even more acutely. Sarah Deming, a member of a revolutionary family that fled the town the day after Lexington and Concord, later recalled "No words can paint my distress" at learning "I was Genl Gage's prisoner—all egress, & regress being cut off between the town & country." Once safely out of town, she recounted that, although many had advised her that Boston would be safer than the siege lines surrounding the city, she "had no faith in their opinion," as she believed that "Boston would be an Aceldama as soon as the fresh troops arriv'd," and that, as the British reinforced their position, "some new piece of soldi[e]ry barbarity, that had been perpetrated the day before, was in quick succession brought in."[11] Deming, like other devout Bostonians, couched the occupation in religious terms—Aceldama, the biblical site where Judas Iscariot hanged himself, served as a common metonym for suffering and bloodshed.[12] Civilians on both sides bemoaned the militarization of conflicts that, though sometimes violent, had not theretofore approached the brutality of full-scale war.

The Battle of Bunker Hill solidified the war footing on both sides, leading to the stabilization of the siege and the consolidation of military rule within the city. On the afternoon of June 17, 1775, an expeditionary force of 2,200 British soldiers engaged 1,200 provincials near the town of Charleston, Massachusetts, just north of Boston, in an attempt to secure the city's northern approach and prevent rebel artillery from firing from the heights of Breed's Hill and Bunker Hill on the peninsula. Although successful in driving the New Englanders from their fortified positions, the British troops lost nearly half their number in one of the bloodiest slaughters of the war. After the carnage, both armies settled in for a long siege, with the British Army awaiting reinforcements and the provincials attempting to force them to withdraw from the town.[13]

As the situation stagnated after Britain's Pyrrhic victory, civilians faced more hardships within the city. Peter Edes, the son of a revolutionary-leaning printer who had fled, remained behind to run his father's shop but found himself on the run from a naval impressment gang a few days after Bunker Hill. As he attempted to escape, the young Edes was apprehended by British soldiers, who subsequently discovered two outlawed muskets in his home. That evening Edes, who described his captors "as harden'd and inhuman as Turks," found himself arbitrarily imprisoned alongside both townspeople suspected of rebel sympathies and the captured veterans of Bunker Hill. In a British military jail, Edes and his fellow inmates suffered multiple abuses at the hands of occupying soldiers, who taunted, beat, and deprived the prisoners of food. After two months' imprisonment, Edes noted in his diary that "73 days confin'd and have had nothing but bread and water allowed us," though eventually the prisoners were given a paltry ration of salt pork, butter, rice, and peas.[14] The printer's son also recorded the harsh treatment of many of his fellow inmates, writing that "the poor sick and wounded prisoners fare very hard; are many days without the comforts of life." Edes recoiled in horror at the harsh medical treatment of wounded Bunker Hill veterans at the hands of the British Army, lamenting that, when surgeons did visit, "some of the limbs which have been taken off it was said were in a state of putrification [sic] and not one survived amputation."[15] For the devout Congregationalist, perhaps the greatest insult was the British soldiers' disregard for the norms of the town's religious community: among entries on starvation, assaults, and poor treatment, one of the most incensed is the young man's description of British soldiers' "continued scene of horrid swearing, obscene talk, and shocking blasphemy." He even complained that "they practice most swearing on the Sabbath."[16] For Edes and other Bostonians, what had begun as a shift in fortune in a continuing contest over authority had transformed into something entirely different.

Edes's experiences in occupied Boston demonstrate the realities of naked military rule in urban areas. What had been a civil offense only a few weeks before the young man was apprehended had become a military matter, to be adjudicated with all the arbitrariness and harsh discipline of the eighteenth-century British Army.[17] Many in Boston experienced similar traumas. And although the provincial forces ultimately forced a British evacuation of the city, the nature of the contest for authority had fundamentally changed during the siege. Whereas before Lexington, Concord, and Bunker Hill various factions had struggled for authority, sometimes violently but just as often peacefully, afterward power in the city resided only in muskets and cannon. It was a transition that would be repeated in port towns across the thirteen colonies, and one that would continue to divide local communities throughout British North America as revolutionary violence gave way to military power.[18]

Like Boston, the city of Newport, Rhode Island, experienced more than a decade of conflict between royal and insurgent authorities in the years leading up to formal occupation by the British Army in December 1776. Even before the Stamp Act protests, Newport had been an epicenter of resistance to British naval impressment, with a mob of around five hundred people burning a boat sent by HMS *Maidstone* to collect sailors in the town. After hearing of the riot in Boston against the Stamp Act, a mob of angry sailors and apprentices gutted the houses of the attorney Martin Howard Jr. and the physician Thomas Moffat, two of the most prominent Stamp Act defenders in the colony, and, like the Bostonians, forcing their designated stamp distributor to resign his post.[19] Also like their near neighbors seventy miles to the north, Newporters continued to protest through the 1760s and early 1770s, spurred on by prominent merchants who incited crowd actions against impressment, taxation, and perceived injustices in customs collection. In 1768, a group of Newporters attacked and burned the newly commissioned HMS *Liberty*, John Hancock's seized ship now refitted as a customs-enforcement vessel, on nearby Goat Island, and in 1772 Newporters were involved in the destruction of HMS *Gaspee*, the next ship to attempt to enforce customs regulations in Narragansett Bay.[20]

Although tensions had been high since the Stamp Act crisis, the outbreak of war exacerbated the situation and led to a full-scale revolutionary occupation of the town. As in other colonies, Rhode Island's revolutionary Committee of Safety declared its intention to seize government property in the town, including the royal customs house. Despite the violence of the 1760s and early 1770s, Newport maintained a loyalist reputation among many revolutionaries. The committee, backed by militiamen sent from economic rival Providence, took control of most of the city's public buildings and placed many of Newport's most prominent citizens under surveillance as suspected loyalists. Although several prominent merchants in the town—such as future signer of the Declaration of Independence William Ellery—joined the revolutionaries, most of the town's traders, fearing loss of their lucrative connections in Britain and the West Indies, either sided with the monarchy or remained neutral in the protest movement. Much of this reluctance to abandon royal rule had to do with Newport's religious pluralism. In addition to the Congregationalists ubiquitous throughout New England, the city had sizable congregations of Anglicans, who sided overwhelmingly with royal authority; Quakers, who abhorred violence; and Jews, who depended on the British Empire's relatively tolerant religious policies for their well-being among a prejudiced population. Many members of these groups, along with Baptists and many religiously "unaligned" people, stayed out of the protest movement or even resisted the efforts of the Sons of Liberty, who largely came from Congregationalist backgrounds, to bring the town's waterfront population into a Boston-style position of fully organized rebellion against royal authority. As late as 1774, in the wake of the destruction of the tea in Boston and the passage of the Coercive Acts, Newport's insurgent leaders still had trouble rallying the majority of their neighbors to the revolutionary cause.[21] Still, by the summer of 1775 the revolutionaries, backed by militia and supported by the Rhode Island Assembly, deposed royal governor William Wanton and installed a regime opposed to royal authority. In the absence of British troops on the ground, the regime took effective control of Newport relatively easily by the fall of 1775.

Although the revolutionary authorities asserted control over the city, the presence of British ships in the harbor halted a complete coup, provided refuge for loyalists, and forced Rhode Island's revolutionary government into an uneasy compromise with the British military. After the destruction of the *Gaspee*, the navy sent a flotilla of vessels to Narragansett Bay to enforce regulations and prevent smuggling. By the fall of 1775, Commodore James Wallace, the fleet's commander, had demonstrated his willingness to use violence against revolutionary authorities. In October his squadron, consisting of four twenty-gun sloops and several smaller craft, bombarded the town of Bristol, Rhode Island, for refusing to supply it with provisions, only ceasing when the town's militia finally agreed to his demands.[22] As in

Boston, the advent of open warfare had turned what had been a multifaceted struggle for authority into one carried out primarily by force. And, as in Boston, this transition deepened already existing divisions among the local population.

The conflict between revolutionary authorities on land and the British navy at sea separated citizens in ways that would continue under British occupation a year later. Wallace's flotilla demanded that Newport supply its ships with bread, salted meat, and beer. This demand put the city in a precarious position: Rhode Island's new regime viewed trade with British military as illegal, yet Wallace had already demonstrated his willingness to take harsh measures against the insurgents. The commodore had more than eighty naval cannons at his disposal, which could reduce the unfortified town, with all of its grand architecture and warehouses full of goods, to rubble in a matter of hours. Further complicating the situation, Newport's merchants and farmers had nowhere else to sell their goods and faced poverty if they did not provision the ships. The dilemma threatened the livelihoods not only of merchants but also of dockworkers, stevedores, and the majority of the population employed by maritime industries. Many in Newport welcomed the presence of the Royal Navy as an alternative to the forceful imposition of revolutionary rule in their city. To avoid the fate of Bristol, Rhode Island's revolutionary authorities agreed to a compromise with Wallace. Nicholas Cooke, the acting governor, gave Newporters permission to trade with the British ships, provided the British landed no troops in the town and that the townsfolk did no more than provide necessities. Cooke also removed Rhode Island troops from the town so as not to antagonize the British forces, but he kept them on Aquidneck Island to keep an eye on the situation.[23] While the arrangement aimed at satisfying both sides and delaying, if not preventing, violence in the streets, it nevertheless put the town's citizens in a delicate position, with revolutionary authorities in control of the city streets but the Royal Navy asserting dominance over the port.

The precarious division of power soon led to conflict. In December 1775, a detachment of Rhode Island militia captured two British officers who had come on shore to arrest deserters from the fleet. Commodore Wallace viewed this action as a violation of the truce between Newport and the British flotilla and demanded the officers be returned, threatening to take hostages from among the town if they refused. The situation put leading citizens, embodied in the Newport Town Council, in the awkward situation

of having to request that the governor release the officers while still professing their allegiance to the revolutionary state. This hedging was a matter of
necessity, as the council wrote in their plea that "the Town is in great want
of wood & other necesaries which will be stopt unless this affair is settled
which will put in utmost distress."[24] Regardless of their political beliefs,
Newport's leading citizens had to make compromises to ensure the physical
and financial well-being of the town's inhabitants.

Customs collector Charles Dudley felt the town's travails acutely in both
his public and private life. Fearing the insurgents would loot the king's
coffers, Dudley fled on board Commodore Wallace's flagship, HMS *Rose*,
with a chestful of the colony's customs records and specie collected from
traders at the port. Despite his position as customs collector and his loyalty
to the Crown, however, Dudley was not a stranger to Newport—he had
lived there for over a decade, married into one of the most prominent
families in the city, owned substantial property, and dealt in mercantile
activity in addition to his customs duties. Under prior circumstances, Dudley would likely have been tolerated—he was not forced to flee, as Martin
Howard Jr. was, during the Stamp Act crisis and seems to have stayed out
of trouble for most of the 1760s and 1770s. Still, the revolutionary takeover
of the town in the fall of 1775 spooked him, and upon being ordered to give
up the customs records and income, he escaped to the *Rose*, calling the
action the "only one honorable measure for me to take" and lamenting to
his wife, Catherine, "In spite of all my discretion to avoid falling under the
power that prevails in this Country, I find myself sep[a]rated from my
D[ea]r Kitty." Over the course of the next few months, Charles exchanged
a series of agonizing letters with Catherine from Newport harbor, unable
to come on shore for fear of arrest by revolutionary authorities. Although
able to communicate and occasionally meet on board the king's ships, the
Dudleys' division represented the bifurcated situation Newport found itself
in—in his initial letter to Catherine, Charles predicted that "many Cares
similar to your own . . . I expect will be the Situation of some of your
female Friends, in Newport 'ere long." [25]

As Charles Dudley sought to protect his sacred duty on board HMS
Rose in Newport's harbor, less than a mile away the rebel administration
began to confiscate his property. As Catherine wrote him bluntly one evening, "Your houses and all the Stocks were yesterday sold," much of it for
less than it was worth, even though the proceeds went to the new insurgent
government.[26] The revolutionary authorities did, however, allow Catherine

to continue living in the couple's house in town (even if it was under new ownership) and to keep her personal effects, as well as a harpsichord, a chaise-style carriage, and ownership of one of the couple's enslaved servants, a man called Tom.[27] As Charles prepared for his departure to Boston and later to Halifax and England in early 1776, Catherine sent provisions on board for him, including pickled vegetables, salted meat, clothing, and other supplies for his sea voyage.[28] In March 1776, he finally set sail for exile in Halifax, and later England, hoping to rebuild his fortunes and writing to Catherine in Newport, "I pray to God I may make the choice [that] will restore us to that happiness of which we have been most cruelly deprived."[29] Charles Dudley thus held out hope for the future, despite having to flee Rhode Island's newly installed revolutionary regime.

Like Dudley, many inhabitants escaped Newport during the period of divided rule, and more left as news arrived in late November 1776 that British troop transports were on the way from New York to occupy the town. The Rhode Island militia, along with the committeemen who had so terrorized the Dudleys and other loyalists, also retreated to other parts of the state, so that when six thousand British and German troops under General Henry Clinton landed on December 8, they found no opposition in a depleted town of less than three thousand.[30] Those who remained welcomed the British troops. The first regiment was met on the wharf by William Wanton Jr., son of the ousted governor, who welcomed their commanding officer into the Newport's colony house, where what remained of the town council formally handed control of the city to British forces.[31] Thus a three-year occupation of the city began virtually unopposed.

Clinton, a veteran of the siege of Boston and future commander in chief of British forces in America, had been ordered to secure the town of Newport and the island it sat on largely for strategic purposes. Newport's harbor, perhaps the deepest in New England, would provide British warships a port to resupply without having to travel all the way to Halifax. The harbor would also provide an ideal place for the fleet's larger ships spend winters: its deep water allowed for the largest British warships of the day, which could displace between two thousand and three thousand tons of water and rode well under the sea level. New York's shallower inner channels could not accommodate these ships, and Admiral Lord Richard Howe deemed Halifax too far away to conduct naval operations effectively in the rebelling colonies.[32]

Newport also served an important role in Britain's overall strategy to defeat the American rebellion. A garrison in the city would serve to keep

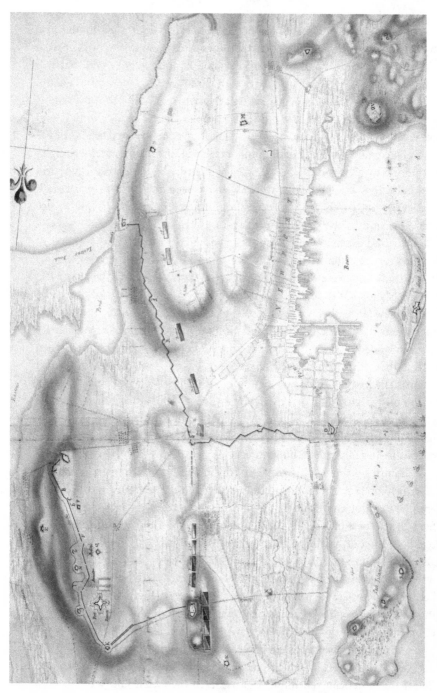

Figure 2. Abraham d'Aubant, *Plan of the town and environs of Newport, Rhode Island, Exhibiting its defenses before the 8th of August 1778.* Courtesy William L. Clements Library.

portions of the Continental Army in New England, preventing them from being deployed in other, more active theaters, and could potentially serve as a staging ground for future campaigns against Boston, still seen by many as the heart of the insurrection. Such campaigns never materialized, but Newport nevertheless remained an important British possession. After taking control of the city, Clinton fortified it with a line of guardhouses, trenches, and dykes, and sent his army into winter quarters in the town's churches, meetinghouses, and abandoned homes. The general himself left for a respite in England in January 1777, leaving overall command to General Richard Prescott. Despite the city's potential as a base for attacks on northern New England, the British Army rarely moved from Newport, although it did defend the town from a combined assault by Continental land forces and the French navy in the summer of 1778. Still, Newport operated as a secondary post to Britain's more important 1776 conquest: New York City.[33]

Like other ports, New York was riven by factions during the 1760s and 1770s—if anything, divisions were far more deeply entrenched than in Boston or Newport, although they proved just as fluid in their loyalties. For a generation before 1765, the landed Livingston and mercantile DeLancey families had vied for power in the colony and the city. Through elected offices in the provincial and city government, prominence in social organizations, and accumulated wealth and patronage, both families wielded considerable influence over the port's commerce and the day-to-day governance of the city. While elite members of the factions held most of the official power, their authority depended in large part on the self-interest of artisans, laborers, and farmers throughout the colony, who switched sides as different parties appealed to their specific needs. To sway people to their sides, both groups engaged in electioneering, sponsored public works projects, and made efforts to persuade neighbors, friends, and fellow city residents to side with their party. By the time of the revolution, competing appeals to the interests of ordinary people had been ongoing for forty years or more.[34]

For many onlookers, the imperial crisis thus seemed like yet another chapter in the continuing struggle for power. Both the Livingston and DeLancey families opposed the Stamp Act and continuing British taxation, but the DeLanceys proved more moderate in their opposition than the Livingstons, squelching early efforts to impose a nonimportation agreement on New York's merchants and restraining extremists in the province's assembly and the city's municipal government. Both sides decried violence, and even the Livingstons attempted to reign in their more radical allies among the town's artisans and laborers after the city's October 1765 Stamp Act riots. Elites in both parties feared that mob violence would loosen their control over the politics of the city, and both attempted to divert and harness the crowd actions that threatened their power.[35] As the contest continued, insurrectionist groups such as the Sons of Liberty emerged as a third, more radical faction, led by figures drawn from the lower and middling sorts. Whereas in Boston and Newport crowd actions had been supported by elites, in New York the Sons created a power base anchored in mob violence, motivated not just by politics but also by tensions between the lower classes and their social superiors. By the early 1770s, factional politics had changed substantially in New York—while debates still occurred in taverns and public spaces, radicals now dominated the streets and competed for influence on the same level as the traditional parties.[36] These crowds also radicalized the traditional groups further, with the De-Lanceyites moving toward full support of the British government and the Livingston faction increasingly abiding by the edicts of the Continental Congress.[37] Fearing that confrontations could erupt into violence at any moment, many prominent New Yorkers, such as the moderate Livingston supporter and attorney William Smith Jr., left the raucous city for country estates or opportunities elsewhere.[38]

By the time the war began, neither insurgents nor loyalists had a clear advantage, leaving the city paralyzed in tension. The unresolved political situation was on full display on June 25, 1775, when on the same day that George Washington visited the city on his way north to take command of revolutionary forces in Massachusetts, popular royal governor William Tryon returned to the city from a visit to England. Despite political differences, both received warm public accolades. Washington supped with radicals in an inn popular among the Sons of Liberty, while Tryon went to a private home for dinner with a group of elite loyalists.[39] Even after Tryon moved on board a merchant vessel anchored in New York harbor for protection against revolutionary mobs, a semblance of royal government continued from his "floating City Hall," and many New York elites continued to push for moderation.[40] Although insurgents had taken control of the armory at the actual city hall and the Sons of Liberty had begun to forcibly repress loyalists, it was not until January 1776, when Washington ordered

Major General Charles Lee to take command of New York with a force of Continental troops, that the rebels could claim control of the city in its entirety. Even still, the British navy retained a small flotilla in the harbor through much of early 1776, providing a place of refuge for dissenters from the revolutionary regime.

When Washington returned to New York in mid-April 1776, it was to a city under full revolutionary military occupation, rapidly building defenses in anticipation of an impending British counterattack on the middle colonies. In the period between the evacuation of Boston and the British invasion of Long Island in August 1776, revolutionary forces imposed a strict and organized military rule over New York City. By July 9, when the general marshalled his troops in lower Manhattan to hear the Declaration of Independence proclaimed, more than twenty-eight thousand men in arms had gathered from across the colonies to resist British rule. In New York, the new Continental Army had begun to form itself into a more traditional military force than it had been in Boston, establishing more rigid discipline and ordering regulations for the behavior of soldiers and officers. It also developed an increasingly sophisticated bureaucracy to recruit, feed, clothe, and arm the citizen-soldiers arriving on Manhattan Island, and to coordinate with both the Continental Congress and the revolutionary government of New York.[41]

The imposition of direct military force—and the presence of thousands of soldiers in arms—had a chilling effect on the city's residents. One inhabitant complained, "We all live here like nuns shut up in a nunnery" due to the curfews imposed on civilians and soldiers patrolling the streets at night.[42] New Yorkers struggled to supply and shelter the growing Continental force, which also consistently found itself short on provisions and weapons. In one instance, Washington's officers went door to door in search of firearms to seize or purchase from locals. The army also brought disease. Although one of Washington's first actions upon arrival in New York was to establish a smallpox quarantine area on Montresor's Island, dysentery ran rampant throughout the army and the overcrowded civilian population.[43] Despite the army's demands, many New Yorkers supported the Continentals' cause—after the reading of the Declaration of Independence on July 9, a mob comprising both soldiers and townsfolk marched up Broadway and pulled down a 4,000-pound equestrian statue of George III that stood in the Bowling Green, disfiguring the king's face and seizing the lead to melt down for ordinance to be used for the army. Still, most residents feared what war would do to their city, and by August 1776 the city had emptied out, with only around five thousand civilians remaining out of a prewar high of five times that number.[44]

Part of the motivation for this exodus was the appearance of the British Army. In June 1776, British forces began arriving in New York harbor for the attack that revolutionary leaders had long expected and that civilians had long dreaded. General William Howe, who had succeeded Gage in command of the British Army, departed Halifax on June 9 with a fleet of 130 ships commanded by his elder brother, Admiral Lord Richard Howe. On June 29, the first of these ships arrived in New York's harbor, sailing past Sandy Hook and into the Lower Bay with no opposition. To the Continentals and their supporters in Manhattan, the flotilla made an imposing sight: one witness exclaimed that "all of London was afloat."[45] On July 2, the Howes began disembarking troops on Staten Island, where the revolutionary militia promptly defected to facilitate an unopposed landing. As the summer progressed, more and more troops arrived, until by mid-August the Howe brothers had amassed thirty-two thousand soldiers and marines.[46]

The two armies soon clashed, and in the ensuing battles the British Army decisively routed the Continentals, taking control of New York City and the surrounding area. On August 22, General Howe landed fifteen thousand men and forty pieces of artillery on Long Island. Advancing quickly toward the fortified town of Brooklyn, the British Army defeated the inexperienced and underequipped Continental troops in a pitched battle on August 27, forcing Washington's soldiers to retreat across the river to Manhattan during the night of August 29–30 to avoid destruction. The British victory was so complete that it left the Continental Army deeply demoralized and eventually earned Howe a knighthood. Two weeks later, elements of the British Army crossed over to Manhattan, again defeating the Continentals and driving the revolutionaries to the northern tip of the island, then across the Hudson to White Plains, New York. After the capture of Fort Washington—the last remaining Continental stronghold in the region—in November 1776, Howe's forces boasted uncontested possession of Long, Staten, and Manhattan Islands.[47]

New York was the first city taken by storm from revolutionary forces, and its citizens experienced a more jolting and destructive transition from revolutionary occupation to British military rule. In addition to psychic trauma, New York's landscape bore the marks of both battle and civil insurrection. Just a week after Howe's victory, a massive fire, possibly started by rebel agents remaining in town—though the cause has never been determined—destroyed nearly one-sixth of the buildings in the city, including the imposing Trinity Church.[48] The fire demoralized an already beaten population and created a housing crisis for both the British Army and the denizens of the port. Still, Long Island's farms and forests provided ready access to provisions, lumber, and supplies, as did nearby New Jersey, where General Howe sent foraging parties and stationed troops in strategic towns. And, as islands, Manhattan, Staten, and Long Islands could easily be defended from attack by revolutionary forces, who lacked serious naval capacities.

As the occupation commenced, the British Army set about rebuilding not only the town's buildings but also its defenses. Almost immediately, General Howe began to fortify Manhattan and the other islands in New York harbor against attack. After the fall of Fort Washington, the last Continental outpost on Manhattan Island, the British inherited extensive defensive works from the Continental Army, which Howe and his chief engineer, Captain John Montresor, improved. All three islands' lines of defense limited access in and out of British-controlled territory, and Howe stationed troops at all ferries, bridges, and wharves to control the movement of soldiers and civilians. New York remained in British hands for the remainder of the war, becoming the royal military's headquarters in North America and the center for directing campaigns over the next seven years. Troop levels rarely dropped below ten thousand soldiers, making New York perhaps the most heavily fortified outpost in North America. While the town never again came under serious military threat, it served as a haven for tens of thousands of loyalist refugees from elsewhere, who by 1783 had swelled its population to perhaps double its prewar size.[49] For the next seven years, New York would be Britain's most important piece of territory on the American continent.

While the British seized Boston, New York, and Newport before rebel governments had time to mature, residents of Philadelphia, Savannah, and Charleston lived for years under armed revolutionary rule. British forces thus had to deal with more entrenched insurgent forces, which in many cases had already employed violence as a method to consolidate their power. In all three cities, rebels deployed troops to seize government buildings and symbols of power, to protect against British attack, and to repress loyalists within their midst. In addition, revolutionaries formed civil governments and systematized their control over the populace. In most cases,

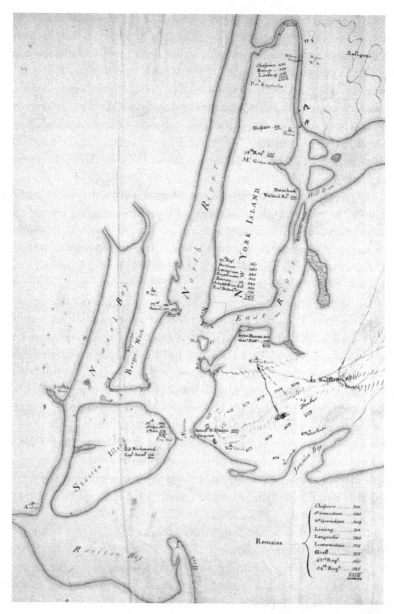

Figure 3. *British Troop Dispositions in and near New York City, Sept. 2d 1781.*
Courtesy William L. Clements Library.

this process involved a combination of military force and civil innovation. Pennsylvania, Georgia, and South Carolina all declared themselves independent states and established new, formal constitutions and codes of law: Pennsylvania in late 1776, Georgia in early 1777, and South Carolina in the spring of 1778. Violence and repression against loyalists and others who disobeyed the new order now took place under the auspices of these new, legally sanctioned states. Although each of these cities had experienced mob actions during the decade between 1765 and 1775, it was not a tradition of violence inherited from tax protesters that drove the use of force by the new revolutionary governments but, as the rebels saw it, legitimate deployment of state power against enemies and dissidents.[50]

By the end of 1776, Philadelphia's revolutionary militia had become a power unto itself in asserting control over the city. Once the war had begun in Boston, thousands of Philadelphians rushed to arms to defend the rights of the colonies. In April 1775 alone, almost eight thousand Philadelphians, largely drawn from the laborers and artisans of the city, rose up and formed themselves into militia companies and battalions. This incipient militia became an institution of radicalization similar to Oliver Cromwell's New Model Army during the English Civil War. Comprising a power base entirely separate from both the Continental Congress and the incipient state of Pennsylvania, militiamen began to assert their own revolutionary principles, calling for the election of their own officers, lobbying for legislation to ease taxes on the poor and middling sorts, and to crack down on those who opposed the revolution or attempted to stay neutral.[51] The militia outstripped its leaders in many respects, leading the vanguard of revolutionary violence.

From the seat of the Continental Congress and de facto capital of the newly declared United States, rebel leaders sought to channel armed revolutionary enthusiasm to suppress loyalists and dissidents and support the revolutionary cause. Although some of the militia's actions, such as raids on suspected loyalists, aligned with the agenda of radical revolutionaries, the militiamen demonstrated an antipathy toward elite congressmen's tendencies toward pomp, ceremony, and luxury. When Congress proposed holding a ball in honor of Martha Washington at the opulent City Tavern in November 1775, militiamen and working-class Philadelphians grew incensed, threatening to destroy the tavern and forcing leaders to not only cancel the ball but to put a moratorium on lavish entertainments throughout the city. The idea that the violence that had been used so effectively

against enemies of the revolution could now just as easily be directed at
congressional elites weighed heavily on the minds of rebel leaders, who
attempted for the next several years to exert control over both the militia
and the Continental Army in Philadelphia.[52]

In part to control popular violence, Congress used Philadelphia as a
staging ground for spectacles that would legitimize the United States in
the eyes of both the world and its own citizens. To reinforce its authority,
Congress took advantage of the violent enthusiasm of Philadelphians by
holding military celebrations. When George Washington left to assume
his command of the army outside Boston, for example, John Adams and
other congressmen arranged for a "great shew" of "Wheelings and Fir-
ings" from the Pennsylvania militia to see the general off. The celebration
of Washington's departure continued with martial music and militiamen
lining the streets of the city. Congress appointed several days of "humiliation, fasting, and prayer," to be observed across the rebelling colonies
in solidarity with the troops and to link their cause to religious beliefs.
Nevertheless, congressional and Pennsylvania officials were unable to prevent rioting by the militia and other armed forces in Philadelphia at the
announcement of independence from Britain in July 1776. Soon after a
public reading of the Declaration of Independence in front of the State
House, a group of Philadelphians stormed the building, tearing down
and destroying the royal coat of arms prominently displayed inside, and
proceeded to attack symbols of the monarchy throughout the city. While
mob actions did not reach the scale of the destruction of George III's
statue in New York, the radical militia nevertheless maintained control of
politics in the town.[53]

A year later, however, Congress proved more adept at using military
pomp and ceremony to reinforce its authority in both Philadelphia and the
nation as a whole. On the first anniversary of the Declaration of Independence, Congress's Marine Committee arranged for a naval procession along
the Delaware River. On July 4, 1777, a flotilla of ships bedecked in Continental banners—and perhaps even flying the newly approved stars and stripes
of the US naval flag—sailed up the Delaware, with sailors well dressed and
aloft. Afterward John Hancock, president of the Congress, along with several other prominent representatives, was rowed aboard the flagship *Delaware*, which fired a thirteen-gun salute—one for each of the new states—as
his boat arrived, to be followed by similar salutes from the rest of the flotilla. Although the procession certainly inspired martial awe among the

population, the form, which closely mimicked naval processions celebrating the birthdays of monarchs during the colonial period, asserted both Congress's authority and its legitimacy as the governing power of a sovereign nation. To further demonstrate the military might of the new nation, Congress used a band of captured Hessian musicians as musical accompaniment to their festivities, which also included a lavish banquet at the City Tavern. Finally, Congress ended the day by solemnly observing a parade of Maryland cavalrymen and North Carolina infantry on their way to the front. Much like military parades in other contexts, the display was meant to inspire a mix of fear, awe, and patriotism. By 1777, revolutionary authorities had learned to use military force to legitimize their authority and even help create the trappings of a new national identity.[54]

Military authority in revolutionary Philadelphia was not limited to parades and ceremonies. The insurgent leadership also turned its armed forces against those who challenged the new republican regime. In perhaps the most forceful assertion of authority over the civilian population prior to the British invasion, Pennsylvania's Supreme Council, with the assent of Congress and the Continental Army, arrested forty of Philadelphia's most prominent Quaker citizens in early September 1777. Although Quakers had been among the most fervent opponents of British taxation during the 1760s and early 1770s, their religion forbade violence and the swearing of oaths, making them unable to either serve in the revolutionary army or swear allegiance to the revolutionary government. As the population and the government radicalized, the Quaker community in Philadelphia came under suspicion as potential loyalists. In August, Continental General John Sullivan presented evidence, almost certainly fabricated, that a Quaker meeting in New Jersey had collected information on troop disbursements and defenses of Philadelphia and passed it on to British forces on Staten Island. On this testimony, the revolutionary army arrested twenty men and, without trial, exiled them to Winchester, Virginia, forcing them to abandon their families and property in Philadelphia. Many in Congress and on Pennsylvania's Executive Council brushed aside protests of the ad hoc imprisonment by claiming it a necessary evil—as Congressman James Lovell put it, drastic actions had to be taken to protect the "Safety of the Union" against those who would "not affirm themselves faithful *Subjects* of it." As the experience of the Quakers illustrates, although the Congress and the state of Pennsylvania had the trappings of a civil government, they nonetheless bore hallmarks of military rule.[55]

Consequently, when British troops arrived in the summer of 1777, they encountered a society already engaged in violent repression. On July 30, General Howe landed with an army sixty miles south of Philadelphia in an ambitious gambit to defeat the Continental Army, seize the rebel capital, and capture the leaders of the rebellion. Although under no illusions that this strike would end the war, the British hoped to demoralize revolutionary troops, force Congress to negotiate under military pressure, and prevent General Washington from moving northward to stop General John Burgoyne's march south from Quebec toward Albany, New York. This latter assault would be supported by a smaller expedition advancing up the Hudson River from New York City under General Henry Clinton, and would cut off the New England states—from whence a great deal of revolutionary manpower came—from the rest of the nascent United States. Between the two campaigns, the three generals sought to divide the rebels from both political leadership and military recruits.[56]

Although Burgoyne's attack failed in the north, Howe's Philadelphia campaign succeeded. On September 11, Washington engaged the British Army at Brandywine Creek in Delaware with eleven thousand men but was utterly defeated, taking more than one thousand casualties and clearing the way for the king's troops to advance on Philadelphia. In the aftermath, Congress evacuated to Lancaster, Pennsylvania, seventy miles to the west, then to York, even further from the capital. On September 26, less than two months from landing at the head of the Chesapeake Bay, Howe's troops marched unopposed into the streets of Philadelphia. On October 9, Washington's counterattack failed to dislodge Howe's forces, leaving the Continental Army to retreat into winter quarters at nearby Valley Forge.[57]

Howe's entry into Philadelphia occurred relatively peacefully, as Congress and the revolutionary elite evacuated well before the first British troops arrived. Unlike New York and Newport, however, the port had not completely emptied out upon British arrival—while many in the city of over thirty thousand had fled, the majority remained, with between sixteen thousand and twenty-four thousand civilians spending the winter of 1777–1778 with nearly fifteen thousand British soldiers.[58] Many likely saw the British Army as welcome relief from the repression of revolutionary forces. Sarah Fisher, wife of one of the exiled Quakers, described the arrival of the first British troops as "a most pleasing sight" in her diary, chiding neighbors who feared the British might burn the town. Most of the population, Fisher observed, were "in very great confusion" at the army's arrival, not knowing what to expect.[59] As in previous conquests, British forces soon fortified the town against attack, in order to prevent Washington's Continentals from launching another assault. The British Army also seized two forts in the Delaware River, forcing the Continental Navy out of the waterway and securing access to the city's port. Howe and his officers took measures to ensure local supplies, sending foraging parties into the Pennsylvania and New Jersey countryside and encouraging nearby farmers to come into town with produce and livestock for the use of the troops. By the onset of winter, the British Army seemed well situated in the new post of Philadelphia, with Washington's defeated army licking its wounds and a humiliated Congress sitting at York making preparations to flee further west should the British Army approach.[60]

Despite another striking victory over the Continentals, however, Howe's occupation of Philadelphia failed to accomplish its tactical objectives. Although he had a superior position and a more-experienced, better-supplied force, Howe made no moves either to attack Washington at Valley Forge or to capture Congress at York, instead limiting military operations to a series of skirmishes over resources in the countryside. Both contemporary observers and later historians have criticized the general's inaction, with many believing that Howe squandered Britain's best chance to win the war. Among the most common critiques by contemporaries was that General Howe fell prey to the luxuries of British North America's most populous and cosmopolitan city, preferring to live a life of ease to a potentially difficult winter campaign.[61]

While these claims may have had some merit, strategic concerns also account for Howe's reluctance to venture from his fortified post. On October 7, as Howe consolidated his control over Philadelphia, General Burgoyne surrendered his entire army, numbering some six thousand British troops, along with German mercenaries and native allies, to Continental Army troops near Saratoga, New York. Although Clinton had been successful in his assaults on the Hudson River, he did not have the manpower to push through to Albany, and the New York campaign had failed almost as spectacularly as the Philadelphia campaign had succeeded. Given this information, which reached Howe in November, the British commander may not have wanted to risk his lone remaining field army in combat, should troops be needed in New York or Newport. Further, news arrived in early 1778 of a treaty of alliance between the United States and France, widening the scope of the war exponentially. Given these reverses, Howe's

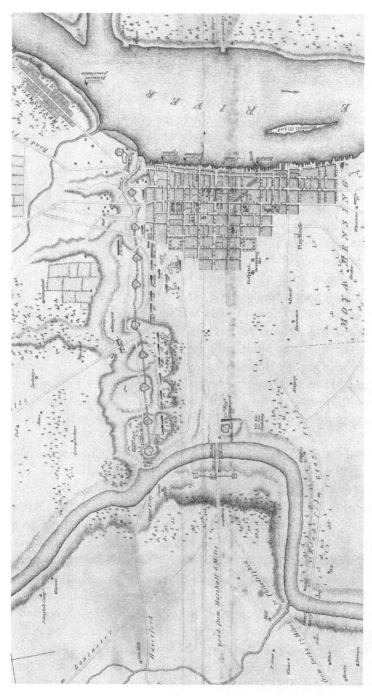

Figure 4. *A Plan of the City and Environs of Philadelphia, with the Works and Encampments of His Majesty's Forces[,] under the Command of Lieutenant General Sir William Howe. K. B [c. 1777–1778]*. London: W. Faden, 1779. Courtesy William L. Clements Library.

decision to keep his troops in Philadelphia seems reasonable as officials in North America and Whitehall—the London palace that housed much of Britain's imperial bureaucracy—considered their next move.[62]

The loss of Burgoyne's army and the French alliance changed the political calculus for the British, refocusing the war on the southern colonies and leading to General Howe's resignation in April 1778. British Secretary of State Lord George Germain ordered the new commander in chief of British forces, Henry Clinton, to abandon Philadelphia in order to free up troops to fight against France in the West Indies. After a bloody retreat to New York, during which the Continental Army consistently nipped at the new commander's heels, Clinton duly dispatched five thousand troops to the Caribbean in October 1778, along with three thousand bound for Florida and another one thousand to fortify garrisons in Halifax, Bermuda, and the Bahamas.[63] Combined with the casualties suffered throughout the campaigns over the previous two years, these departures left Clinton with less than two-thirds of the nearly thirty-five thousand men Howe had commanded a year earlier, and those were spread between garrisons at New York and Newport—too few men, the new general feared, to defend either port, let alone wage an offensive campaign. Although the empire continued to raise more and more troops for the war effort, ultimately increasing the standing army to more than a hundred thousand men by 1781, British forces never again fought in North America in the numbers they had between 1775 and 1778. Rather, Germain dispatched the new regiments to the West Indies, Gibraltar, India, and Canada, while Clinton's army shrank due to disease, desertion, and attrition at the hands of rebels. Not even six months into his command, Clinton became so frustrated with the situation he offered his resignation to the king.[64]

After the evacuation of Philadelphia, the Revolutionary War took on an even more divisive character, as fighting moved south and the conflict drew a wider array of men and women from all walks of life. Toward the end of 1778, Germain sent Clinton secret orders to wage a new kind of war in the former southern colonies, ordering the general to capture the provinces of Georgia and South Carolina, where, he was assured by intelligence from loyalist refugees, inhabitants chafed at revolutionary rule and demonstrated a "general disposition to return to their allegiance."[65] The ambitious campaign would rely not just on British troops but also on large bodies of civilian loyalists thought to be willing to fight for the Crown, along with

Creek and Cherokee Indians and, most controversial of all, escaped slaves, who were to be offered their freedom in exchange for service. A precedent for all of these tactics already existed. Loyalist militias had fought with the British from the beginning of the war, playing key roles in defending garrisons and in key battles throughout 1777 and 1778. The regular army had also recruited heavily among loyalists in New York and Philadelphia to make up for losses in the first years of the conflict. Native troops had made up a large proportion of Burgoyne's army, though most had fled west or been killed in retaliatory attacks after Saratoga.[66] Virginia's last royal governor, Lord Dunmore, had offered freedom to enslaved people who fled their rebel masters, and blacks who had made their way into occupied New York, Philadelphia, and Newport were allowed their freedom as a matter of British military policy. The new southern strategy, however, called for the use of all three forces on a scale never before undertaken in America.

The campaign began with an attack on Savannah, Georgia. Once Georgia was secure, Clinton sent a larger force to seize Charleston, South Carolina, and from thence the entire state. With both provinces firmly under British control, Clinton and Germain hoped that they would be able to redress shortages of lumber and provisions on the West Indian sugar-producing islands, as well as support further military action in the French Caribbean and, potentially, Spanish America. The conquest would also deprive the revolutionaries of a rich source of income and provisions for the war effort, and might even lead them to seek a negotiated peace. Although Clinton lamented his force's diminished role in the war, should the new strategy succeed it had the potential to put an end to fighting in North America and allow the British Empire to focus all of its attention on subduing France, which George III and his ministers regarded as the far more dangerous foe. To begin this undertaking, in mid-November 1779 Clinton dispatched Colonel Archibald Campbell, with a force of 3,500 men, to Savannah.[67]

British leaders had reason to expect speedy success in Georgia, whose former royal governor, Sir James Wright, had remained popular even as imperial authority wavered elsewhere. During the 1760s and early 1770s, Wright won acclaim from Georgians for effectively organizing defenses against native attacks and even forcing the Creeks to cede land to the colonists. Wright's political acumen allowed him to stave off the worst of the Stamp Act protests in Georgia and to keep the radical protesters in check for most of the imperial crisis, though he lamented "the Civil power obstructed" by the extralegal committees and councils that eventually formed in the state.[68] As a result of Wright's successful politicking, the controversies roiling the rest of the colonies did not have much effect in Georgia until news of Lexington and Concord reached Savannah in early May 1775, sparking popular insurrection. Between May and July, revolutionaries seized gunpowder and military stores from public storehouses around Savannah, and some particularly bold insurgents destroyed twenty-one cannons in the town's fort to prevent the firing of a salute in honor of the king's birthday.[69] Sir James could not prevent these acts, nor could he stop the convening of a provincial congress, the formation of a local committee of safety, or the raising of a rebel militia. Still, he continued to negotiate with local revolutionaries, keeping the peace until January 1776, when armed insurrectionists took total control of the government, arrested the governor and his council, and darkened the door of royal clerk Henry Preston. A month later, Wright escaped and fled aboard HMS *Scarborough*, then anchored off nearby Cockspur Island, and in March departed for Halifax and then to England, where he joined a growing community of colonial governors and royal officials in exile. Where politics had failed to oust the royal government, insurgents in Georgia had resorted to force to accomplish their revolution.[70]

Once rid of the royal governor, Georgian revolutionaries used organized violence to establish the province as an independent state. The first priority of the new government was the repression of loyalists, who still made up, by one Savannah resident's calculation, "two out of three" people in the state.[71] Under Georgia's first constitution, established on February 5, 1777, the assembly passed laws, similar to those in other new states, to imprison, exile, and strip of their properties those who would not swear allegiance to the revolutionary cause, or even those who showed inadequate enthusiasm for the rebellion.[72] Although many loyalists fled in the wake of Wright's departure, many more migrated to nearby British East Florida during the early months of 1777. Many of these refugees formed small militia units or joined bands of Creek and Cherokee Indians to harass the revolutionary forces on the new state's borders. After a failed Continental invasion of Florida in the summer of 1776 drove more refugees into the province, Governor Patrick Tonyn launched a series raids against the state's southern borders, organizing loyalists and regular troops to burn plantations, seize livestock, encourage enslaved people to escape, and force Georgia's new assembly and the Continental Army to divert troops from the northern campaigns to patrol the border.[73]

In addition conflict with loyalists and Floridians, Georgia's revolutionaries used armed force to deal with challenges from Native Americans and
the state's enslaved population. Tensions with the native Creeks flared up
in March 1776 with the killing of thirty natives on Tybee Island, and again
in the summer of 1778 with a Creek raid in western Georgia leading to the
deaths of twenty white militiamen. While the Creek never went to war with
Georgia or the new United States on a large scale, they nevertheless posed
a threat that drained resources from the state and required a permanent
military force on the frontier. Georgians also feared slave insurrections, inspired by British policy in the north. Further, the Floridian raiders
and Creeks often kidnapped slaves when they plundered Georgia
plantations—in one attack during the spring of 1778, a group seized more
than two hundred enslaved people from farms in the interior before retreating back across the Florida border. Sufficient forces, then, had to be kept
on the state's border to prevent escapes and organized violence by insurrectionist slaves.[74]

Despite its small population, Georgia fielded impressive military might,
though it often proved insufficient to deal with the threats faced by the
revolutionary state. According to one estimate, four thousand white men
served in the militia, although only half that number could be called up at
any given time. Given Georgia's prewar white population of twenty-three
thousand, the four-thousand-man militia accounted for at least 20 percent
of the population, and likely accounted for the majority of white men who
supported the revolutionary government. In addition to the militia, Georgia
fielded a regular Continental battalion of four hundred men in 1776 and
several militia and regular units drafted in the Carolinas to aid in its
defense. The cost of keeping so much of the population in arms proved
enormous. In addition to taking up most of the revenue collected by the
Georgia Assembly, in the summer of 1777 the Continental Congress devoted
$600,000 for Georgia's defense, and in 1778 increased this budget to $1
million. With such sums and manpower devoted to defense and repression,
revolutionary Georgia lived under a curtain of military rule—directing and
raising money for the army took up virtually all of the assembly's time
between 1777 and 1778, and almost all families had someone serving in the
armed forces at any given time.[75]

Even with so much of Georgia's population in arms, Colonel Archibald
Campbell's small force of British soldiers found easy success against Savannah, and after the conquest he quickly instituted his own military regime.

Landing his troops just south of the city in December 1778, Campbell found the town well-fortified but defended by fewer than two thousand men. Aided by intelligence provided by a former slave of Sir James Wright, the British expedition outflanked the Continental defenses and surprised Savannah's defenders from the rear of their lines. On December 29, Campbell took the town with only twenty-six casualties, killing 100 Continental soldiers and Georgia militiamen and capturing 450 more. Upon taking the city, the colonel gave orders for the raising of a loyalist militia and offered rewards for the capture of rebel soldiers. Joined and superseded in command by General Augustine Prevost, who had marched north from East Florida in mid-January, Campbell moved toward Augusta—Georgia's second largest city and a major fort in the western part of the state—taking the mostly empty town on January 31.[76] Soon after, Prevost gathered a force of British regulars, loyalist militia, and escaped slaves to invade South Carolina, reaching the outskirts of Charleston in early May 1779 and preempting a planned Continental counterattack. Soon after, most Continental troops and rebel militia retreated north of the Savannah River. By July 1779, when Sir James Wright returned to the city to resume his governorship, British troops controlled almost the entirety of low-country Georgia, although battles continued to rage between loyalist and rebel militias in the western backcountry.[77]

After its capture, Savannah played an integral role in the attempt to resurrect royal rule in the southern colonies. Although Sir James Wright returned to a city diminished from its prewar population of around 3,200, it soon became a thriving port once more, providing a safe haven to British ships en route to the Caribbean and allowing trade to resume between Europe, the mainland colonies, and the West Indies. Sir James also restored civil government to the town and the province, administering oaths of loyalty, reopening the royal courts, and making preparations to elect a new colonial assembly. With the help of military engineer Captain James Moncrief, Wright and General Prevost successfully defended the town from a combined Franco-American assault in the fall of 1779. During the siege, which culminated in a brutal attack on October 9, more than two hundred armed ex-slaves fought for the British, and hundreds more served to shore up defenses, load cannon, and support other defenders of the town. After the British victory, blacks became increasingly involved in military operations in the south, and encouraging their desertion from rebel plantations became military policy for the remainder of the war.[78] Further, the capture and successful defense of Savannah proved to General Clinton that the southern strategy could succeed. As a result, British leadership began preparing in early 1780 for an assault on the more populous and strategically important city of Charleston, South Carolina.

Of all the port cities occupied by the British, Charleston experienced the longest period of revolutionary government, much of it through force. During the imperial crisis preceding the war, insurgents took de facto control of the government of South Carolina as early as 1771, when Lieutenant Governor William Bull vetoed a tax bill put forward by the assembly that included a sizable donation to the English radical John Wilkes. From then on, the assembly refused to pass any further legislation, leaving the government of the province in the hands of extralegal revolutionary committees and councils. As a result of this impasse, nearly all of the powerful low-country planters who dominated the provincial assembly supported the revolution once violence broke out, and the transition to full republican rule was quickly accomplished. In addition to controlling the assembly, Charleston's leaders used their positions as the heads of a society governed by strict racial hierarchy to quell dissent within their own ranks: slaveholders had to hold a united front or risk rebellion and ruin. By September 1775, threats against his life forced Governor Lord William Campbell, only recently arrived, to flee to a warship stationed in Charleston's harbor. After an unsuccessful attack by General Clinton and Earl Charles Cornwallis on June 28, 1776, the state of South Carolina remained largely at peace—at least against internal enemies—until Prevost's invasion of 1779, marking one of the longest periods without formal warfare in any of the thirteen colonies.[79]

Like its neighbor to the south, revolutionary South Carolina became a highly militarized society, and for many of the same reasons. As in Georgia, slaves constituted a majority of South Carolina's population—of the approximately 175,000 residents of the state, 104,000 were enslaved. Threats of slave rebellions constantly vexed the state's leaders, as did the threat posed by Native Americans. The Cherokee, South Carolina's Native American neighbors to the west, launched raids along the borderlands beginning in July 1776, devastating towns and farms and forcing the Carolinians to send large forces of militia to stop them. Like Georgia and other colonies, the government also pursued systematic repression of loyalists within the state, one that increased in intensity as the war in the north wore on. Many in the western part of the state remained loyal to the king, embodying in loyalist militias and waging a guerilla war against revolutionary South

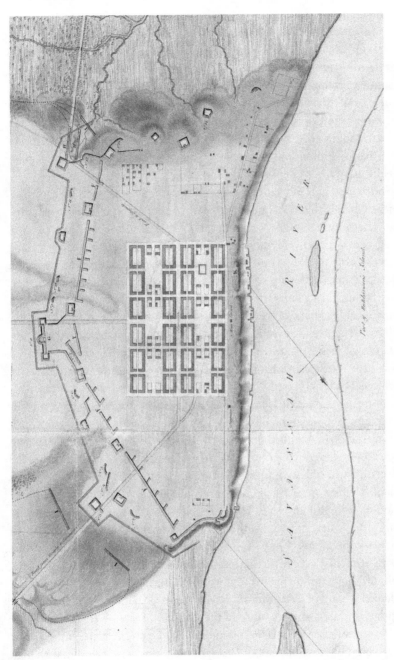

Figure 5. *Plan of the Town of Savannah, with the works constructed for its Defence [. . .]*, c. October 1779. Courtesy William L. Clements Library.

Carolinian forces from the mountains and swamps of the backcountry. These threats, combined with the ever-present possibility of a renewed British assault on Charleston, forced South Carolina's new government to adopt a military posture despite its ostensibly peaceful situation. The state of South Carolina recruited tens of thousands of militiamen to defend its borders, and Charleston itself became the headquarters of the Southern Division of the Continental Army, responsible for defending the port and its surrounding areas from British attack. The city soon became home to more than five thousand Continental soldiers, the largest force of regular revolutionary troops deployed outside of the North before 1780.[80]

South Carolina proved more successful at defending itself than revolutionary Georgia, likely because of its larger population size and economic base. The militia soundly defeated the Cherokee in the summer of 1776, taking captives and marching deep into the tribe's territory and forcing them to come to the peace table. Prominent revolutionary leaders in the state also subverted many supporters of the Crown, either calling on their racial prejudices to enlist them in the war against the Cherokees, or co-opting local leaders and absorbing formerly loyalist militias into the rebel military structure. The constitution of 1778 greatly increased the representation of western settlers, giving them 40 percent of seats in the new legislature. South Carolinians also managed to successfully repress slave rebellions. Although South Carolinian blacks had no bordering British colony to flee to, as the Georgians did, revolutionary authorities nevertheless embarked on a series of repressive acts against supposed insurrectionist plots by slaves, including one by led by Thomas Jeremiah, a free black man executed for allegedly distributing arms and gunpowder to slaves across the low country to aid in a future British invasion. Still, South Carolinians remained either in arms or in fear of armed repression throughout the period of revolutionary rule. This militarization was especially apparent in Charleston, where up to six thousand Continental soldiers crowded in beside a population of approximately twelve thousand, and strong fortifications stretched across the harbor and around the northern neck of the town. Although not formally occupied, militarization and military coercion remained a part of Charleston's revolutionary experience well before the British Army arrived once more in the summer of 1780.[81]

Revolutionary vigilance was vindicated when General Clinton's fleet arrived on the sea islands east of Charleston on March 29. Clinton, with high hopes for subduing the South's most populous port, had been preparing for this campaign for months, abandoning the 7,000-man garrison of Newport and utilizing a 3,600-man reinforcement from England to create an assault force of nearly 9,000 soldiers and marines. Landing his troops on James Island on April 1, Clinton marched unopposed to Charleston, where he besieged the city and the 6,000 Continentals and militia defending it. After monthlong siege cut off food and water to the city, and the British navy in Charleston harbor forced the nearby Fort Moultrie into submission, the revolutionaries surrendered on May 12. In one of the greatest British victories of the war, Clinton took 5,266 soldiers and militiamen prisoner and seized nearly 6,000 muskets, 311 artillery pieces, and 49 merchant vessels lying in the harbor. Denying the Continental Army the honors of war, the general imprisoned ordinary soldiers and released officers on parole within the city, hoping to exchange them for the British and German troops taken prisoner at Saratoga. Soon after Charleston's surrender, Continental resistance folded almost completely in South Carolina. After granting parole to Continental and militia officers who promised to lay down their arms and issuing entice-ments for loyal civilians and escaped slaves to take up arms and fight for the British, Clinton sailed back to New York on June 8. In his stead, the com-mander in chief left his longtime subordinate, Lieutenant General Earl Charles Cornwallis, in command of approximately 6,300 troops in South Carolina, with orders to collect as many loyalists as possible and secure the allegiance of the entire province to Great Britain.[82]

Cornwallis largely succeeded in his task, and by midsummer of 1780 revolutionary forces had mostly abandoned South Carolina. Marching northwest from the city in August 1780, Cornwallis defeated a larger Ameri-can force near the town of Camden, South Carolina, forcing the Continen-tals into a disorderly retreat into North Carolina. Cornwallis also secured military posts across the western portions of the state, reopened the port of Charleston to European and West Indian trade, and seized rebel plantations everywhere. Ex-rebels and those who wished to remain neutral flocked to Charleston to seek British protection, and by the end of the year the British position seemed so secure that Cornwallis decided to move the bulk of his army into North Carolina, hoping to capitalize on British victories and loyalist support to subdue the remnants of the American army south of New York.[83]

With the fall of Charleston in 1780, each major port city had fallen under British control at one time or another. But military rule was not a

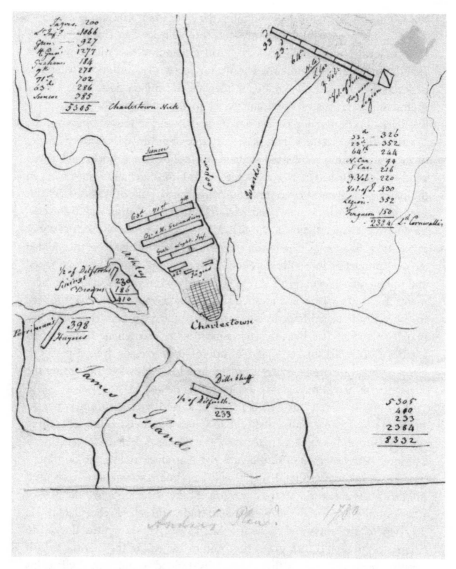

Figure 6. *Distribution and Strength of [British] Corps [in Charleston], 1780.*
Courtesy William L. Clements Library.

novelty. British armies had come on the heels of a revolutionary government that had imposed its authority through force of arms. Circumstances
differed, often vastly, by region and time period. In the earlier occupations
of Boston, Newport, and New York, the struggle for authority between
rebels and royalists had been ongoing when British troops instituted military rule, whereas in Philadelphia, Savannah, and Charleston revolutionary
authorities had held power for years before British occupation began. Still,
British rule was something different. As Peter Edes found when he was
arrested in Boston during the summer of 1775, the British Army dispensed
with the pretenses of civil government, placing civilians fully under a harsh
regime of military justice. Now, offenses that would have been punished
with a fine or a day in the stocks under civilian rule now carried imprisonment, whippings, or even death. As they imposed these harsh new realities
on American civilians, British troops often doubled or even outnumbered
the local populations at times, creating a logistical nightmare for the officers
and officials in charge of feeding, housing, and clothing both civilians and
soldiers. Further, orders from home, especially in the later occupations,
demanded that commanders reconcile those Americans willing to swear
allegiance to the Crown and create in occupied cities safe havens for persecuted loyalists in rebel-controlled areas.

Despite the importance British officials attached to currying favor with
local populations, army officers and ordinary soldiers alike only vaguely
understood the intricacies of the situations in which they found themselves.
Officers, while sometimes aware of local populations' dispositions, often
were too busy caring for their men or setting up supply chains to deal with
civilian matters unless it fell within their explicit duties. The commanders
in chief, William Howe and Henry Clinton, concerned themselves primarily
with obtaining military glory, chafing at Lord George Germain's orders to
solicit the support of local populations. Although both men fancied themselves peacemakers, neither took time to fully understand the nuances of
urban politics. Thus, while they did make moves to coerce civilians to sign
loyalty oaths in each city they captured, Howe and Clinton did little to
ameliorate the divisions that they found in occupied cities—indeed, they
often took advantage of them to solidify the Crown's position. Subordinate
officers largely followed suit: although they delighted in socializing with the
colonial elite and pursuing entertainments such as balls, concerts, and
plays, they largely saw themselves as warriors rather than agents of peace
and reconciliation. Ordinary soldiers mingled with civilians on a much

wider basis, but the strict military hierarchy to which they belonged prevented them from transmitting knowledge gained from these connections
to their superiors. The British Army thus proved, with a few exceptions,
ineffective and largely uninterested in civilian matters.[84]

In the absence of both concrete knowledge about city populations' tem-
perament and a policy to deal with civilians who came under their authority, British commanders relied on a cadre of former colonial officials and
elite loyalists to provide intelligence and administer military towns. Using
these civilians in a quasi-military manner, Howe and Clinton set up ad hoc
civil administrations. Under officials such as Andrew Elliot, a former tax
collector who managed the port and headed informal civil courts in New
York, and James Simpson, a former attorney general who created the powerful board of police in occupied Charleston, these regimes grew increasingly sophisticated throughout the war. As time went on, they worked their
way into the structure of martial law and became hybrid civil-military
administrations whose agendas often differed from those of the British military officers ostensibly in charge of the occupied cities. For ordinary people
living under military rule, these imperfect power-sharing arrangements created conditions in which their own experiences often belied the assurances
of those in power and ultimately forced civilians to turn to themselves,
rather than royal authorities, to get by—ultimately eroding what at the
outset seemed an all-encompassing occupying force.

CHAPTER 2

Collaborator Regimes

In each city under British occupation, military commanders worked with former officials and prominent loyalists to give inhabitants a stake in the success of renewed royal rule. Although many of these people had been exiled, imprisoned, or otherwise insulted by the revolutionary governments, they still knew their communities well, and worked in good faith to convince their neighbors to support the occupation regimes. Many argued for the reinstatement of full civil government and the restoration of colonial representative assemblies, although no occupied area except Georgia ever achieved this status. Under military supervision, though, civilians and soldiers collaborated to create temporary governments capable of dispensing justice, providing poor relief, and taking on many other municipal tasks. In doing so, these civil-military regimes sought to convince residents of port cities that restored royal rule was not only tenable but preferable to revolutionary government.

The experiences of Ambrose Serle, personal secretary to Admiral Lord Richard Howe, explicate how many of these civil-military partnerships formed. Over the course of six days during the spring of 1777, Serle spoke to, entertained, and dined with dozens of British officers, elite loyalists, and ousted colonial officials. On May 12, 1777, he took a long walk to visit the upper Manhattan villa of Andrew Elliot, former customs collector of the colony of New York. The next day, he dined with former South Carolina attorney general James Simpson. On May 14, he supped with several of the military officers responsible for administering the British occupation of the city, including former governor William Tryon, now a general in the loyalist corps responsible for the town's defense. Four days later, Serle had a long evening's conversation with his close friend Joseph Galloway, a former speaker of the Pennsylvania Assembly and an original member of the Continental Congress who had ultimately sided with the British cause. Galloway himself had just returned from a visit to Elizabeth Franklin, whose husband, William, languished in a New Jersey prison after his ouster as royal governor of that province.[1] The week was typical of Serle's experience during the first half of 1777, which, aside from official duties, consisted mostly of conversations, carriage rides, lavish dinners, and late-night drinking sessions with a vast array of well-to-do loyalists and British Army officers.

Serle's social activities reveal the vibrant social circle formed by the mingling of the military elite and gentlemen loyalists from across the rebelling colonies, most of whom had held political offices at one point or another. At first glance, fraternization between these two groups seems incidental. Most men who populated occupied New York's elite social scene shared similar educations, ambitions, and tastes in literature, food, and wine. Serle seemed to enjoy at least a few of his new companions on a personal level, going for long, meandering walks with Joseph Galloway in New York and, later, carriage rides along the Schuylkill River in Philadelphia.[2] However, Howe's secretary spent most of his free time discussing politics with the colonial officials he encountered, often debating the finer points of Anglo-American relations until late in the evening.

The civilian acquaintances Serle made in the first months of New York's occupation, especially the former officials, would go on to play crucial roles in occupation policy throughout the war. General Sir William Howe appointed Andrew Elliot superintendent of imports and exports, then head of the police for New York, effectively giving him control over much of the civil policy for a majority of the city's seven-year occupation. Later in the war, Elliot secured an appointment from George III as New York's lieutenant governor and ended the conflict as the province's last royally sanctioned governor. Galloway became superintendent of police during the short-lived British occupation of Philadelphia from September 1777 until June 1778, retreating to London after the British evacuation of that city and becoming a consultant on American affairs to various imperial policy makers through the 1780s. When the British Army turned its attention south in 1778, James Simpson shaped civil policies for the occupations of Georgia and South Carolina, and for the first year of military rule in Charleston he headed up the administration. The network of former officials, loyalists, and officers that emerged in the first months of New York City's occupation became the basis for leadership in occupied zones throughout the rebellious colonies.

Several of the military officers who populated New York during the early months of occupation also became leading figures in crafting occupation policy throughout the war. General Sir William Howe, the brother of Serle's employer, had taken over as commander in chief of the British Army a year earlier in the midst of the occupation of Boston, and would go on to coordinate occupation policies in New York, Newport, and Philadelphia, consulting frequently with prominent loyalists and former officials such as Tryon, Elliot, and Galloway.[3] Major General Daniel Jones, with whom Serle, along with Governor Tryon, had "much Conversation about the Cruelties shewn by the Rebels to the loyal Subjects" in early December 1776, later secured an appointment as military commandant of New York City, a post he held until 1779 and in which he worked closely with Elliot.[4] Henry Clinton—himself knighted in 1777—went on to succeed Howe as commander in chief of the British Army in America, overseeing changes in occupation policy in New York and implementing new administrations in Savannah and Charleston.[5] Major Nisbet Balfour, with whom Serle and Galloway dined in May 1777, would three years later become military commandant of occupied Charlestown, partnering with Simpson in creating perhaps the most ambitious occupation regime of the war.[6]

As the army entered new territories, occupation regimes evolved so that successive administrations reflected the experiences of previous ones, as well as local conditions and changing strategic goals. While the administration of occupied Boston was hurried and ad hoc, sympathetic members of the local elite cooperated with the British military in order to govern the town, and the army began to make haphazard attempts to involve ordinary townspeople in the occupation regime. When British troops garrisoned New York, military officers and prominent loyalists began for the first time to deliberately consider the ways in which port towns under occupation could not only provide bases for military campaigns but also zones of refuge for persecuted loyalists and bastions of royal rule to encourage loyalty among the larger population, many of whom were far from stalwart in the revolutionary cause. The occupation regimes of Philadelphia and Newport mimicked the civil administration of New York and developed in conversation with one another. Observing the weaknesses of the limited civil powers granted to loyalist officials in New York, Newport, and Philadelphia, the

British Army restored full civil government when it conquered Georgia, restoring Governor Sir James Wright in Savannah and reestablishing the provincial assembly. Despite high hopes, Sir James's government proved less effective than the military in administering territory. The occupation of Charleston one year later reflected lessons learned from all five previous attempts at military rule, resulting in a civil-military partnership on a much grander scale than anywhere else.

In different contexts, occupation administrations in all six cities aimed to give Americans a stake in military rule. The regimes that developed along the North American coast each sought to instill loyalty in the surrounding areas by providing financial and social incentives to cooperate and return their allegiance to the Crown. To that end, occupation governments took measures to maintain order in the streets of these ports and to minimize conflict between soldiers and civilians. They recruited civilians as to act as constables, overseers of the poor, and in other municipal capacities rendered defunct by military rule. Officials also used civic and military resources to improve public works, clean streets, and provide other services. These administrations embarked on large public works programs and regulated the institution of slavery in ways that they hoped would align with local sensibilities. In short, occupation governments incorporated a wide range of local residents in a cooperative civil-military structure, and large numbers of urbanites, even those who had rebelled against the Crown, accepted this compromise and collaborated with British military authorities.

Despite their best efforts, however, in the long run these regimes failed to convince ordinary people to acquiesce to restored royal rule. Although they gave many ordinary citizens a stake in the success of British military government—and attempted in good faith to actually improve the lives of the people living under them—these regimes proved increasingly unresponsive to the struggles taking place at the ground level. Although they provided work, aid, housing, and access to courts in exchange for allegiance, occupation governments could not alleviate many of the problems of life within a military garrison. Violence, shortages, and exploitation continued despite the best efforts of occupation regimes. By the end of the war, even those with the most faith in the civil administrations—including some of those who actually participated in the regimes—had come to regard them as illegitimate. This abandonment was not due to a lack of effort or planning on the part of the civilian and military officials who headed these governments, but rather to the fact that the everyday experiences of Americans belied their promises.

To keep order when the onset of violence sparked a hostile siege of Boston, General Thomas Gage sought to foster close collaboration with the American elite to maintain peace within the city. Siege conditions split families, created food and fuel shortages, and threatened the lives of both civilians and soldiers. To mitigate these hardships, Gage consulted frequently with the town's selectmen and even the revolutionary Committee of Safety during the first months of the war. In these negotiations, British officers and local elites reached several compromises that benefitted both sides.[7] Coordination between occupying forces and Boston civilians continued under General Howe, who replaced Gage in early 1776. Whereas Gage had sought to facilitate the movement of patriots out of the city and loyalists into it in order to shore up security on both sides, Howe sought to engage the citizenry remaining inside the town. In a proclamation printed in October 1775, Howe called for the embodiment of Boston's loyal male citizenry into companies "for the Preservation of Order & good Government within the Town of Boston."[8] These companies were to be led by members of the local elite, who were issued weapons and rationed on the same terms as the British Army.

For their part, Boston's civilians also made efforts to cooperate with the military during the siege. Appended to Howe's proclamation was a declaration of association created by several "quiet & obedient subjects" in the town, who declared it their duty "to contribute our aid in promoting the peace, order, and security of the town." Peter Oliver, Foster Hutchinson, and William Brown, the Bostonians appointed in the proclamation as leaders of the civilian defense companies, were also prominent signatories of this association.[9] Oliver, Hutchinson, and Brown were not ordinary loyalists. Each had connections with the former colonial government: Oliver, for example, had been the colony's chief justice, and Hutchinson was another high-ranking magistrate and the brother of a former governor.[10] Howe's proclamation represented not only outreach to the population but also positive response from the city's influential loyalists. By allying himself with vestiges of the former colonial regime and empowering its former officials, Howe hoped both to give the occupation a sense of legitimacy and, more importantly, to give loyalists who remained in occupied Boston a stake in the regime. For those on the fence about their allegiance, these actions demonstrated that British rule might, in fact, become more inclusive and responsive to the needs of local populations once the crisis had ended.

The extensive collaboration between Boston's military government and the town's civilian elite became a model for other cities under British control. With the occupation of New York in November 1776, however, collaborations between civilian leadership and military officials became more formal. Once the garrison had been established, former officials and elite loyalists from across the thirteen colonies fled to occupied New York hoping to help the British war effort and possibly recover their lost positions. These members of the American gentry sought out connections with the gentlemen of the British Army and Royal Navy, and the political collaborations that would shape the face of occupation throughout the war evolved from the interaction between the two groups.

Civilian participation in occupation regimes primarily took the form of police systems, which existed in every occupied city from New York onward. Headed by superintendents drawn from the ranks of the old colonial government and staffed by other Americans loyal to the Crown, the police took on many of the duties of municipal bureaucracies, cooperating with the military to carry on essential city functions. These governments managed departures and arrivals of ports, regulated imports and exports, granted licenses for taverns and other businesses, made efforts to curb street crime, prevented fires, and promoted public works. Although structures differed from city to city, these bureaucracies formed the basis for deeper collaborations between the military and civilian loyalists. Despite the fact that police officials remained dependent on the military for enforcement of their power, these administrations organized large numbers of people under their auspices and, for the most part, effectively governed occupied cities and their populations.

Andrew Elliot, the chief civil officer in occupied New York, was typical of the leaders of these regimes. Leading collaborators tended to be people in the middle ranks of the imperial bureaucracy who had maintained moderate positions prior to the war. Elliot immigrated to Philadelphia from Scotland in 1746 at the age of eighteen, and became the customs collector for the Port of New York in 1764. Despite his position as a royal official, Elliot sympathized with many New York merchants in their protests against the Stamp Act and the Townshend duties during the 1760s, and had used his office to grant liberal terms to the city's traders, with the approbation of successive royal governors and with an eye toward mollifying both the mercantile community and the imperial administration. As a result, Elliot was able to collect taxes effectively while maintaining the affection of many New Yorkers well into the revolutionary period. He did not flee the city until March 1776, several months after the governor had repaired to the harbor and well after New York had been occupied by Continental troops. As the revolution raged, Elliot received multiple assurances of safety by influential merchants, and even members of New York's revolutionary provincial congress. While ultimately forced to flee to New Jersey before returning when General Howe's forces occupied the city, Elliot nevertheless retained some trust among the city's businesspeople and a good reputation with Crown officials. For Howe, then, he must have seemed an ideal choice to act as a mediator between the military and the city's civilian population.[11]

New York's occupation government began to take shape in the summer of 1777, when Howe appointed Elliot as superintendent of imports and exports. As the chief civil officer of the city's port, Elliot became responsible once more for enforcing customs regulations, inspecting vessels arriving and departing, and seizing contraband.[12] Later given the additional title of superintendent general of the police, Elliot also exercised a wide range of civil authority, trying misdemeanors in an ad hoc civil court, regulating taverns, and organizing fire companies, among other duties.[13] To aid the superintendent in these duties, Howe appointed two deputies, along with an assortment of clerks, searchers, warehouse keepers, and other functionaries.[14] By 1781, thirteen people in addition to Elliot claimed full-time employment in the office of the police, and dozens more worked for the administration part-time.[15] Beyond these direct employees, hundreds of civilians received aid in the form of subsidized housing, rations, or public works contracts from the police. New York's office of police had become a complex bureaucratic structure to complement that of the military in governing the city.

Under these auspices, Elliot's administration performed a wide variety of municipal tasks that would have earlier fallen to New York's colonial government. The civil establishment took on poor relief, forming a vestry, or council of leading citizens, to rent out vacant houses—typically those of New Yorkers who had left the city before the British conquest—and to administer funds allocated for charity.[16] This organization, under the supervision of Elliot's police, wielded considerable power as collector of rents owed for houses of absentees. As the superintendent later recounted, "a small Proportion" of abandoned houses were "occupied by Gentlemen

Refugees of Character and Fortune, whose Circumstances made such aid absolutely necessary." Other buildings the regime "set aside for the use of the Army, Public Department, Military and naval Store Houses, &c&c." The majority, however, were "put under the direction of Forty of the Principle Inhabitants of this Town"—the vestry—"and rented out" to people in need. However, public welfare did not stop at subsidized housing. Rent money paid to the civilian administration went toward "assisting a number of indigent Families that must have starved or been supported by government," as well as "maintaining in an Alms House about 300 Aged and infirm Poor, together with the Orphans of the Refugees and Military." Elliot's police not only functioned to enforce loyalty to the occupation regime but also to help those who had embraced it.[17]

In many cases, the occupation administration interceded with the military in favor of civilians. In the spring of 1778, rent collectors found a group of soldiers' wives living in a house that a civilian wanted to rent, and convinced the commanding general to order "the acting barrack master to turn the soldiers wives out of this house, that it may be rented."[18] Collectors also exercised a great deal of discretion in terms of when to collect. Although George Elizer, a free black man who lived with his family at 60 Wall Street, willingly paid the half-yearly rent of £5 for his "very miserable house" in March 1778, the rent collector determined that "the money ought to be returned him" due to the poor condition of the dwelling.[19] Fence Reilly, who lived in a vestry house at 21 Dock Street, had his rent reduced in consideration of soldiers also quartered there who "rob'd him of effects to the amount of £40."[20] Like Elizer and Reilly, many New Yorkers found themselves under the care of the vestry. By the end of the occupation, New York's civil government rented out 260 houses owned by residents residing outside the lines to persons and families in financial distress. These houses brought in an annual rent of just over £3,155.[21] Considering that many of these houses likely contained multiple families and were rented and re-rented several times over the course of the occupation, it stands to reason that the vestry wielded a great deal of authority in occupied New York.

Beyond those who rented vestry houses, New York's wartime civil government benefited hundreds civilian contractors and others in need of employment. Between April 15 and July 31, 1783, the city's occupation administration dispensed just over £5,357 from public accounts for various expenditures. Of this, £1,514 went to the commissioners and overseers of the poor, £1,582 went toward salaries of officers "acting under proclamations" of the military government, and the rest went to repairing houses, street maintenance, lighting, and other municipal concerns. Much of this money came from rents, license fees, and other traditional sources of municipal revenue. In addition to more than £3,000 brought in by the rent of vestry houses, the city counted £22 from tavern, grogshop, and inn licenses and £210 from rents on the Brooklyn ferry. This money was dispensed under the official authority of New York's military commandant but reflected extensive cooperation with the police. By the spring of 1783 the civil-military administration of New York had not only authority over a great deal of resources but also a finely tuned system for accounting and distributing these monies to the population, reflecting the sophistication of the enterprise.

Through the power of the purse, New York's civil-military administration touched the lives not only of those in positions of power but of thousands of city residents of lesser means. In addition to those who received direct charity or rent relief from the vestry, civil officers received compensation for such activities as inspecting taverns, collecting rents, enforcing regulations on the price and size of loaves of bread, and serving as justices of the peace, among other duties.[22] Other contractors received money for providing services such as street cleaning and building repair.[23] Presumably, these men were not doing the work themselves but employed dozens or perhaps hundreds of laborers who drew their pay from the government disbursements. Other workers were paid directly. The city's occupation regime paid an F. Bottecher three pounds, eight shillings, and six pence for "erecting a privy" on the grounds of Mayor David Mathews's house.[24] William Black received sixteen shillings for "fixing Pulleys" on the doors to the police office.[25] James Rivington, printer of the loyalist-leaning *Royal Gazette*, made a small fortune from the occupation government, collecting money for printing advertisements on behalf of Elliot's police and supplying the administration with stationery and ink. The printer was the preferred vendor throughout the occupation, though the regime also paid for advertisements in a rival paper, Hugh Gaine's more moderate *New York Gazette and Weekly Mercury*.[26] Other purveyors received money or goods that went directly to their workers. In the summer of 1783, Moses Pitcher and several other people received payments for rum provided to a crew of African American workers employed in cleaning the streets.[27] The wide spectrum of New Yorkers and refugees that benefited from money dispensed by the city's administration gave thousands of people a stake in the success of British occupation.

In addition to activities in its own right, the office of police cooperated extensively with New York's military hierarchy. Elliot's powers as superintendent of police were enumerated and reinforced many times by the city's ranking officers. Major General Daniel Jones, the commandant of New York when Elliot received police powers, delegated many different responsibilities to the civilian office. In July 1778, Jones asked the superintendent to form a city watch made up of civilians in each of the various wards to maintain order in streets that were quickly filling with refugees from the countryside.[28] In the months that followed, Elliot received the authority to regulate woodcutting privileges, oversee chimney sweeping, award licenses for taverns, and set rates for cartage in the city.[29] These powers represented a large part of the running of the city, gave the office of police authority over a wide variety of civil employees and, through fees and fines, potentially provided a great deal of money to draw on as well.

Jones also granted Elliot and his fellow magistrates discretion over whether or not to send petty criminals to the military for court martial and potential exile from New York. In doing so, the commandant conceded that not only were civilian authorities better at administering municipal functions but also at dispensing justice for American civilians. Jones's order emphasized this distinction, calling the magistrates of police "better Judges of their [disorderly inhabitants'] Character than officers that compose a Court Martial."[30] Elliot decided, along with the military, what would happen to those criminals. According to Jones, the ultimate punishment would be to turn such "disorderly inhabitants" out of the lines, exiling them to the mercy of hostile revolutionary governments. Other punishments included flogging, recommended for unruly slaves and servants whose labor could still be valuable, and impressment into the navy, which Jones recommended for "all able bodied Men white or Black that may be guilty of petty crimes."[31] Although military officers actually carried out these sentences, Elliot's police apparatus referred the cases to the military, giving the superintendent and his associates a great deal of power over the behavior of New York's civilians. An opponent of the regime might find him- or herself exiled for a minor offense, while a supporter's crimes might be overlooked.

As the war continued, the military depended more and more on New York's civilian police to administer the city. Jones's successor, General James Pattison, turned to the police to take care of nearly every civil matter of which he received complaint. These functions ranged from road repairs to cleaning up rotten fish to suppressing illegal distilleries.[32] Going beyond orders giving the police jurisdiction over inhabitants apprehended by the city watch, Pattison ordered that magistrates, in conjunction with military officers, meet once a week to determine what to do with inhabitants brought into the main guard by military patrols as well.[33] Further, Pattison demonstrated a willingness to enforce civil decisions with military force. In writing to a debtor who refused to pay the judgment ordered by the civil administrators, Pattison declared that he was "determined to support the authority of the Magistrates of Police," and threatened "disagreeable consequences" should the debtor not pay up.[34] Elliot's regime had become an integral part of the occupation government of New York; one that functioned efficiently, received support from the military, and wielded actual power in conducting the business of the city.

New York's police system provided a template for officials and their loyalist allies to build upon in planning the administrations of other occupied zones. When he appointed Joseph Galloway as superintendent of imports and exports in occupied Philadelphia in December 1777, General Howe took parts of the commission verbatim from Elliot's equivalent appointment in New York. As in New York, Howe granted Galloway extensive powers to regulate Philadelphia's port and a staff of deputies and other minor officials to aid him. As he did with Elliot, Howe later made Galloway superintendent of police, adding a great deal of civil power to his appointment. New York's regime so deeply informed the formation of civil government in occupied Philadelphia that Galloway's orders explicitly referenced—and in some cases were taken verbatim from—those given to Elliot months earlier.[35]

Like the former New York customs collector, Galloway had a background that positioned him as a potential mediator between British military authorities and a wary population. A longtime political ally of Benjamin Franklin, Galloway had taken a moderate position during the imperial crisis, sympathizing with colonial discontent but never losing his faith in royal rule. In 1774, Galloway represented Pennsylvania at the First Continental Congress, where he proposed a constitutional compromise that moved within one vote of adoption by the colonies, and the language of which made its way into the Declaration of Colonial Rights produced by that body. Despite election to the Second Continental Congress, Galloway retired from politics in mid-1775, refusing to go along with moves toward independence and rebellion, despite Franklin's personal appeals. Torn between his friendships and his loyalty to the king, Galloway did not declare for one side or the other until November 1776, when he finally left his rural Pennsylvania farm for a British encampment in New Jersey. Once he arrived in British territory, the former Continental Congressman made his way to New York and became a trusted advisor to General Howe, eventually accompanying him to Philadelphia to take up the civil administration of the occupation less than a year after he had left his home.[36]

As the British military ruled over both New York and Philadelphia in the winter of 1777–1778, the two cities' civil governments developed in tandem. While both remained arms of the military, they also provided a way for civilians to influence policy within the chain of command. The British Army needed not just the labor of these loyalist bureaucrats to implement policy but their advice and wisdom on local affairs as well. In his initial instructions to Elliot, General Howe concluded by noting that "the Office of Superintendent being intirely [sic] new, it is impossible to foresee the difficulties that may arise in the Execution of it," and asking Elliot to continue to keep him informed of his progress and forward to him any suggestions for improving efficiency in occupation government.[37] Howe's instructions to Galloway bore the same direction, soliciting the new superintendent for "any Observations that your Experience may suggest, for rendering the Plan more perfect."[38] Howe would not have included these instructions, nor would he have created the superintendencies of police, had he not needed the counsel as well as the cooperation of these loyalist officials.

The correspondence between Elliot, Galloway, and Howe in the months after their appointments reveals the extensive collaboration between the commander in chief and the heads of the civilian administrations. In July 1777, Elliot sent Howe a draft of policies intended to facilitate importation of supplies and exportation of goods out of New York City.[39] Though busy with the Philadelphia campaign, Howe nevertheless responded in December of the same year, advising Elliot that he could not "admit of any Exportation whatever from the Port of New York to Great Britain, Ireland or the West Indies which you are to make the Rule of your conduct in future," although exports to Newport, Philadelphia, and other British posts in North America were acceptable.[40] Four days after Howe's reply to Elliot, Galloway reported detaining a ship with a cargo of barrel staves bound for the West Indies. As the ship turned out to be a transport in the royal service,

Galloway posed the further question of whether such regulations applied to vessels employed by the military.[41]

Policies for export and seizure of vessels continued to take shape as Galloway's and Elliot's administrations evolved. In January 1778, Elliot also detained a vessel, the brigantine *Betsy*, for attempting to smuggle salt out of New York. Since an officer of the navy had actually detained the vessel, Elliot queried whether or not the condemned goods should be considered a prize of war, or whether, as with a customs seizure, the illegal provisions aboard the *Betsy* should go into the city's resources. If a prize, the vessel and its cargo would be returned to Great Britain for sale; if a customs case, they would remain in New York. Further, continuing the policy discussion, Elliot asked Howe to reconsider allowing New Yorkers to export to the West Indies, as he feared not doing so would cripple the city's already weakened economy.[42] In his response, Howe claimed that he had restricted exports due to Parliament's Prohibitory Act of 1775, which continued to impose an embargo on American ports as a punitive action meant to suppress the rebellion.[43] When Elliot objected further in February, Howe consulted Galloway in his capacity as a legal expert.[44] Although military and civilian priorities were not always compatible, Howe, Elliot, and Galloway made deliberate, good-faith efforts to solve problems and create effective systems of municipal governance. As they did so, occupation regimes evolved not unilaterally but as the result of constant conversation between high-ranking military officers and civilians.

Even after the British withdrawal from Philadelphia and Howe's resignation in the spring of 1778, later occupation regimes—most notably that of Charleston, South Carolina—followed New York's example of collaboration between former civil officials and the military. In planning and execution, Charleston's police system went far beyond what had existed previously in occupied America. In order to maintain control over the newly conquered state of South Carolina, British Army officers and their loyalist supporters imagined, as one early memorandum authored by former South Carolina attorney general James Simpson put it, "a plan of more general jurisdiction . . . than what is proposed by Mr. Elliott [*sic*]" in New York.[45] To maintain control of the entire province, the officials proposed appointing an intendant general of police to not only preside over Charleston but also to empower intendants of police in any region under British control. The intendant general would assign three or more intendants of police for the Charleston district, who, along with the intendant general

himself, would make up a political advisory council to the city's commandant and, when necessary, the general commanding British forces in South
Carolina. The intendants of police would have the power to appoint constables in their districts and would "execute the duties usually exercised by
justices of the Peace, church wardens, [and] overseers of the poor or high-
ways."[46] As proposed, the statewide board of police would exercise wide-
ranging powers of civil administration in both the capital and the
hinterlands.

As with Elliot and Galloway, James Simpson's background and temper-
ament prepared him to mediate between civilian interests and the military
rulers. Born in South Carolina, Simpson had risen from clerk of the governor's council to acting attorney general of the province in the years before
the revolution.[47] Despite his high position in the royal bureaucracy, however, Simpson's name nevertheless appears on the roll of a voluntary militia
company associated with South Carolina's revolutionary Council of Safety
in October 1775, indicating that, in the beginning of the rebellion, Simpson
had at the very least recognized the authority of the insurgent government.[48] Nevertheless, Simpson refused to sign an oath of allegiance to the
revolutionary state, and a subsequent one to the new government of the
United States in the summer of 1776, resulting in his exile. After short
sojourns in New York and London, Simpson returned to North America in
the aftermath of the British conquest of Georgia, venturing into revolutionary territory and reconnoitering the planters of South Carolina in preparation for the planned invasion. After making his report to Clinton, Simpson
became secretary to the commander in chief's council in New York, where
he worked closely with loyalist officials like Andrew Elliot.[49] It was during
this period that he likely formed his plan for civil government once the
province was retaken, taking careful note of Elliot's successes and missteps.
Finally, he accompanied Clinton to Charleston and became superintendent
of the city's police after the surrender of the revolutionary garrison. His
prior experience with both the state's population and the British military
regime of New York no doubt guided him in his task.

South Carolina's police explicitly intended from the outset to convince
civilians to become loyalists. The proposal for a new government concerned
itself not only with maintaining civil order but also with "calming the
minds and conciliating the Affections of the People." As such, it strove to
appear as nonpolitical as possible. According to Simpson's plan, appointments to the board of police and other public offices should be based on

merit rather than political allegiance. As the superintendent put it, "Their fitness for the Duty will be what is most material," while "their Political opinions will be of no Consequence."[50] By allowing persons of any political persuasion to act as intendants of police, the British encouraged elites and petty magistrates who had supported the revolutionary government to return to their loyalty by offering them a stake in the British administration.

In a further attempt to sway public opinion, Simpson's plan also granted the civilian board of police extensive power to regulate slavery, allowing intendants to mediate between masters and slaves and to capture and return escaped slaves to their former owners—so long as those owners avowed their loyalty to the king.[51] Since there remained a great number of self-emancipated slaves under the protection of the British Army, their potential peaceful return to former masters could be a powerful tool in inspiring loyalty among the enslavers. If a slaveholder played by the rules and accepted the intendants of police as a legitimate civil authority, he had a better chance to regain his property. Granting the police authority over slavery also affirmed the importance of the institution in the state, quelling the fears of many—at least temporarily—that the British Army would be a vehicle for blacks to gain their freedom. The plan explicitly protected the institution of slavery—and slave property—in the postrevolutionary imperial government of South Carolina, assuring wavering slave owners that their investments would be safe.

The regime that Simpson supervised reflected many of his earlier ambitions, although it never reached beyond Charleston. In addition to the superintendent, the board of police also comprised Robert Powell, a prominent merchant; Alexander Wright, a wealthy planter; and Colonel Alexander Innes, former secretary to the royal governor of South Carolina and an officer of the city's British garrison.[52] The members of the board drew salaries paid by the British Army, performed a wide range of civil functions, and exercised broad powers to regulate slavery. For much of 1780 and 1781, the police also acted as an advisory council to the city's military commanders. In January 1781, Charleston's commandant wrote of Simpson that he could not describe "how much I have been Obliged to this Gentleman's Attention and Abilities in Conducting the police and adjusting much of the very complex business of this Town and Province."[53] Even if the board fell short of the early planners' grand vision for a province-wide government, it reflected many of the innovations proposed to encourage loyalty and maintaining order.

The occupations of Newport and Savannah also incorporated police systems, although their roles are not as clear as those in New York, Philadelphia, and Charleston. In Newport, former lieutenant governor Joseph Wanton Jr. took on the role of superintendent of police, though surviving records do not speak to the extent of Newport's office of police beyond the employment of a clerk, a messenger, and an office cleaner.[54] In Savannah, the British military established a board of police immediately after the conquest of the city, primarily to deal with estates and enslaved people abandoned by fleeing rebels, but it was also empowered to license taverns and administer the city in ways similar to the police offices of New York and Philadelphia.[55] This body only lasted two months, however, as the British Army quickly reestablished civil government in conquered Georgia. Still, its officers remained the de facto power behind the civilian government throughout the occupation of Savannah.[56] Police systems thus formed a cornerstone of British occupation policy.

Still, institutional avenues other than police bureaucracies also thrived in cities under British Army rule. To win hearts and minds in Georgia, British authorities experimented with the restoration of a full civilian administration—territory captured from the former revolutionary state would be regarded as belonging to a restored royal colony rather than as occupied territory. Although it would never be repeated elsewhere, the restoration of full civil authority in the province was intended as an experiment that would eventually encompass the rest of occupied America. Lieutenant Colonel Archibald Campbell, the officer in charge of the expedition to Georgia in the fall of 1778, carried with him express authority from General Clinton to reestablish full civil power both in Georgia and, if his expedition could effect it, in South Carolina as well. Campbell's orders even contained "provisional Appointments to the Governments of those Provinces to be produced & carried into Execution," should the lieutenant colonel see any opportunity to "encourage & maintain any considerable proportion of the Inhabitants in a Return of Loyalty to their Sovereign and of affection to their fellow Subjects."[57] For military planners, the conquest of Georgia and its reintegration into the British Empire might have inspired other rebelling colonies to return to their loyalty in hopes of a swift end to the rebellion.

Although Campbell never took up the governorship of Georgia for himself, his early administration paved the way for the reinstatement of colonial government. Upon the conquest of Georgia and the flight of the

Continental Army from the province, Campbell and his naval counterpart, Commodore Hyde Parker, issued a proclamation promising protection to Georgians who swore their loyalty to the king.[58] In March 1779, three months after the conquest, Sir James Wright received orders from White-hall to return to Georgia and resume his position as governor. Wright arrived in mid-July and took power from Campbell's replacement, Briga-dier General Augustine Prevost, proclaiming Georgia officially at the king's peace and recalling many of his former subordinates—including the colo-nial lieutenant governor and chief justice—to their duties.[59] While Sir James did not find himself in a position to restore the full legislative power of the province of Georgia by immediately calling for an assembly, his leadership did take such steps as appointing justices of the peace, taking measures to control the spread of smallpox, and administering loyalty oaths.[60] Although tenuous, Wright's government showed the potential to, as Campbell put it in a report to Lord George Germain, "rend a Stripe and Star from the Flag of Congress" and return Georgia to royal rule.[61] In this sense, both military and civilian elements shared many of the same goals and collaborated to achieve them.

During the 1779 siege of Savannah, Georgia's civil and military officials united in the defense of the town, showing remarkable cohesion. In his report to Germain, Wright wrote that, when faced with a demand for sur-render from the French admiral Count D'Estaing, "it was the Unanimous opinion & Resolution of the *Civil* and military [authorities] to defend the Town," which delighted him, as the governor had "*strong* Reasons to appre-hend and fear the Contrary."[62] Sir James's emphasis on the civil govern-ment's commitment to protect the city is significant. While he heaped praise on the military in his letters to Whitehall, other accounts of the siege of Savannah suggest that General Prevost, at least initially, waffled and even attempted to negotiate honorable terms for the surrender of the city.[63] The town was ill-provisioned for a siege, and French and Continental troops heavily outnumbered the British garrison. As D'Estaing stressed in his sur-render demand, the same French army now preparing to besiege Savannah had met with great success in the West Indies, and the admiral menacingly reminded the town's defenders "how much Lord McCartney had suffered by not capitulating in Grenada" upon his force's arrival.[64] Seen in this light, the civil government's enthusiasm for defending the city may have tipped the balance in favor of defiance over surrender. Further, Wright and his council exercised their authority to employ several hundred of the slaves and free blacks in their power to help build fortifications and recruited volunteers from among the population and merchant ships. Wright also took an active role in directing the town's defense. He and his lieutenant governor lived in the military camp for the duration of the siege and may even have been present at the decisive assault on the redoubt at Ebenezer, Georgia, where a final assault by French and Continental troops was repulsed after a bloody struggle.[65] Civil-military cooperation not only supported the defense of the town but was essential to victory in the siege of Savannah.

After the successful defense of against the French and Continentals, Wright's government came to resemble the prior colonial administration even more. In January 1780, Wright and his administration presided over the first legal trials in British Georgia since the onset of the war. As the governor reported to Lord Germain, the court convicted three people of misdemeanors and treasonous activities, with another three on the docket for the next court. Wright expressed his desire that "the Judgments and Sentences" of the court would "Strengthen and Support Government," which Wright assured his superior "at Present Stands in Great Need of it."[66] The new civil government of Georgia continued to take steps in early 1780 to secure its hold on the population. In April, Sir James issued writs of election for a new assembly, cementing his restored government's legitimacy and enabling him to begin to pass bills and make changes to Georgia's colonial laws. Although much of the legislation stalled, the assembly still took up such issues as crafting policies to punish known rebels and to help impoverished loyalists.[67] By 1781, Wright's government wielded enormous influence over the lives of Georgians.[68]

Although such detailed accounts do not exist for other occupied cities, traces of how occupation regimes touched residents' lives remain, and in all occupied zones these connections ran deep. In Philadelphia, British officers issued orders strictly enforcing the prices for various foodstuffs even before the army was fully in control of the city and its surroundings.[69] Such regulations mimicked the assizes, maximum prices set on essential goods, that city governments regulated in peacetime.[70] In Newport, the occupation administration regulated the sale of liquor in the town and even went so far as to issue permits to residents allowing them to hunt and fish.[71] In Charleston, the board of police assessed the levels of currency inflation during the war, indexing the cost of living in terms of a number of common provisions and suggesting measures to curb soaring food prices.[72] The collaborative regimes that administered military rule thus reached far beyond the loyalists who served directly to affect the lives of thousands of ordinary Americans. By taking on many of the responsibilities of prior municipal governments, occupation regimes made a powerful case for the viability of restored British rule.

Following James Simpson's suggestion, occupation administrations took an active role in regulating the institution of slavery, attempting both to mollify loyalist slaveholders and find a military use for the thousands of enslaved people who fled behind British lines in hopes of freedom. British commanders had since the onset of the war used the promise of freedom to lure slaves away from plantations and into British lines.[73] In occupied New York, the civil-military government quickly moved to protect slaves who had fled rebel masters. In 1779, the commandant of the city declared, "All Negroes that fly from the Enemys Country are Free—No Person can claim a right to them—Whoever sells them shall be prosecuted with the utmost severity."[74] The regime vigorously enforced this regulation. When Newporter George Brinley encountered a slave belonging to his brother in the streets of occupied New York City in the fall of 1781, he attempted to send the man back to Rhode Island, then occupied by the French, but lamented that "he declines going, and the Commandant will not compel any Blacks to Return."[75] In protecting blacks who had fled to British lines in hopes of freedom, New York's civil-military government was both protecting loyal subjects and encouraging more slaves to abandon their patriot masters.

In the occupied south, slave policies became more nuanced, as administrators attempted both to maintain a crucial labor source and to persuade Americans to swear their loyalty to the Crown. In doing so, the occupation regimes of Charleston and Savannah balanced the promise of freedom for slaves who fled patriot masters and the need to return runaways who belonged to loyalists. Charleston's police ruled that former rebels could reclaim their slaves "if, by dutiful and peaceful Behavior, they manifest an attachment to His Majesty's government."[76] Slaveowners who would reclaim their property also had to pay a fee of "one shilling, per day for the time they have been fed" at government expense.[77] In Savannah, the governor and council used enslaved people who had absconded from estates owned by rebels to mitigate the losses of many loyalists, and as an encouragement to those who had fled to return and resume the running of their plantations.[78] In both cities, the civil-military government used labor from confiscated, refugee, and newly freed slaves to improve public works and construct defenses.[79] Further, both civil governments collaborated with the military to suppress potential slave rebellions. In the summer of 1781, Charleston's civil government recommended that the city's commandant send soldiers to discipline the slaves on a nearby plantation upon receiving reports of their "ill behavior and insurrectious [sic] conduct . . . towards their overseer."[80] The occupation regimes of Savannah and Charleston thus defended and enforced the institution of slavery to a much greater degree than did that of New York, in keeping with the sensibilities of the local white population.

Despite its guarantee of the security of slave property for loyalists, Charleston's occupation regime nevertheless took measures to protect those slaves and free blacks who fled behind British lines from harsh treatment and, in the case of free blacks, reenslavement. In addition to having to prove loyalty to reclaim slaves, the administration required owners to promise not to punish slaves who had run away from their plantations. The board was adamant that "care must be taken to prevent the Negroes from being punished by his Master for . . . leaving his service to join the King's Army."[81] The board of police also took measures to prevent fraudulent sale and seizure of slaves. In the summer of 1780, the board observed that "several Negroes the property of diverse Persons Inhabitants hav[e] been carried off . . . by Masters of trading vessels and others," most likely for sale in the West Indies. The administration responded to this problem by issuing an edict demanding that all outgoing vessels submit detailed registers of their cargo, granting the harbormaster—the official in charge of pilot boats—the power to board and inspect ships at random, and imposing a fine of a hundred pounds sterling for each illicit slave discovered on board a ship.[82] Even transactions between civilians came under scrutiny. When Ann Timothy petitioned the administration for permission to sell a few of her slaves in September 1780, the board required her to advertise the slaves' names three times in the newspaper to ensure that no one else had a claim to them.[83]

Charleston's occupation regime also protected free blacks in the city. In July 1781, the board of police heard the complaint of James and Thomas Hayman, two free black fishermen. The Haymans claimed George Pagett, a pilot in the harbor, had "run them down in their canoe with his Pilot boat." In response, the board ordered Pagett to appear before them in its next meeting to answer the suit. When the pilot did not appear when the board met three days later, having "secreted himself to avoid being summoned," the board ordered the harbormaster to produce Pagett if he reported for work and ordered his apprehension by constables if he appeared in the streets.[84] While the pilot never appeared, the board's willingness to prosecute demonstrated publicly the regime's commitment to protecting those residents, black or white, who swore loyalty to the Crown. By using the structures of military rule to seek justice, people like the Haymans claimed for themselves a stake in the regime's success. Even as the administration sought to protect the institution of slavery, it made moves to protect individual enslaved and free blacks—especially those who had affirmed loyalty to the Crown.

In a further effort to encourage city residents to support restored British rule, occupation regimes embarked on extensive public works projects. New York's civil administration spent thousands of pounds sterling maintaining streets, repairing buildings, and maintaining public water pumps.[85] Charleston's board of police used funds seized from rebel estates and its supply of unclaimed slave labor to provide relief for the poor and fund burial ground expansion, street sanitation, and bridge and ferry repair.[86] The regime even attempted to improve public education in the city. In September 1780, the board of police advertised for a schoolteacher "whose principles are unquestioningly loyal . . . to undertake the charge of the Provincial free school in which the principles of Grammar and the Greek and Latin languages are to be taught."[87] In Savannah, Governor Wright himself directed the construction of a new road near his plantation just outside of town.[88] In Newport, public works took on a different tone, as the administration tore down derelict houses in order to provide fuel and construction materials.[89] As with other interventions, by addressing many of the problems of wartime life, public works projects sought to give urban populations a stake in the success of the occupation regimes and the eventual restoration of royal government.

Civil-military cooperation did not always come easily, and clashes occurred frequently between civilians and soldiers in conducting municipal duties. In Philadelphia during the winter of 1778, members of the civilian city watch complained of "shamefull and unGentlemanlike treatment" at the hands of British officers in charge of military patrols.[90] In occupied New York, the operator of a Brooklyn ferry petitioned the commandant of the city for relief after a British colonel had commandeered his vessel and, when the ferry master complained, "push'd him several times on the Breast" and "very nearly push'd him off the wharf into the Water."[91] Governor Wright complained multiple times about the army's recalcitrance to the edicts of his government in Savannah, writing in the summer of 1780 that the military still had not accounted for the property it had seized a year and a half earlier in the conquest of the city—likely, many officers chafed at having the spoils of war reclassified as part of the public treasury.[92] Such incidents of conflict were inevitable under military rule and occurred at all levels of the collaborative regimes.

Through petitions, complaints, trials, and court orders, occupation regimes often adjudicated civil-military conflicts in peaceful and constructive ways. In dealing with the officers who had offended the Philadelphia city watch, for example, General Howe declared in his general orders that he could "scarcely believe that officers and Gentlemen are Capable of being Guilty of such illiberal outrages," promising to punish severely any soldier caught abusing the watch and decreeing that "all patroles are to give every kind of Protection & assistance to the Civil Officers appointed to protect the peace and good order of the Garrison."[93] Other interventions on behalf of civilians came in response to individual requests. In the summer of 1779, New York's commandant exempted a Mr. Geyer from having an officer billeted in his home on the basis of a "plea of humanity" directed toward him. In March 1780, the city's commanding officer addressed several "irregularities" in the barrack master's office at the behest of several inhabitants of the city. In August of the same year, perhaps as a result of an investigation into those irregularities, the commandant exempted all captains of the city watch from having soldiers quartered on them.[94] In these cases, military officers protected the civilian components of occupation regimes, taking sides against their fellow officers and soldiers.

Police apparatuses also became adept at managing civil-military conflicts. When Captain Collins of HMS Camilla balked at paying the ships' carpenters in Charleston harbor ten shillings a day for repairs, he laid his case before the city's board of police, which arrived at a compromise between the two parties and, in the process, set the standard rates for such work going forward.[95] In New York, the commandant and the office of police created a policy for resolving disputes between citizens and soldiers, consisting of "a Board composed of three officers of rank in His Majesty's Army, and the principal magistrates of the city"—namely, Andrew Elliot and his deputies.[96] Adjudicated through the system of petitions, executive actions, and court decisions, conflicts between military and civil components of occupation regimes were more analogous to tensions between aspects of prerevolutionary colonial governments, which factions were constantly fighting for power and obtaining redress through legal avenues.[97]

The preponderance of these conflicts should not necessarily be taken as evidence that occupation regimes were dysfunctional but as a measure of the similarities they bore to what had come before. In late colonial America, power in the seaports rested in many different and often competing sources of authority. Although the specific structures differed, in each city mayors, aldermen, sheriffs, and colony-wide officials—both appointed and elected—had all vied for authority in these cities since the late seventeenth century. And, as the eighteenth century wore on, these multipolar municipal governments became more and more prone to factional rivalries. New York's politics through the 1760s, for example, were dominated by the competing DeLancey and Livingston families. Philadelphia's civic institutions found themselves divided between proprietary and royalist parties. And, as late as 1774, Charlestonians used the civil courts of South Carolina to debate the powers of local and imperial officials to maintain "the internal police" of the city. Each of these factional rivalries was characterized not only by elites jockeying for power but also by artisans, laborers, and other ordinary citizens aligning themselves on both sides based on their interests. And such disputes produced innovations such as almshouses, hospitals, and harbor safety regulations, among other outcomes. Urbanites thus not only tolerated but expected a degree of productive conflict within their municipal politics before the occupation regimes took hold, and the continuation of these conflicts—and their resolutions—by the regimes may have acted in their favor in the eyes of the population.[98]

Despite their efficacy—or perhaps because of it—occupation administrations drew the ire of a select class of former colonial officials, especially those passed over for official positions under military rule. William Franklin, formerly the governor of New Jersey, and Martin Howard, former chief justice of North Carolina, criticized the occupation regime in New York for failing to meet the needs of thousands of refugees and for failing to marshal loyalists into a coherent military force. Franklin eventually formed his own association of loyalist refugees to act independently of the British military hierarchy.[99] Former officials in Charleston also criticized that city's occupation regime. Although they both took up posts on the board of police, former lieutenant governor William Bull and former chief justice Thomas Knox Gordon privately maligned the administration. Bull pleaded with Lord George Germain for reinstitution of his full civil powers—as Sir James Wright had received—writing that he could only maintain tranquility "under the protection of His Majesty's Royal favour and former Government by known Laws." Gordon complained that Charleston's board of police lacked legal training and thus could not act as a legitimate court of law—a valid critique, perhaps, but for the former chief justice one driven more by outrage over the loss of the perquisites that accompanied the magistracy than concern for the well-being of the body politic.[100] Even Wright, restored to his governorship in Georgia, complained that his patronage powers were insufficient to maintain his station.[101] To listen to these officials, the occupation governments constituted at best an ad hoc expedient to full civil power, and at worst an illegal abuse of the British constitution.

Although these criticisms may have had some merit, largely they reflected the frustrations of the officials themselves rather than major shortcomings in the occupation regimes. Franklin, Howard, and dozens of other former officials from the thirteen colonies resided in New York but never achieved a place of power within the occupation administrations.[102] Despite their prominence in New York's wartime society, these former officials were outsiders looking in when it came to administering the city. In Charleston, even though Bull and Gordon held official positions in the occupation regime, they did not design it, and Germain rejected the changes they attempted to make once they arrived.[103] In both cases, relatively minor colonial officials—customs collector Elliot and acting attorney general Simpson—had designed and implemented the occupation administrations in tandem with military officers, displacing their former superiors in the civil administration. Prominent loyalists like Franklin and Howard found themselves largely pushed out of administering restored British rule. Thus, the criticisms leveled by these higher officials do not reflect the actual workings of these civil-military governments but rather the complaints of a recently and unexpectedly disenfranchised element of the colonial elite.

Despite the harsh criticisms leveled by alienated elites, many ordinary Americans accepted the reality of royal rule and participated in occupation regimes. In addition to the hundreds who participated in these administrations, thousands of Americans cooperated with military occupation simply by acceding to its authority. Judging by loyalty oaths collected at various points, majorities of Americans living in occupied cities were willing to collaborate with their military rulers. In the winter of 1776–1777, some 2,970

New Yorkers signed oaths of loyalty to the king. These oaths promised that signatories would "disavow, renounce, and disclaim" the revolutionary government, while promising "Submission to His Majesty's government."[104] Since New York's population fell to a wartime low of five thousand residents in the aftermath of the initial British invasion, the signatories of these oaths likely represented a majority of residents who remained.[105] This proportion may have been even higher than the number suggests, since adult men constituted the majority of signers and likely represented their entire families. Former governor William Tryon, who took charge in distributing the pledges, triumphantly reported to Lord Germain that New Yorkers took these pledges "without a shadow of coercion," and that the enthusiasm of the people was such that even if the troops were to quit the city "there would not be the least risk of a Revolt."[106] In Charleston, by the summer of 1781, almost two thousand residents had signed similar oaths of loyalty. Since the city's population of about eight thousand during the war included a high proportion of slaves, who before the war accounted for more than half of the city's residents, and, again, adult men signed the majority of oaths, signatories likely accounted for a substantial majority of the city's free population.[107] The act of declaring their allegiance caused oath signers to take an active role in the daily operation of military rule, and the oaths signified the extent of power of these military administrations.

Still, these regimes ultimately failed, for reasons that both their originators and their critics failed to recognize. The collapse of these governments cannot be traced to a lack of cooperation between the British military and local civilians. In each city, officers made efforts to reach out to locals, and in all cases they worked closely with sympathetic elites to craft civil policy. Occupation regimes brought in people of all walks of life and gave them a stake in the success of British military rule. And, despite inevitable conflicts and the complaints of ex-officials, they largely succeeded in their endeavors. Civil-military administrations managed municipal services, undertook public works programs, dispensed justice, and peaceably solved conflicts between civil and military components of the government. Still, they were unsuccessful at fundamentally convincing ordinary citizens of their legitimacy. Everyday experiences of exploitation, social instability, violence, starvation, and other privations undermined even the most well-planned and evenhanded attempts at military government. Explaining the failure of occupations thus requires going beyond the political structure of military rule to examine more closely the experiences of ordinary people within the occupied cities.

CHAPTER 3

Within the Lines

The arrival of British troops gave city dwellers the chance to reinvent themselves in new and potentially liberating ways. The British Army offered tens of thousands of African American slaves the chance to control their own destinies by fleeing the plantations, farms, and households of rebel masters and taking refuge behind British lines. As these ex-slaves filtered into occupied zones, they remade their lives and created new societies within the larger occupation society. Many women found empowerment in their capacities as purveyors of accommodation, food, and clothing, and as social and sexual partners for British soldiers. These roles took on new significance when combined with the weakened economic and social position of local men in occupied cities, and allowed women to assert a greater degree of economic and social independence than previously permissible in colonial society. Opportunity was not limited to those most disenfranchised under the old regime. Poor whites, middling craftspeople, and even some elites also took the opportunity that the arrival of the British military afforded to raise their standards of living, make larger profits, and forge valuable social connections. For thousands of civilians, military rule represented a chance to change the trajectory of their lives for the better.

As Americans remade themselves in occupied towns, members of the British military imposed their own values, which were part and parcel of the reinventions that occurred. Officers and ordinary soldiers instituted distinct versions of military culture, which civilians appropriated in unexpected ways. Officers went beyond organizing lavish balls and theatrical productions in occupied cities, integrating themselves into local society when they attended local churches, participated in dinner parties, took tea with members of the colonial gentry, and courted single women. Ordinary soldiers incorporated themselves into non-elite society when they lived alongside lower-class Americans, moonlighted to supplement their army pay, and socialized with civilians in taverns. Soldiers' wives operated illicit grog-shops, gambling dens, and brothels that served both military and local clients. Officers and common soldiers also brought negative aspects of military life to occupied cities. Gentlemen at war dueled, drank to excess, gambled compulsively, and racked up large debts they often left unpaid. The rank and file engaged in street brawls, large-scale looting, and drunken acts of violence. Both classes of soldier lived not only alongside but also within civilian communities, and military culture mingled with civilian customs to create a coherent, if unstable, occupation society that mixed elements of both.

Despite the opportunities for reinvention that military society offered many Americans, those who participated in it took enormous risks. Violence pervaded occupation society, with assault, rape, and even murder a daily threat. Further, the opportunities for reinvention that many residents eagerly seized held the risks of almost unimaginable catastrophe if they failed. African Americans who freed themselves by joining the British faced the constant threat of reenslavement if they strayed outside of the lines, encountered former masters or their agents in the streets, or were kidnapped by British officers for sale elsewhere. Women who claimed social freedoms in occupied society lost many of the protections that prewar society had afforded them, leaving many open to economic exploitation and sexual assault with little recourse to defend themselves. Even white men who took advantage of the opportunities occupation afforded for refashioning their lives faced ruin if they lost their protectors, with many facing loss of property and even trials for treason in areas controlled by revolutionaries. Consequences could thus be dire for those who took advantage of occupation's promise.

The ever-present tension between reinvention and ruin lent occupied cities a frenetic, almost desperate character—that of a world gone mad, where possibilities seemed limitless yet everyone lived constantly on the brink of disaster. This atmosphere spawned bizarre spectacles, such as an event held in Charleston in January 1782. On a chilly winter night in the besieged city, British officers and newly freed black women participated in a night of revelry that would have been unthinkable in other circumstances. The women, most of whom had fled plantations to take advantage of the promise of freedom behind British lines, went out, according to one observer, "dress'd up in taste, with the richest silks." At precisely eight o'clock in the evening, officers in gilded carriages escorted them to "a very capital private House," where they all enjoyed a supper that "cost not less than £80 Sterling" before dancing until nearly four o'clock in the morning.[1] Though likely funded by British soldiers, the managers of the ball were "three Negro Wenches," the former slaves of prominent revolutionary leaders. These women went to so far as to "assum[e] their Mistress's names" on invitations to the levee, signing the cards with the surnames Pinckney, Roussell, and Fraser.[2] The event outraged many onlookers outside the city, with one correspondent describing it as evidence of the "state of shame and perfidy the Officers of that once great Nation (Britain) has arrived to."[3] Perhaps to defy their critics, the British officers who organized the event christened it the Ethiopian Ball.

The Ethiopian Ball encapsulates the nature of occupation society, both in the strange possibilities it suggests and in the dangers involved in acts of defiance against the old social order. The black women who participated had reinvented themselves in occupied Charleston. In addition to liberating themselves from slavery, these people took on new identities, using clothes, rituals, and even names to declare their new status as free women. The form of the ball reflects military custom, in which officers entertained themselves when armies were idle for the winter with lavish theatrical productions, dinners, and dances, almost always in the company of local women. While they did not typically depart so radically from social norms, these celebrations often took on symbolic meaning, as gentlemen officers competed with one another to display their urbanity and make subtle political points.[4] The Ethiopian Ball, then, suggests how a disenfranchised group could appropriate military custom to achieve its own ends.

An equally important aspect of the ball was the precariousness of the event for both the soldiers and the women who participated in it. Despite their radical refashioning of themselves, the African American women were in the power of British officers; and even in their fine silks, they faced the threat of economic exploitation and sexual violence. Further, the event took place only months after the surrender of a large British force at Yorktown, Virginia, had all but sealed British defeat, lending the event a note not only of defiance but of desperation. The officers who danced and drank with ex-slaves on that January night likely suspected they would soon have to cede the city, and probably the entire North American continent, to the revolutionaries. While the impending withdrawal might damage the officers' careers, it threatened ruin for the ex-slaves who took part. Freeing oneself was dangerous in the best of circumstances, and many newly freed people saw in the impending British defeat a near-certain return to the state of bondage they had so recently escaped.[5] This unstable and even desperate cast defined the event—and life within the lines of occupied Charleston —as much as its opportunities for change.

The quotidian experience of this social instability—despite the dizzying opportunities that it brought for many—fostered insecurity, which helped to doom attempts by military rulers to restore British authority. As men and women of a variety of backgrounds reinvented themselves within the lines of garrisoned ports, they experienced viscerally the dangers of violence and exploitation, and ultimately risked losing not only their newly gained freedoms but also what they had had before. These fears were realized in their most extreme when the British Army evacuated Philadelphia and Newport in 1778 and 1779, leaving behind many who had taken advantage of occupation to the mercies of vengeful revolutionaries, but persisted even where British forces maintained control. As with the occupation regimes themselves, on a day-to-day basis peoples' experiences reinforced the reality that the opportunities brought by a restored British rule came at dire peril. Ultimately, this vulnerability prevented many from fully embracing the promise of military rule and formed the first cracks in the structure of military occupation.

African American slaves had perhaps the most to gain, and the most to lose, in occupation society. The American Revolution constituted a massive self-emancipation event, as tens of thousands of slaves across the thirteen colonies fled their masters in hopes of making a better life behind British lines. As rumors of freedom spread and the British Army moved across the countryside on campaign, slaves across New England and the mid-Atlantic flocked to the king's forces, filling the streets of occupied New York and Philadelphia.[6] When the army moved south, the numbers of escaped slaves increased more than tenfold, with tens of thousands of bondspeople from plantations in Georgia and South Carolina making their way to occupied Savannah and Charleston.[7] When they arrived in occupied cities, these escaped slaves began the process of creating new, free lives by pursuing employment, starting families, and traveling great distances in search of new opportunities.

The experiences of Boston King, a South Carolina slave who freed himself by running away to occupied Charleston, explicate the ways that many slaves refashioned themselves in occupied America. King fled his master's residence, about forty miles from the city, sometime in late 1780. According to an account he published after the war, the British Army welcomed him "readily," and the newly freed King "began to feel the happiness of liberty" almost immediately upon coming into the occupied town.[8] After succumbing to smallpox, recovering, and serving for several months as a servant to a British officer on campaign in the South Carolina backcountry, the ex-slave returned to Charleston and signed onto a privateering vessel that sailed up to the Chesapeake Bay, where King and his shipmates "were at the taking of a rich prize." When the ship paid off in New York, King settled in that city, at first attempting to find work in his trade as a carpenter, but "for want of tools was obliged to relinquish it, and enter into [domestic] service."[9] Despite having to sell his services as a manservant, King still exercised his freedom in choosing his masters, abandoning two men for having paid him too little or not at all. Between 1781 and 1782, King married another ex-slave, and together the couple managed to earn an income enabling them to survive.[10] When a whaleboat King was working on was captured by revolutionary forces, he escaped from a Connecticut jail and returned to New York, where he lived until the British Army evacuated the city. Evading recapture once again, the Kings left with the troops, eventually settling in Nova Scotia.[11] By the time King and his wife left in 1783, they had established themselves as free people and escaped forever the bondage into which they were born.

King's journey reveals how crucial urban centers controlled by the British Army were to achieving that liberation. These sites served not only as beacons of hope for African Americans living in the countryside considering the possibility of escape but also as accessible destinations, served by familiar roads and waterways by which fleeing slaves could travel. Boston King and those like him would surely have found it more difficult to reach a remote garrison fort, for example, than the capital and primary port of the colony. While slaves from nearby farms and plantations flocked to the army as it moved on campaign, thousands more arrived in the occupied territories, sometimes traveling hundreds of miles to do so.[12] Further, the sort of reinventions that took place in cities would not have been possible in rural areas. Because they were newcomers, cities allowed ex-slaves to become anonymous, escaping both their masters and their former states of bondage by blending into a teeming crowd of others seeking similar transformations. Such an act would have been unthinkable in less-populated rural areas, or in military fortifications, where escapees were more often reenslaved than liberated. The massive slave insurrection sparked by the American Revolution, then, would not have been conceivable without these sites.[13]

Once formerly enslaved men and women arrived in occupied cities, they built new lives in occupation society. Like King, many of these people found work as officers' servants, and many others became paid laborers on fortification projects, wagon drivers and stevedores in the supply train, or soldiers.[14] Some even took multiple jobs: in the summer of 1780, an officer commanding the ferry boats between Paulus Hook and New York City complained that "a negro man belonging to the Boat . . . is often absent, being employed as a Drummer" in a loyalist regiment.[15] Self-emancipated blacks integrated themselves into the organization of the British Army, and in so doing forged new identities. In civilian life, King's attempts to find remunerative work also fit in with the experiences of newly freed slaves in occupied society. Although King could not find work as a carpenter, escaped slave craftsmen in occupied New York formed a vibrant sector of the city's economy, with many finding remuneration.[16] And when Boston King took to the sea in a privateer and whaleboat, he followed the examples of hundreds of African Americans and whites who sought opportunities offshore.[17] Finally, when King and his wife boarded a vessel leaving New York in 1783, they joined at least 2,775 other escaped slaves whom the British Army took with them when they evacuated the city.[18]

Even when occupation regimes thwarted escapees' quests for freedom, many used military policies, combined with the mobility and confusion generated by occupation society, to improve their lives within slavery. Not all escapees benefited from British policies promising protection from rebel masters. The slaves of loyalists and those not in rebellion were not eligible for freedom behind British lines. Occupation regimes often put in place policies to reassure loyal slaveholders of the security of their human property. Still, a great many slaves belonging to loyalists ran away from their masters in the chaos that surrounded British occupation, and many were able to use occupation society to their advantage, if not to achieve freedom than to improve their lives and assert new privileges. In Charleston, the board of police created an opportunity for even the slaves of loyalists to better their lives. Before issuing a certificate entitling a would-be owner to claim an escapee, the occupation regime decreed that "the Owner must make a solemn promise not to resent the Behaviour of the slave for having left his service." To enforce this amnesty for runaways, the board pursued an even stronger policy of rescinding protection from those owners who went on to punish their restored slaves in spite of their promises not to. Indeed, the occupation regime ordered that if "the slave punished, or any other slave belonging to [that owner] should afterward desert from him, he should not meet with any assistance to get him returned."[19] Even when ex-slaves were ordered to be returned to their former masters, British policy allowed escapees who had attempted to free themselves to retain some of the dignity they had achieved in occupation society.

The British Army continued to protect slaves and ex-slaves under their power during the closing days of the war, when masters began to reenter occupied cities to try to find their bound servants. As the evacuation of Charleston loomed in late 1782, a board of British officers and loyalists met to adjudicate the claims of escaped slaves and their former owners, who had come to the city to reclaim them. Overwhelmingly, the board sided in favor of the freedpeople, obstructing the attempts of their enslavers to retrieve them and even causing several loyalist members to resign from it in disgust.[20] Such policies were in keeping with the British Army's overall ambivalence toward the institution of slavery, which often worked to the advantage of self-emancipated people in spite of official policies. When envisioning southern society after its conquest by British arms, General Clinton went so far as to muse, "Why not settle the Negroes on forfeited [rebel] Lands after the War? Perhaps they would be a check on the others— and tis possible just the contrary."[21] While his idea never came about, Clinton's thought exposes the radical possibilities for change in the lives of slaves that the British Army brought and reflects countless smaller changes that actually did take place.

Beyond official policy, the chaotic nature of occupation society made possible negotiations for better treatment between masters and their slaves. Communities of free blacks that arose in occupied cities allowed newly arrived escapees to simply blend into a larger crowd of other refugees and strangers, and masters were not ignorant of the unlikelihood of ever recovering their value. Still, former owners often continued to hold spouses, children, and other relatives, giving these newly freed people some incentives to remain or return. As a result, masters and their former slaves in New York engaged in complex negotiations, in which owners often conceded items such as deferred freedom, better treatment, and even monetary compensation for their labor in exchange for returning to service.[22] In many ways, these negotiations paved the way and provided a model for the gradual process of emancipation in the northern states over the following decades.

Some slaves even used their residence in occupied areas to negotiate for freedom in rebel-held zones. In the spring of 1777, a slave named Jinnie fled occupied Newport and obtained official, written recognition of her freedom by Rhode Island's revolutionary government. In 1778, Rhode Island's revolutionary governor, Nicholas Cooke, issued Jinnie a certificate declaring that "the Bearer . . . made her escape from Rhod[e] island in march 1777 while the Enemy were in Possession of the Same," and granting her "Permission from the Governor and Counsel of the Sta[te] of Rhod[e] island to go where she thoght propper [sic] to get her living."[23] Presumably, Jinnie had been enslaved either by a civilian or an officer living in Newport. Likely, she received her certificate of freedom in exchange for information on conditions on the British-controlled town.[24] In receiving a written declaration of her status, Jinnie leveraged her escape from occupation society to shed her past and reinvent herself as a free woman.

Although written arrangements were rare, newspaper advertisements for escaped slaves printed in Savannah, Georgia, hint that informal negotiations between masters and slaves occurred with some frequency even in the South. Many such postings contain language offering forgiveness to runaways should they return home. The former master of a young ex-slave called Hercules promised that "if he will come home he shall be forgiven."[25] The titular owner of a black woman named Eve, "well known in Savannah" but "lately seen in Charlestown," similarly assured that "if she returns of her own accord she will be forgiven."[26] While such enticements had peppered runaway-slave advertisements before the war, occupation gave these particular escapees a better bargaining position. After escaping their masters, both Hercules and Eve had returned to occupied Savannah. Since to print advertisements in a loyalist paper their owners must have taken oaths of loyalty to the British government, Hercules and Eve had no legal right to the freedom they claimed. Had they been captured by either revolutionary or British authorities, they would have been forcibly returned to slavery. Still, by virtue of their knowledge of the town and ability to travel, they retained some bargaining power. Seen in this light, the promises of forgiveness in these advertisements, and in countless others in both Savannah and Charleston, acknowledge the new free identity that these people had built for themselves even while attempting to return them to bondage. In this way, even those escapees who were reenslaved retained some of the refashioning that they had forged under occupation.

Still, African American slaves who took advantage of occupation to free themselves or better their circumstances lived under constant threat of exploitation and reenslavement. In Charleston and Savannah, unscrupulous merchants and corrupt British officers kidnapped many runaways and smuggled them in ships to the West Indies. The problem got so bad that Charleston's board of police issued an order against ships' captains caught with such people aboard.[27] The practice also occurred in northern ports, though on a smaller scale. In a vessel given special permission to leave Philadelphia, merchant Tench Coxe put aboard a slave named James, who he hoped would fetch a high price in the island of Grenada.[28] While James's origin and status is unclear, it requires no stretch to imagine him as one of the many refugees who fled behind British lines in hopes of freedom. While such freedom could be obtained, ex-slaves had to be on perpetual watch lest it slip away.

Other self-emancipated people faced coercion and reenslavement inside occupation society. While men and women who escaped from patriot masters could legally claim their freedom, in practice they were often abused and coerced into labor by the military. The British Army conscripted thousands of such people, forcing them to build defensive works and perform other menial tasks to support the military. Although in some instances ex-slave conscripts received pay, most did not, and almost everywhere the army showed little concern for their welfare.[29] Boston King recalled that, upon being struck with the smallpox soon after his entry into Charleston, military officials confined him in a quarantine camp with hundreds of other black refugees in very unsanitary conditions and with little food and water.[30] Many died in such circumstances. Newly free people employed by the army faced not only disease and death but also reenslavement.[31] During his time serving in South Carolina, a loyalist officer beat King and attempted to assert ownership over him, threatening that "if you do not behave well, I will put you in irons, and give you a dozen stripes every morning."[32] While King was able to escape this fate, the threat of losing the freedom they had fought for hung over all ex-slaves who served with the British military.

While enslaved people may have enacted the most radical transformations, women living in occupied cities also claimed for themselves a greater degree of economic and social independence than they had previously exercised. Women acted as landladies, laundresses, cooks, and purveyors of all kinds of goods for military personnel. Because men were often absent or unable to pursue their trades due to suspicion or embargo, these activities gave women a greater degree of economic independence than they had heretofore enjoyed. Women in occupation societies also became desired commodities as social and sexual partners for British soldiers and sailors. While some refused such advances, others leveraged this attention, along with the weakness of their male relatives, to assert a greater degree of social independence than they had exercised previously.

The absence and lack of power of male relatives facilitated women's social advancement. In occupied Newport, many men were simply absent, having joined the army or fled the city as British troops arrived. Ezra Stiles, a Congregationalist minister who had himself left at the onset of British occupation, calculated that only 260 "men with families" remained in Newport in late December 1776. From this estimate, Stiles calculated that "fewer than *five hundred Families* perhaps not above 350" were left, concluding that "it is therefore most probable that there is but one Quarter of the Inhabitants left shut up in the Town."[33] The minister's calculation likely underestimated the remaining population, as he based it only on male heads of household. Although some entire families left, most of the evacuees were male, and many of these men left their children and female relations behind. Even under occupation, Newport may have seemed safer than life in the countryside, and leaving women in town proved a useful strategy in protecting property from harm under military rule.[34]

Other women remained because of political belief or even to take advantage of occupation society. Mary Almy, for example, remained in Newport and operated a boarding house for British soldiers while her husband, Benjamin Almy, became a captain in the Continental Army. Despite their marriage, the Almys disagreed on politics, with Mary espousing loyalist sentiments throughout the war. During the 1778 French and Continental siege of Rhode Island, for example, Mary Almy wrote, "I am for English government, and an English fleet. I care not who takes the Frenchman."[35] Far from being impoverished by her husband's departure, Mary thrived in occupied Newport, operating her business and continuing to support the Crown, even while her husband fought against it.[36] While the politics of most women who remained are not as clear, many others likely embraced the occupation regime even as their male relations fled it.

Military rule stripped many of the men who remained in Newport of their livelihoods and diminished their social prominence. Men had to obtain written permission before leaving or returning to Aquidneck Island for any reason, or, according to standing orders, they would be "considered as an Enemy & treated as such." Further, male residents had to register their small boats with the British military and obtain written permission to fish or hunt wildfowl.[37] As many Rhode Islanders had productive lands in other parts of the colony or made their money on seagoing trade, these restrictions effectively limited many men's ability to generate an income for their families.

Political suspicion also limited male opportunities. Newport resident Fleet Greene, who kept a diary throughout the occupation, recalled that the town teemed with secret informers who helped the British Army enforce its policies. Greene commented after the occupation that "by their Reports the Jails and Prison ships were continuely [sic] Crowded with the Namable Inhabitants." Any hint of sympathy with the rebel cause was sought out and punished. Greene records that one particularly harsh military commandant "Abuses the Inhabitant Friends to Liberty in a Most shocking Manner, Not suffering them to talk in the Street."[38] In October 1777, British authorities rounded up sixty-one of these "friends to liberty," all men, and interned them on board the *Lord Sandwich*, a prison ship floating in Narragansett Bay, for refusing to sign an oath pledging to defend the town against attacks from the revolutionaries.[39] In order to escape such a fate, men in occupied Newport had to be especially circumspect about what they said and to whom, as well as in their movements and activities. Because of these restrictions, the conditions of occupation limited the effective social power of many men in occupied society.

Women moved much more freely than men under British occupation and used that freedom to make up for many of the restrictions placed on their male relatives. Almost every other week in the nonwinter months, Greene noted the arrival and departure of boats sailing under a flag of truce and ferrying women and children between British-occupied Newport and the revolutionary mainland of New England.[40] Although standing orders required that "such women and children as chuse [sic] to go off the Island" be identified and searched by British officers, in practice this happened only rarely.[41] These boats offered women a way not only to move between zones of control but to trade and obtain vital supplies for their families on either side. Further, women in occupied Newport had almost unfettered access to the prisons. When the army transferred seventy-three prisoners from the provost jail to a prison ship in the harbor, they were "followed by Great Numbers of Women & Children."[42] Family support probably played a large role in keeping prisoners alive under harsh conditions, and women's relative freedom of movement and economic agency allowed them alone to provide this support. Even undertaken out of necessity, this mobility thrust women of all classes into a much more public role in society than they had ever taken before.

Newport's women also achieved a degree of economic independence by providing food and lodging to British soldiers during the three-year occupation. While stationed in Newport, Captain John Peebles of the Scottish grenadiers breakfasted daily with his aged landlady, a widow who the Scottish officer described as a "civil body." Although many householders had little choice in quartering officers for the winter, their room and board did provide an opportunity for income. When Peebles's regiment left Newport at the end of January 1777, he recounted that "tho I overpaid her she did not seem to be satisfied."[43] Women lower on the social scale also found opportunities to profit by the army's presence. Captain Peebles described Sal Leak, proprietor of "a house of Pleasure" in Newport, as "a well look'd girl about 30" who was "spoke of by everybody in town in a favourable manner."[44] Prostitution, which had flourished with Newport's prominence as a major Atlantic port, continued to thrive under occupation. At least some of Newport's women thus actively profited from the presence of the British Army.

Elite women in occupied societies found themselves in demand as social and sexual partners for British officers. As gentlemen in the eighteenth-century anglophone world, officers needed a female audience for whom to display their masculine, urbane qualities. Fresh from the conquest of Savannah, British Lieutenant Colonel Archibald Campbell begged a commander of the Continental Army to "please acquaint the Ladies, who had abandoned their houses at Savannah, that they have certainly been taught with other wild conceptions, to form the worst impression of British officers," imploring them to return to town.[45] Such requests stemmed from the officers' vision of themselves as gentile conquerors who needed to interact with gentlewomen to counteract the more brutal aspects of war. A poem published in a Newport newspaper further elaborated on this point. In a work titled "To the Ladies of Rhode-Island," an anonymous officer mingled military imagery with feminine virtue. In the opening stanza, the poem praises "Ye gentle Nymphs . . . More powerful far than Caesar's Arms." Later, after detailing the horrors of war, the officer-poet declared, "Tis yours, fair Maids! While Youth abounds / 'Tis yours to heal our bleeding Wounds."[46] In this officer's formulation, as in many others, women became essential in alleviating the horrors of war for gentlemen soldiers.[47]

For American women, the interactions that military society facilitated also brought exciting new possibilities. During the war, New York became infamous among revolutionaries for elaborate social spectacles and the frequent courtships that occurred between British officers and elite civilian women. As headquarters for the British Army, the city became for many critics a symbol of British predation on American women. Hannah Lawrence, the twenty-one-year-old daughter of a Quaker merchant, became disgusted by the courtships between officers and civilian women. An aspiring poet, she turned her pen against the use of Trinity Church as a promenade ground: "This is the scene of gay resort / Here Vice and Folly hold their court / Here all the martial band parade / To vanquish some unguarded maid."[48] The composition, left anonymously on the steps of the church, caused a stir in the city, and she followed it up in April 1780 with another satirizing the destruction of a part of Trinity's churchyard to expand the promenade: "Enlarge the walk to which the fair / In shining nightly throngs repair / The female size, by hoops increast / Demands a tomb or two at least."[49] While for Lawrence such activities provided an opportunity to hone her satirical wit, other observers took a harsher view of courtships between British officers and local women. In Philadelphia, where a similar scene emerged during its brief occupation, several women who carried on relationships with British officers became pariahs after the occupation ended, subject to intimidation and even punitive action on the part of the restored revolutionary government.[50] To critics, socializing with British officers marked at best a frivolous dalliance, and at worst treason against the revolutionary cause.

Still, occupation society in New York could be a thrilling, potentially liberating place for many women, especially those of elite and middling backgrounds. As young Elizabeth Tauncey described New York in the spring of 1782, "This is to be sure for young Ladies who love gaiety, a most delightful place."[51] In addition to entertainment, many women used the courtship culture to break free from patriarchal family structures. Although she criticized it in her poetry, Hannah Lawrence herself eventually joined in this scene, marrying Jacob Schieffelin, a young lieutenant in the British service, in the summer of 1780. She did so in defiance of her family. As Lawrence noted in a journal she kept of her courtship, her brothers were "extremely averse to this union," and her father was "alarmed at the risk . . . in marrying so great a stranger." Her father even went so far as to threaten to expel Hannah from the local Quaker meeting if she went through with her nuptials. Still, Lawrence married her beau in a secret ceremony, and the couple departed New York soon afterward for British Canada.[52] In doing so, she asserted her independence from her male relatives, in a way made uniquely possible under occupation.

The newly minted Hannah Schieffelin was not alone. Newport's Anglican Church registered more than a dozen marriages between officers and civilian women and several baptisms resulting from those unions over the three years of that city's occupation.[53] Such relationships became so common that, when preparing to evacuate the city in late 1779, Newport's commandant left strict orders for women to be kept out of military camps, under threat of immediate death for soldiers found sheltering them, to prevent desertions.[54] William Rawle, a young loyalist law student who was a friend of Hannah Lawrence before her marriage, found the extent of courtships with British officers unsettling and occasionally scandalous. Rawle wrote of a fourteen-year-old New York girl who, "finding marriages so very fashionable . . . eloped with a Hessian officer," leaving her parents "inconsolable."[55] Newcomers could be especially susceptible to such seductions—soon after her arrival in New York, a sixteen-year-old girl whom Rawle described as "one of the plainest little mortals, all awkwardness and simplicity . . . eloped with a Captain in the army," horrifying her family, who had "guarded her with the most peevish caution."[56] Such relationships frustrated Rawle's romantic aspirations—the young student complained vociferously about the "the Lord's and Sir George's, and dear Colonel's" of the town monopolizing eligible romantic partners.[57] Still, many of these young women used the presence of soldiers to escape the rule of their parents and find eligible partners elsewhere—partners who, like Hannah Schieffelin's new husband, could open up new possibilities in their lives.

Not all courtships involved British soldiers, nor did all result in marriage. Elizabeth Shipton, daughter of a loyalist family in Flat Bush, Long Island, fell in love with Continental prisoner of war Aquila Giles, eventually marrying him in 1780. And, although Giles's status as a prisoner had restricted him to New York, the union allowed the couple to leave for his

Maryland plantation—on learning of their nuptials, a British commander friendly with the Shiptons promised that "Should Major Giles be left out of the present exchange of Prisoners of War, a Parole to go out shall be solicited for by me agreeable to Mrs. Giles desire."[58] Marriage could, thus, not only allow new spouses access to British territories but also vice versa.

Some women in occupied America also found advantage in staying single. As Elizabeth Shipton Giles's friend Elizabeth Tauncey wrote to her in 1782, "Marrying does not seem to be much the Fashion," despite "a good many matches talked of."[59] Likely, many women who took advantage of the opportunities to assert the greater social independence that occupation provided did not relish the thought of potentially giving up that newfound independence by marrying. By simply participating in the vibrant social world of occupation society, however, women experimented with new, potentially empowering freedoms unimaginable before the imposition of military rule.

The independence that women claimed for themselves under military rule came with persistent danger. While the absence of many men allowed women a greater degree of social freedom, it also stripped them of protection from the rougher aspects of garrison life. Assaults occurred almost immediately when British soldiers came into contact with American civilians. In the winter of 1775–1776, a private soldier in the Fifty-Ninth Regiment beat a Boston woman, "Mrs. Morris," nearly to death.[60] Civilian women in occupied cities also found themselves vulnerable to rape. Ezra Stiles recounted early on in the occupation of Newport that "the Soldiers ravished two Lying-in Women."[61] During the occupation of Philadelphia in the winter of 1777–1778, two wagon drivers in the British service attacked, robbed, and sexually assaulted Catherine Stone and Isobel Mitchell, local women who had signed on as servants to a local officer. The soldiers nevertheless took them from the street and "dragged them towards the Playhouse," where they locked Stone in a cellar and "beat her with a Stick" and began to rape her, though a passerby interrupted them and the women escaped.[62] In the summer of 1778, three soldiers returning from an oyster-fishing expedition on Long Island stopped at the home of Phebe Coe, a local widow, and demanded refreshment. After she fed them, the soldiers threw her out of her own house, and one began to sexually assault her mentally disabled, bedridden daughter. When Coe reentered the house and protested, the soldier "laid violent hands on her, threw her on the Bed," and proceeded to rape her as well.[63] Such incidents almost certainly occurred more often in occupied society than has been recorded in the documentary evidence. Captain John Peebles described in his journal the conviction of a soldier in Newport for rape in December 1776, noting sadly that "there have been other shocking abuses of that nature that have not come to public notice." The Scottish officer took such crimes with a fatalistic attitude, remarking that "hard is the fate of many who suffer indiscriminately in a civil war."[64] Even if martial society brought with it opportunities for women to refashion themselves, the military's casual attitude toward violence against them opened up new risks as well.

The threat of violence in occupation society could be just as devastating on women as the assaults themselves. Even where rape cases were tried by court-martial, victims often faced pressure to forgive their attackers. John Dowling, an English soldier convicted by court-martial of a rape in Newport, had his sentence commuted after "intercessian having been made by the injured party, in favor of the prisoner."[65] Two soldiers who raped Elizabeth Johnstone during the battle of Long Island also had their sentences commuted at their victim's behest.[66] Such recantations and pleas for leniency occurred with some frequency in civilian rape trials during the eighteenth century, usually due to a complex combination of community ties, social pressure, and intimidation of victims by the friends and family members of their attackers.[67] In occupation society, these actions took on an even more sinister aspect. The comrades of soldiers convicted of rape had in their power the ability to destroy the lives of these women through physical intimidation, deprivation of food or supplies, or even destruction of their homes. Threats of implied violence against women could thus have as much or more of an effect on their lives as that violence itself.

Implied violence had the potential to constrain the hard-won independence that women claimed in occupation society. Elizabeth Drinker, a well-to-do Quaker woman living in Philadelphia during the occupation, successfully dissuaded several officers from quartering in her home during the early months of military rule, using her social position and the absence of her husband to beg off such requests.[68] However, things changed for Drinker when a drunken British captain burst into her home in late November 1777, demanding food and drink, brandishing his sword, cursing, and eventually carrying off one of Drinker's maidservants. This event had a profound effect on Drinker, who wrote in her diary that night that "tis not near one in the Morning and I have not yet recovered from the fright."[69] The next month, when a young major came to request lodgings at the household, Drinker accepted his offer. According to her diary, the officer had persuaded her by arguing that "it was a necessary protection at these times to have [an officer] in the House."[70] Drinker's fear of violence against herself and her family, made real by the intrusion of the drunken officer weeks earlier, compelled her to give up some of her independence and to open up her house to a British soldier. Although the young officer who moved into the Drinker household proved mostly inoffensive, his presence lessened the independent authority that Drinker had taken for herself.

In addition to violence, women in occupied America became vulnerable to economic hardship. The very absence of men that enabled the unprecedented social independence women took on also left many, especially those unused to labor and without skills, destitute. In New York, the commander in chief's office was inundated with petitions for support from such women. Refugees found themselves particularly prone to financial ruin. Margaret Brush, whose husband had escaped imprisonment in revolutionary Boston only to die in British New York, pleaded in January 1779 that his death had left her unable to purchase food for herself and her daughter or to even leave the city for her former home.[71] A Mrs. Beasley, whose sons had left to fight in loyalist regiments, also begged for rations on account of her three small children.[72] Hundreds of other female refugees with no male support petitioned or were recommended for relief during New York's seven-year occupation.[73] Even those with local roots suffered. When her husband left New York to pursue other opportunities in 1783, one previously well-off woman complained that her circumstances became so bad that "for days together I could not command a shilling to provide myself a common fish dinner."[74] Military rule could bring destitution to women as easily as the independence it facilitated. Still, thousands of women of varying backgrounds reinvented their lives under military rule.

Occupation society provided new opportunities not only for women and slaves but for men of all social positions as well. Although many white men were absent serving in the military, exiled due to earlier political activities, or imprisoned as suspected rebels, many managed to reinvent in an attempt to better their positions. Members of the elite who remained in occupied society could often leverage their loyalty to achieve wealth and power in occupied society at the expense of those forced into exile by their political beliefs. Middling merchants and tradesmen found new avenues for profit in occupation society, providing for the needs of soldiers and officers, speculating on essential goods, and engaging in privateering adventures. While opportunities for lower-class people may not have been as great, many still found ways to benefit from occupation society, squatting in abandoned houses, taking advantage of the army's demand for labor, and enjoying the excesses of military society.

Elite men who remained under military rule could often rise far and fast in occupation society. At the onset of the occupation of New York, Andrew Elliot was a customs collector—a relatively low-level rung on the ladder of Britain's imperial bureaucracy. Within two years of the British conquest of Manhattan, Elliot had become the de facto head of the occupation regime's civil government, wielding more power in New York City than any colonial official before him. By the end of the occupation, the erstwhile imperial bureaucrat had risen even higher, receiving a royal appointment as lieutenant governor of the entire province in 1780 and, after the resignation of Governor James Robinson in the last months of the war, ending his American career as the last royal governor of New York.[75] In addition to gaining political power, Elliot also used his position in occupation society to arrange advantageous marriages for his daughters. In 1779, his daughter Elizabeth married William Schaw, the Baron Cathcart, who served on General Clinton's staff. In 1783 another of Elliot's daughters, Agnes, married Sir David Carnegie, a baronet, also stationed in occupied New York. Even Elliot's stepdaughter, Eleanor, married well, uniting in a 1784 London ceremony with Admiral Robert Digby, whom she likely met in occupied New York. After the war, Elliot used these family connections to weather his losses in property in New York and Philadelphia and obtain a comfortable rural retirement in England, where he lived until his death in 1797.[76] Occupation thus changed the course of Andrew Elliot's life for the better.

Elliot was not the only former minor official who rose to power during the occupation. Joseph Galloway, superintendent of police in occupied Philadelphia, also used occupation conditions to raise his stature. When the British Army occupied Philadelphia, Galloway became the highest-ranking civil official in that city, although his rise stopped suddenly when the army evacuated Philadelphia earlier than expected. Still, he enjoyed a comfortable retirement in England after the war and even received a pension for his services to the British government.[77] James Simpson, whose highest rank before the war was acting attorney general of South Carolina, leveraged connections forged while in exile in New York to become the superintendent of police in occupied Charleston, wielding similar authority to Elliot and Galloway in that city and potentially even more over the rest of conquered South Carolina.[78] Former low-ranking officials such as Elliot, Galloway, and Simpson used the conditions of occupation to rise above their former stations and amass greater political power and wealth.

Those who succeeded often appropriated the rituals and cultural practices that the British Army brought to occupied zones. As groups of civilians took action to change their circumstances, they did so in the context of a military culture with its own rituals and values. Even where elements of military culture had the potential to marginalize Americans, residents of occupied cities incorporated themselves and subverted them to fulfill their own ends. This process occurred gradually, over the course of hundreds of thousands of everyday encounters. Military theater, officers' and gentlemen's clubs, and a vibrant party scene became sites of interactions and understanding between officers and well-to-do civilians, in which civilians wielded more and more power. For those of more modest means, street and tavern life, drinking, and practices of desertion and evasion of military authority united common soldiers and ordinary townspeople. As military personnel and civilians came together to form a unique society, opportunities and dangers abounded for both.

Some of these interactions took place on a literal stage. In each occupied town, military officers organized acting troupes, in which they performed for one another and for the entertainment of prominent townspeople. In New York, British officers organized a vibrant theater scene that lasted through the entire seven-year occupation.[79] Officially a charity for army widows and orphans, the "Theatre Royal" mainly functioned as a place for officers to display their gentility and refinement and a venue for wealthy New Yorkers and British officers to socialize. Theater seasons ran from winter through early spring, with biweekly or monthly offerings, and performances drew a wide variety of people. At its peak, the popular comedy *The West Indian* drew an audience of nine hundred in January 1778.[80] Although officers took on most roles, local men and women participated as well, especially in the female parts. For the season-opening production of Henry Carey's *Chrononhotonthologos* in 1779, a newspaper advertisement boasted that all of the female parts would be portrayed by "young Ladies and grown Gentlewomen, who never appeared on any Stage before."[81] Often, the women who took these roles were reputed to be officers' mistresses, such as a "Mrs. Williams," who played many roles in 1778 and 1779, including Desdemona in *Othello* and Charlotte in *The West Indian*.[82] Despite its charitable pretenses, the Theatre Royal put on lavish public entertainments, complete with expensive costumes, opulent boxes for which high-ranking officers and civilians paid hundreds of pounds sterling, and a cadre of civilian ticket takers, caterers, and boxkeepers to serve the actors and their audience.[83] The accounts of the theater demonstrate that, despite incomes of around £4,000 in ticket sales in both 1778 and 1779, it never donated more than £220 to the widows' and orphans' funds, with the rest going toward "expenses."[84] As the occupation of New York wore on, the Theatre Royal became a pillar of elite sociability.

While not in as grand style as that of New York, other cities possessed military theater scenes as well. In Philadelphia, which boasted perhaps the most sophisticated theater outside of New York, Major John André and other officers organized a vibrant theater company that staged sixteen performances between January and May 1778. Plays included staples of the late eighteenth-century English stage, as well as farces and two productions of William Shakespeare's *Henry IV, Part I*. The company drew actors from the officer corps of various British and German regiments, with elite local women playing many of the female parts.[85] In Savannah, military theater seems to have been more inconsistent, though officers did put on a double bill of *Jane Shore* and *The Mock Doctor* in September 1781, and possibly other plays throughout the three-year occupation.[86] Charleston and Newport appear to have been bereft of organized military theater, though there is evidence in Charleston of civilian attempts to organize plays, which may have had cooperation from military officers.[87]

Theater played an important role in military society during the era of the American Revolution. Organizing and acting in plays allowed officers to display their gentility and refinement, and to compete with one another in a nonlethal arena. In addition, performances, and their reception in print, represented a way for officers across the British Empire to express their political views and to weigh in on the deep political divisions in the empire without transgressing their place as servants of the king.[88] Performing officers often added prefaces and additional scenes to the texts of plays in order to convey meaning or display authorial prowess.[89] Plays could even mark officers' allegiance to one particular general over another, or one philosophy of war over another. As one scholar has speculated, the performance of the play *Douglas* in Philadelphia on the day General Howe departed his post and Clinton assumed command of forces in North America may well have marked a shift in the officers' loyalties and a shift from Howe's positions of attempting reconciliation with rebels to Clinton's advocacy of military conquest.[90] As texts and performances rich with metaphor and ambiguity, plays allowed officers and civilians to indirectly challenge the military hierarchy while maintaining their allegiance to it.

Theater in occupied cities also provided opportunities for women to assert independence and embrace the social opportunities that occupation brought. In accompanying officers to plays, women engaged in a courtship ritual within military society. Many these women did so independently of their male relations, which made such attendance not just a part of the elite marriage market but a public statement of independence and changing social conditions. The women who acted alongside British officers displayed their embrace of the new social possibilities of occupation even more publicly. Often, actresses in these productions were the actual or reputed mistresses of the officers involved. The "Mrs. Williams," who performed with New York's Theatre Royal for at least two seasons was the mistress of a Major Williams, having gone so far as to assume his surname.[91] The reputed mistress of a British officer played Lady Randolph in the production of *Douglas* that marked Henry Clinton's ascension to command.[92] Even where actresses were not involved with officers, their performances nevertheless signaled publicly their embrace of the opportunities of occupation society. In this way, elite American women subverted a military theatrical tradition that had the potential to subjugate them and used it to assert a newfound social independence.

While gentlewomen integrated themselves into military society by performing in and accompanying officers to the theater, the men of the American gentry mingled with officers in social clubs. As they had before the war, clubs formed an essential part of male-male sociability in both military and civilian elite society. In the military, officers regularly pooled their money and set up social clubs to pass idle time in garrison. During the winter of 1776–1777 in Newport, Captain John Peebles participated in one such organization, in which about a dozen officers from his battalion "agreed to meet twice a week, on Saturday Evenings[,] play cards & sup; & on Wednesdays to dine."[93] Civilian gentlemen's clubs also remained a part of occupation society. Newport's civilian "Fellowship Club" continued to meet into the occupation and likely incorporated members of the occupation force into its ranks, as did the Newport Marine Society, a social club comprising the city's most prominent merchants. In February 1777, at the outset of the occupation, the society delegated three members to "wait on Lord Percy and General Prescut [*sic*]," the two senior British officers in the garrison, "and present Each of them the Articles of the Fellowship Club," inviting the generals, and likely other officers, to join in their events.[94] The Saint Andrews Society, a charitable group formed in 1729 by Scottish immigrants in Charleston, elected the city's superintendent of police James Simpson as its president in 1780, and inducted Lieutenant Colonel James Moncrief, the British Army's chief engineer, and General Alexander Leslie, commander in chief in South Carolina, into the fellowship in subsequent years.[95] By incorporating military officers into elite social clubs, civilians co-opted military sociability and used it to forge valuable connections.

Elite connections in occupied towns extended beyond theaters and club meetings to encompass dinners, balls, tea parties, and other more informal entertainments during which martial and civilian society merged. At lavish dinner parties, officers mimicked genteel civilian customs by entertaining their subordinates, using these occasions to show off their refined tastes and largesse. During his visits to New York, Philadelphia, and Newport, Ambrose Serle attended many such suppers, rubbing shoulders with the elite of the British Army and of local society.[96] Levees and balls also occurred frequently, typically funded by subscription to which officers contributed a small sum and which American women attended gratis. Captain Peebles recalled one such event in Newport, in which around fifty women, consisting of "a few good looking Girls, some ugly women [and] the rest but middling," danced and dined with 150 officers in a private room of a local coffeehouse until midnight one January evening in 1777.[97] Such events became common in occupied ports, and advertisements for assemblies and dances frequently appeared in newspapers.[98]

Opportunities for elite socialization abounded in occupied society, and local civilians took on hosting duties as often as military officers. Even church became an opportunity for soldiers and locals to interact: on accompanying his battalion to religious services in Newport in December 1776, Captain Peebles observed that "some pretty looking Girls" came out to worship with the army.[99] Private homes also offered their services to facilitate officer-civilian socialization. A Mrs. Crawley frequently advertised her home as a meeting place, offering to "do every Thing in her Power . . . to conduct an Assembly" for "the most respectable Gentlemen of the Army and Navy." For her trouble, Crowley charged these honorable gentlemen the small fee of one dollar per head, with women entering for free.[100] Sarah

Wanton, the wife of a former lieutenant governor of Rhode Island, often hosted teas and dinner parties for British officers at her Newport home—the men no doubt attracted both by the hospitality and the prospect of meeting the Wantons' two teenage daughters, both of whom eventually married into the army.[101] By hosting and facilitating these events, civilians like Mrs. Crawley and Mrs. Wanton appropriated military culture for their own ends, be they profit or social betterment.

While civilians facilitated small-scale entertainments, wealthy officers continued to stage the most elaborate celebrations. Some of the grandest events, such as ceremonies marking monarchs' birthdays, provided even greater opportunity for military and civilian elites to come together. These events could be quite elaborate. In one instance, Baroness Fredericke Riedesel, the wife of a German general stationed in New York, found herself guest of honor at a ball celebrating the Queen of England's birthday. The levee took place at the home of former governor William Tryon and consisted of the flower of the British officer corps and the civilian New York elite. Although several months pregnant, the baroness nevertheless found herself "obliged to open the ball with one of the generals by a formal minuet" and proceeded to dance "several English dances" before eating a fine supper "under a canopy" and retiring to bed at two o'clock in the morning.[102] New York saw even greater celebrations when the teenaged Prince William Henry, at the time serving aboard a British man-of-war, visited the city in the fall of 1781. New Yorkers marked the future King William IV's visit with a series of fetes, balls, a parade, and a flurry of celebrations lasting days.[103] While such grand events occurred relatively rarely compared to the more commonplace small assemblies, teas, and dinners that made up the mainstay of military sociability, these events combined to create a unified elite society in occupied America.

The nature of elite society in occupied cities provides the context for the infamous wartime entertainment known as the Meschianza. An event held outside Philadelphia in the summer of 1778 to mark the impending departures of General Sir William Howe and his brother Admiral Lord Richard Howe from America, the Meschianza was perhaps the most elaborate celebration ever staged in North America. Planned by Major André, who engineered much of the previous winter and spring's theatrical season, the event consisted of a sailing regatta down the Delaware River, a medieval tournament complete with triumphal arches, and a dinner, ball, and fireworks display afterward at a local country mansion. During the tournament, which made up the mainstay of the entertainment, British officers dressed as medieval knights and jousted with one another for the favor of Philadelphia women dressed in mock-Turkish garb. After the contest, which ended in a tie between the self-styled "Knights of the Blended Rose" and the "Knights of the Burning Mountain," the ladies bestowed laurel wreaths on their champions, and the entire company proceeded to feast, drink, and dance until four o'clock in the morning.[104] The cost of the event was enormous, more than £3,000, and reveals much about military society in its sheer opulence. According to Captain Peebles, who attended, the bulk of the expense fell to "21 or 22 Subscribers," and "it cost each Subscriber £140." These sponsors also sold tickets to make up the expense, as the supper alone was said to have cost 900 guineas.[105] Although it marked a low point in the war, coming on the heels of the Howes' recall and General John Burgoyne's defeat at Saratoga, New York, the Meschianza represented the single greatest incarnation of military entertainment during the Revolutionary War.

Viewing the Meschianza in the context of elite occupation society invites a reconsideration of its significance. The event achieved legendary status in the English-speaking world soon after its conclusion, primarily through the criticisms of General Howe's detractors and the publication of André's account of it in the 1778 Gentleman's Magazine in London, and scholars have long sought to unpack its complexities.[106] Most interpretations emphasize the actions of the officers, with the American women involved in the celebration portrayed, at best, as willing objects in a subjugation play—symbolically representing the conquest of America—or as pawns in a larger political debate in the British Empire.[107] In the deeper context of occupation society, however, the women's participation reverses course. Like the participants in the Ethiopian Ball, the elite women who participated in the Meschianza transformed themselves and their circumstances under occupation. As they bestowed favors on some of the most prestigious members of the English gentry, these women used military ceremony to their own benefit, positioning themselves at the apogee not only of a provincial town like Philadelphia but also of a cosmopolitan empire. In this act of reinvention, the Meschianza throws into sharp relief the slow processes of integration that occurred in countless dining rooms, coffeehouses, and church halls throughout occupied America.

While events such as the Meschianza occurred at very high levels of the social spectrum, ordinary soldiers also mingled with their civilian counterparts, forming similarly mutual societies as they moonlighted as laborers,

Figure 7. Ticket for the Meschianza, c. 1778. Courtesy Library Company of Philadelphia.

Figure 8. Sketch of a Meschianza costume, c. 1778. Courtesy Library Company of Philadelphia.

socialized in taverns and brothels, and lived alongside one another in the streets of occupied ports. Although these did not have the structured nature of interactions between officers and the elite, these societies nevertheless thrived as soldiers and civilians found common ground. However, while civilians most often sought to better themselves through military society, soldiers more often tried to take advantage of civilian life for their own gain.

Upon arriving in occupied territories, many soldiers remarked on the rich prospects of the new towns they encamped in. On observing New York in the wake of the invasion in September 1776, junior officer Loftus Cliffe wrote to a friend, "I never saw a more beautifull Country[;] Peaches and Nectarines grown upon Hedges, so plenty that even all the Soldiery were not able to consume them." Cliffe continued to remark on the ready availability of good land, writing that if he could "save money out of [his] three and sixpence [salary]," he would "make some advantageous purchases."[108] Frederick MacKenzie of the Royal Welch Fusiliers remarked on the "many fine and well cultivated Islands" and "beautiful bays and inlets" visible from his post in Newport.[109] Stephan Popp, an enlisted man in the Ansbach-Bayreuth regiment of German mercenaries, remarked that Long Island "is a very fertile land, produces much fruit and drink and has a fine cattle industry," while Rhode Island "has little woods, but fish and crabs are caught in abundance, and many support themselves with such work." Of the people in Newport, Popp gushed that "the inhabitants are mainly rich people" and "the women are very beautiful and shapely, almost like the gods in attractiveness."[110] Johann Döhla, another transplanted German, marveled that "New York is a large, beautiful, rich, and splendid port city," where "most of the inhabitants . . . eat and drink from silver tableware." The young man was also astounded at New York's diversity, describing how "Jews and Christians marry together without giving it any consideration," and marveling at the "many Irish living in New York; also many Germans, and many blacks."[111] Such a scene of diverse prosperity would have been strange and likely enticing for the young man from war-torn, economically depressed central Europe. While the Germans perhaps wondered the most at circumstances in America, soldiers from all backgrounds found tantalizing economic and social opportunities in occupied territories.

Although few records exist of how ordinary soldiers took advantage of the opportunities they found under military rule, cases where soldiers deserted their ranks suggest how many attempted to integrate fully into civilian society. Fueled by the ready availability of work and encouragement by local civilians, desertion ran rampant in occupied towns, as soldiers attempted to rid themselves of the restrictions of army life and take advantage of the opportunities for reinvention that occupation society offered. Although perhaps not on the same scale as escaping from slavery, fleeing military society was nevertheless a desperate act, as recaptured deserters faced hanging if convicted by court-martial. Often, such acts were spurred by dissatisfaction with military discipline. After enduring a particularly harsh punishment for being drunk on duty one night in May 1779, private Nicholas Eggars of the Royal Welch Fusiliers secreted himself in "a cave dugg [*sic*] for the preservation of Roots" in the Bowery neighborhood of New York. The unfortunate soldier subsisted on potatoes stored in the cave for seventeen days before two townspeople discovered him and turned him in to the authorities.[112] More often, however, locals aided soldiers in their attempts to flee army life. In the winter of 1779, a deserting soldier borrowed "an old coat & a Hat" from New York resident John Stewart, who may or may not have been privy to the man's scheme.[113] Entrepreneurial city residents often encouraged desertion to gain the labor of the escaped military personnel. In Philadelphia a year earlier, a court-martial found the master and boatswain of the merchant vessel *Rose* guilty of enticing seamen from HMS *Zebra* to work aboard his ship. The boatswain had apparently gone aboard the *Zebra* while the ship lay at anchor in the Delaware River, recruited several sailors, hidden them in the home of a sympathetic Philadelphia resident, and entered them into the *Rose*'s rolls as ordinary deckhands.[114] While such aid may have come with the potential for exploitation (deserters often found themselves blackmailed by their new employers to avoid recapture), for many British sailors and soldiers participation in civilian society yielded their only opportunities to escape harsh military life.

Fearing the consequences of deserters taking up arms against their former comrades, the army hierarchy imposed harsher and harsher punishments for the crime. As early as the summer of 1774, General Thomas Gage ordered that those soldiers who abandoned the British Army in America "will not be considered in the light of a deserter only, but also in that of a Traiter [*sic*] and Rebel to his King and Country."[115] Although the penalty for treason, as for desertion, remained death, a traitor could be executed without court-martial, stripping the deserter of his right to defend himself, and his officers of their right to mitigate the sentence. Punishment for civilians caught aiding in desertions could also be severe. In the fall of 1778, a

Long Island man convicted of attempting to aid deserters from the garrison received a heavy fine and, worse, one thousand lashes with a cat-o'-nine-tails outside the courthouse.[116] For someone unused to military discipline, the flogging must have been particularly harsh and perhaps even life-threatening. Other punishments placed civilians directly under that military discipline. In Philadelphia, a military court sentenced Thomas Buck, one of the men convicted of helping sailors desert from HMS *Zebra* in Philadelphia, to serve as an ordinary seaman on a man-of-war, a disastrous change in circumstances for a civilian mariner.[117] Despite the harsh punishments that the military justice system inflicted, however, residents of occupied towns continued to aid deserters throughout the war. As late as the spring of 1782, a council of high-ranking officers in Charleston complained of "alarming instances of desertion" among the German regiments stationed in the city, crediting the trend to "their having been so long stationed" there and forging "connexion[s] . . . with the Inhabitants of the town."[118] Wherever the army went, soldiers colluded with inhabitants to desert from the British service and remake their lives in America.

While British commanders feared that rebel sympathizers would seduce their soldiers, most often deserters simply wanted to escape military discipline and improve their prospects in life. According to testimony at his court-martial, Private John Winters of the Fifty-Ninth Regiment "was seduced away by the persuasions of an Inhabitant of Dedham, near Boston," sometime in 1774 or 1775. Two years later the deserter was found working in a Manhattan tavern. Although he attempted to rejoin the army when the British landed on Staten Island in the summer of 1776, enlisting with a Scottish loyalist regiment, old acquaintances soon revealed his previous desertion and the unfortunate Winters suffered death for abandoning his regiment. Despite this harsh sentence, Winters's occupation as a "servant to a man who kept a public house," as well as his attempt to reenlist in the British service in a loyalist regiment, suggests that his desertion did not carry ideological motives.[119] Rather, like many other deserters from occupied towns, Winters had attempted to better himself through the opportunities offered in port cities.

Soldiers' wives, who traveled with the army in large numbers, also took advantage of the opportunities on offer in occupation society by opening up grogshops to serve both soldiers and townspeople. As early as the summer of 1774, British commanders in Boston had to take measures to prevent these women from opening these illicit operations, ordering that a particular barn near the British encampment be declared off-limits to both soldiers and their wives, "as they have been found selling spirituous liquors there contrary to repeated orders."[120] During the winter of 1774–1775, British commanders reported frequent "complaints of soldiers['] wives, keeping dram shops in the different parts of the town."[121] In Newport during the winter of 1777–1778, the commanding general restricted wives from opening such businesses, observing that "the great drunkenness that prevails among the Soldiers, proceeds from the Soldiers['] wives being allowed to keep little shops not of the districts of their Regiments."[122] Dangers associated with these illicit shops went beyond mere drunkenness. On one particularly bad night in Boston, two soldiers died from ingesting "poisonous liquors" at a shop run by camp followers.[123] Despite their risk, these small operations persisted throughout occupied America, plying both common soldiers and lower-class colonists with a ready supply of liquor and providing opportunity for the mixing of both societies.[124]

As the concerns over dramshops run by soldiers' wives suggests, drunkenness pervaded occupied society. Soldiers on garrison duty, recovering from injuries, and in winter quarters often drank to excess, sometimes with disastrous results. In addition to the Boston soldiers who drank themselves to death, excessive imbibing caused arguments, brawls, and even murders. While stationed in Boston in early 1775, Frederick MacKenzie of the Royal Welch Fusiliers recorded that drunkenness among the soldiers contributed to "many irregularities" in military discipline.[125] The abuses MacKenzie alluded to could be severe and persisted throughout the war. In one particularly heinous case in the fall of 1779, William Whitlow of the Forty-Fourth Regiment murdered his wife in a drunken rage aboard a troop transport floating in New York harbor. Although testimony clearly proved him to be inebriated—not an acceptable defense in typical proceedings—the court acquitted Whitlow on the basis of temporary insanity.[126] Such instances demonstrate how commonplace and accepted drunken violence was in British military society in the eighteenth century.

Officers too got drunk, gambled to excess, and frequently resorted to dueling to settle disputes. Because their class status, officers had even more ready access to alcohol than did their men. Regulations restricting the sale of spirits to common soldiers often made exceptions for wine and other drinks intended for consumption by the officer class.[127] While these beverages constituted an important part of elite male sociability, some officers overindulged. In the winter of 1778, John Miller, an ensign in a loyalist regiment composed of volunteers from New Jersey, lost his commission after being accused by his commanding officer of having been drunk on duty.[128] Other drunken offenses led to worse outcomes. In occupied Charleston during the spring of 1781, Lieutenant Anthony Allaire of the Loyal American Regiment killed a fellow officer in the British service in a duel that began as a drunken argument over dinner in a tavern.[129] Officers in cities under military rule thus found themselves as prone to drunken altercations as enlisted men.

Violence within the military was not limited to drunken rages but also occurred with great frequency among sober officers, soldiers, and army personnel, often with very little cause. In the winter of 1777, Captain Luther Pennington of the Coldstream Guards killed Captain John Tollemarshe of HMS *Zebra* in a New York tavern following an argument that began when the naval officer began to hum a tune that Pennington found disagreeable.[130] In the fall of 1780, Private Patrick Egan of the Sixty-Third Regiment met his end in a New York street brawl between soldiers in his unit and royal artillerymen, one of whom fatally stabbed him with a bayonet.[131] In the winter of 1781, John Lindon, a private in the Twenty-Second Regiment recovering from his wounds in New York, shot his wife while perfectly sober and in front of several witnesses when she threatened to leave him.[132] Even divorced from the liquor on which it was often blamed, violence pervaded military culture, as both officers and soldiers fought with one another incessantly.

For all the opportunities it brought, then, occupation society was a violent, unstable one, and those who embraced it in search of new opportunity faced grave dangers. As civilians integrated themselves into military society, they also became vulnerable to the violence and risk inherent in under military rule. As they asserted their social independence, women faced the risk of sexual assault, doubly so as the very absence of male relatives that allowed their social independence also left them without the protections patriarchal society afforded. Even where women avoided physical violence, they remained prone to economic privation in occupation society. African Americans who fled slavery faced an even more precarious situation, constantly vulnerable to reenslavement and exploitation by British soldiers.

Even more devastating perhaps than the violence inherent within military society, however, was the potential social ruin for many Americans who bound their fortunes to that of the British Army. As the army invested and evacuated ports because of strategic and political concerns, it both made and destroyed those Americans who depended on it for reinvention.

The fragile gains ordinary people made under occupation depended entirely on the success of British arms, and dissolved almost instantly when British forces withdrew from areas it occupied. Americans discovered this hard fact when the British Army strategically evacuated Boston, Philadelphia, and Newport in the midst of the war, and thousands of people followed them away. These people were not hangers-on but rather those who had gained the most from British occupation and could not remain safely when the cities reverted to revolutionary rule. They included Joseph Galloway, who never returned to his native Philadelphia after his short rule as superintendent general.[133] The Wanton family, who had been at the center of occupied Newport's social scene, also had to leave its home when the British evacuated that city in the winter of 1779. Joseph Wanton Jr., who had been lieutenant governor of Rhode Island before the revolution and served as superintendent general of the police during the occupation of Newport, died impoverished in New York two years later.[134] Thousands of other Americans who had claimed the opportunities for reinvention that occupation brought also had to flee, creating a refugee crisis of epic proportions. Thousands more, unable to follow their benefactors, saw those opportunities disappear as the British pulled out and left them behind to fend for themselves.

The devastating effects that the evacuations of Philadelphia and Newport had on those who had bought into the British military's promises of reinvention and opportunity hammered home to many living in other occupied cities just how precarious their positions were. Their experiences also bore out this reality, as men and women of all backgrounds frequently experienced harassment, violence, exploitation, and other dangers, even in the best-run occupied ports. This realization caused many to reconsider their allegiances to the restored royal regimes, and ultimately most men and women living in port towns under military rule began to hedge their bets by maintaining ties to both sides. Far from hypocrisy, these ties allowed ordinary people to alleviate the privations of military rule while ensuring that, whichever side came out on top, they would avoid the fate of Galloway and the Wantons. Still, these connections—proven necessary by hard-won experience—undermined British authority even in the places that the king's army felt most secure.

CHAPTER 4

Starving amid Plenty

Occupation imposed harsh living conditions, even as British Army officers and their civilian collaborators went to great lengths to reconnect port cities to the wider economy of the British Empire. Imported luxuries flooded occupied zones as occupation regimes encouraged merchants to reconnect with counterparts in England and Scotland and to resume shipping the manufactured goods and commodities that had made the trans-Atlantic trade so lucrative before the war. On a local level, however, military rule interrupted vital links with the countryside, making it difficult to feed the civilian populations of each town, let alone the army and navy personnel and refugees crowded into occupied zones. As consumer goods like tea, ceramics, and printed cottons reappeared in shop windows and exports flowed out to Europe and the West Indies, residents struggled to obtain the everyday necessities of life. The result was a strange paradox in which citizens of cities awash in luxury goods and hard currency experienced—many for the first time—the privations of starvation, overcrowding, and lack of fuel in harsh winters.

British occupation restored American ports to the larger economy of the British Atlantic.[1] Many urban merchants, whose prewar livelihoods had depended on importing manufactures from England, embraced the chance to reopen the trade in consumer goods from Europe, while British manufacturers and firms relished the chance to return to what had been one of their largest markets. For their part, many ordinary residents of occupied cities delighted at the prospect of access to goods that had been cut off both by boycotts and parliamentary acts. Further, being able to supply consumer goods created a powerful incentive for British regimes to entice residents of occupied cities to support the Crown. Because of these pressures, manufactures came into occupied cities from a very early period, at times even selling for far less than they did before the war, much to the distress of merchants on both sides of the Atlantic.

Despite the plentiful supply of consumer goods, occupation caused severe shortages of food, fuel, and shelter in port cities, forcing many residents to turn to desperate measures to subsist. Army personnel severely strained local resources. Soldiers and their families, as well as refugees seeking safe haven behind British lines, often doubled or even tripled prewar civilian populations. At the same time as urban centers found their supplies of food and fuel stretched by increased population, zones of control made getting provisions from the surrounding countryside difficult in the best of circumstances, and impossible in the worst. Even where the British Army exerted control over outlying areas, raids, plundering, and lack of production limited the ability of the countryside to feed enlarged urban populations. Although supplies periodically arrived from England, they fell short of the needs of the occupied territories. Finally, overcrowding and harsh winters in the northern cities combined to create widespread housing and fuel shortages. The army's presence lowered the quality of life for everyone living in under military rule. Scarcities forced residents of the occupied zones to violate British policies in a number of ways. Almost all inhabitants of occupied cities, even vehement loyalists, maintained regular communication with friends, relatives, and acquaintances in rebel-held areas, using these ties to trade for necessities or, in some cases, a means of escape. Those who did not engage in such endeavors circumvented occupation regimes in other ways. Many also resorted to theft, hoarding, poaching, or squatting to scrape together enough to survive. In one way or another, ordinary men and women—even those who supported British rule wholeheartedly—had to circumvent occupation regimes in order to survive.

That residents of occupied areas had to turn to illegal means to survive undermined faith in British rule more generally. As citizens of port towns maintained trading ties with friends and relatives on the rebel side of the lines, and increasingly turned to unorthodox and even illicit tactics to meet their day-to-day needs, they learned by experience that, despite the potential economic benefits of a restoration of the empire, the king's representatives either would or could no longer supply basic necessities to his subjects. Just as social instability had been a double-edged sword that provided both opportunity for reinvention and ruin, the economics of occupation, which should have been a point of strength, became a weakness that helped to hasten people's growing belief in the illegitimacy of British authority in North America.

When British forces arrived in the port cities, merchants on both sides of the Atlantic seized the opportunity to quench Americans' long-suppressed hunger for English products. In Newport, Rhode Island, dry goods merchant Stephen Ayrault began writing to his contacts in Europe a mere three days after the British landed, advising a business connection that he would soon resume orders of metalware.[2] A month later, Ayrault wrote to two different former associates in Britain, assuring one that, although the war had "prevented [his] send[in]g for Pewter as Formerly," invoices for new stock would soon be forthcoming. The Newport merchant urged another supplier to send goods "p[e]r first Opportunity Hence as it is probabl[e] there will be Ships coming out in the spring."[3] A mere two months later, European imports began to arrive in Newport, with retailers advertising goods such as Madeira wine, Irish linens, Barcelonese handkerchiefs, wine glasses, wax, playing cards, and a wide variety of other manufactures from Europe.[4] Such imports may have begun even earlier. Captain John Peebles, the grenadier stationed in Newport during the winter of 1776–1777, recalled visiting several shops along the wharf looking for "some trimmings for a great Coat," though he remarked that the prices seemed quite high.[5]

Other ports saw a similar influx of imported goods almost immediately after British soldiers arrived. In New York, advertisements for imports began to appear in local papers in November 1776, again about two months after the conquest of the town. At his store in Maiden Lane, Patrick Reid boasted of freshly imported men's linen shirts, port wine, Glasgow beer, printed handkerchiefs, Russia duck cloth, and a variety of other items for purchase.[6] In December 1777, three months after the British entered Philadelphia, John Stevenson offered for sale several items recently imported on the ship *Ceres*, including Irish linens, needles, stationery, pewter plates, and tinware.[7] Robert Taylor, another Philadelphia merchant, advertised silk petticoats, ladies' cloaks, hats "with remarkable good lace," and a variety of coats "all made in the newest fashion."[8] The threat of a French fleet in the West Indies and the attempted invasion of Georgia by French and Continental forces slowed resumption of imports to Savannah, but merchants nevertheless began to service the port once the waters became safer. By the winter of 1781, residents and soldiers stationed in the city could purchase

West Indies rum, yards of broadcloth and corduroy produced in English textile mills, Indian chintz, and other goods.[9] In Charleston, South Carolina, resumption of trade occurred perhaps most rapidly. By July 1780, only a month after the British Army took the city, merchants advertised imported books, beaver hats, Jamaican rum, Spanish sugar, and "London Quality" Madeira wine for sale at auction to the highest bidder.[10]

Occupied cities began to export goods as well, most markedly in the southern ports of Savannah and Charleston. Part of British strategy in invading Georgia and South Carolina had been to restore the vital flow of rice, lumber, and other commodities to West Indian sugar plantations, and southern merchants duly began shipping supplies to the Caribbean soon after British rule resumed. In September 1780, only five months after the British conquest of Charleston, James Simpson reported that a large mercantile convoy stood ready to set sail and that "the value of the several cargoes, will amount, as I am well informed, to above one hundred thousand pounds sterling."[11] Exports of raw materials from Savannah resumed as well. Just before the British evacuation, a committee of Georgia loyalists calculated that "from the 1st of Janry 1780 to 1 Janry 1781 not less than 100 Vessels Enter'd in & Cleared from the Port of Savannah, a great part of w[hi]ch were loaded with Lumber & Naval Stores."[12] In response to this uptick in trade, the reconstituted Georgia Assembly even went so far as to propose a bill to impose "certain Duties upon all Goods, Wares, & Merchandizes whatsoever, which may be exported from this Province" to support the war effort.[13] Occupation and the restoration of trade thus had the potential to enrich both the local government and merchants.

Although exports from northern cities never resumed in any meaningful way, war plunder and surplus imports stimulated New York's oceangoing economy. Privateers, who sailed not only from New York but also from occupied Philadelphia and Newport, could apply for licenses to sell goods seized from rebel vessels in London if there was no market in the British-occupied North American ports.[14] In addition, merchants in New York found themselves possessed of, as superintendent Andrew Elliot put it, "quantities of British manufactures that had been imported chiefly by the Virginia and Maryland merchants" before the commencement of the war, for which there was little demand in the city. Beginning in 1779, the occupation regime allowed these goods to be shipped to Canada or the British West Indies, selling them and returning with cargoes of food and fuel. The regime made this move in order to save warehouse space and prevent losses by the merchants who held these goods and to bring in supplies of badly needed provisions for New York.[15] Thus, even if raw materials from occupied northern areas never flowed back to the mother country, the city's merchants did benefit from some opportunities to export goods to Europe and the West Indies.

While exporters had to rely on the beneficence of the military governments, if they played their cards right they could make a great deal of money, as the success of Philadelphia merchant Tench Coxe proves. Early in the war, Coxe had been forced from his native city because of his outspoken support for the king. When the British Army captured Philadelphia, Coxe returned and embarked on an ambitious mercantile business, leveraging social connections made among loyalists in New York to garner special licenses to export and reap large profits importing goods from Europe and the Caribbean. A distant familial relationship to superintendent Joseph Galloway and friendships with many of the regime's customs officials gave Coxe advantages that other importers lacked. After six months of military rule, the young trader bragged that in that time he had sold "consignments from New York, Mad[ei]ra, Britain, & the West Indies to the amount of £30,000."[16] Very much a man on the rise, Coxe rubbed shoulders with high-ranking British officers and civil administrators, frequently attending dinners, balls, and plays put on by Philadelphia's military elite. Many of these soldiers and officials likely came out to celebrate the young merchant's marriage to the daughter of a wealthy loyalist family, which Coxe's biographer describes as "one of the highlights of the city's social season."[17] In many ways, the occupation made Coxe's fortune.

Even with commerce restored and a lucky few merchants generating wealth for themselves, Americans often found the economic landscape different from that which had existed before the war. By the end of the first year of Newport's occupation, Stephen Ayrault had successfully resumed his import and retail businesses but found that he could not make as much profit as before the war, complaining to partners in England that "many Articles are much over charg'd" and even canceling some of his invoices.[18] Local merchants also faced the threat of adventurers from Britain who swept into these ports and often undersold long-established businesses. Merchant Samuel Carne reported that many of the new importers and retailers in Charleston came from Scotland and had never done business in South Carolina before the revolution.[19] Philadelphia's merchant community also saw an influx of newcomers from New York and Britain.[20] In

Georgia, during the fall of 1780, the legislature passed an act to impose additional duties on "Goods, Wares, & Merchandize Sold at Auction." The bill was sparked by complaints by shopkeepers "that everything was sold at Auction" by "Transient Persons & others" who "undersold them without contributing any thing towards the support of Government &c."[21] Georgia's bill echoed similar measures taken by occupation administrations in New York and Philadelphia, responding to similar complaints from both merchants and consumers.[22] Resumption of trade and a plentiful supply of cheap manufactured products did not necessarily benefit Americans living in occupied zones as much as they had hoped at the onset.

Still, trans-Atlantic trade lent economic and social vitality to occupied cities. Residents could see evidence of the economic rejuvenation physically in the streets of the towns themselves. Shops selling luxuries of all sorts also popped up all over occupied Philadelphia's wharf.[23] Such places promoted socialization between British soldiers and American civilians. In May 1778, just before British evacuation, Captain John Peebles recalled spending a pleasant afternoon in Philadelphia "shop[p]ing with the Ladies."[24] Quantities of British manufactures and the intermingled society that they fed had the potential to sway the population toward the British side. In New York, an informant wrote to Lord George Germain in the spring of 1779 stating, "This place is now become the Center of Trade with America, & people are building houses very fast."[25] A similar scene greeted visitors to Charleston a year after its conquest by British arms. On his return to Charleston in February 1781, Lieutenant Governor William Bull remarked with pride that "buildings are rising out of the ashes of that part of the Town burnt two years ago [during a British assault]."[26] In the same month, Charleston merchant William Burrows wrote to a friend, "You wou'd be greatly surprised if you was to walk thro' Broad-Street & along King Street to see the Number of Stores & Shops[;] . . . we have great plenty of all kind of goods."[27] The return of commerce and manufactured goods caused many residents to hope that occupied cities would soon return to the prosperity they had experienced before the war.

While the port towns were awash in imports, a lack of everyday necessities plagued territories under military rule. The British Army, which at times numbered as high as thirty-six thousand soldiers spread across North America, required a great deal of food and fuel. This demand outstripped what could be supplied from Great Britain, Ireland, and Canada, and in many places also left the surrounding countryside bare. Civilians found themselves even worse off than the military, as prices of essentials skyrocketed. In the midst of these shortages, the civilian population of each occupied city had to house the British garrisons, who crowded into churches, public buildings, and private homes. These soldiers often caused major property damage and very rarely paid sufficient rent. In short, military occupation stretched the resources of occupied zones to the breaking point.

Food shortages haunted military life in North America, with British troops always struggling to find enough to feed themselves. Although soldiers never starved, food stores, vital for long periods of campaigning, remained insecure throughout the war.[28] The demand for resources was immense: an eighteenth-century army of thirty-six thousand required at least 13,500 tons of food a year.[29] Competing zones of control made relying on the countryside for supplies problematic, and supplies from Britain were unreliable and susceptible to spoilage en route and corruption once they arrived in North America. Poor equipment and a counterproductive policy of destroying nearby farms and livestock herds to deprive the Continental Army of supplies worsened the problem. Although the ad hoc measures generally supplied the army, they often left little food remaining for civilian populations. Hunger threated both military and civilian populations in occupied areas, though in very different ways.

In their attempts to create a stable supply of victuals, British Army commanders solicited the produce of local farmers. Local supplies of fresh provisions depended on these farmers, some of whom lived within British lines but who, for the most part, resided in the no-man's-lands that emerged in between zones of British and Continental control. In each city, the occupation regimes set up public markets to encourage farmers and others from the countryside to come in and sell their produce to meet the army's needs. These exchanges were tightly regulated and controlled to benefit both traders and the army. In New York, such markets fell under the control of the superintendent of police, who took great care to encourage participation and prevent fraud. To reward farmers for coming in to sell their goods, the office of police allowed those who wished to come over from rebel-held New Jersey. The city's commandant ordered blank passes to be printed and issued to commanders of posts across the river in New Jersey, who could then issue them to "such People as you think may be trusted with Boats to attend this Market," as well as "such Persons as you may think proper to allow to pass with Country produce to this City."[30] To prevent fraud, the occupation regime guaranteed compensation for anyone whose produce was stolen or taken out of the city and continued earlier municipal practices of banning "hucksters"—unauthorized traders—from taking part in the city's public market, under penalty of exile.[31] The regime hoped that these measures would convince farmers in outlying areas that a trip to New York to sell produce would be secure and profitable.

However, markets in British-occupied zones may not have been as appealing to American farmers as military leaders hoped. As in earlier municipal governments, maximum prices were strictly controlled, though military administrators, more concerned with feeding their troops than the economic health of the community, proved to be much stricter than colonial city councils. In Newport, the commandant issued strict price limits for both fish and farm produce brought to market beginning in the summer of 1777. According to these regulations, a codfish could not sell for more than one and a half pence per pound, while a pound of pork or beef was "not to exceed" seven pence.[32] Inability to profit from increased demand may have prompted some Americans to stay home rather than take their produce to market. Further, trade between occupied zones and no-man's-land held risks for both sides. Americans who came into the lines from outside were constantly under suspicion by both sides. During the occupation of Philadelphia, General Howe complained that "divers ill disposed persons have under pretence of bringing in provisions . . . taken by force the property of several of his Majesty[']s loyal subjects."[33] Other traders fell victim to profiteers, who met them just outside of town, bought their produce, and sold it in Philadelphia at a markup.[34] Americans living in areas controlled by rebel forces could face dire consequences if they were caught supplying British forces. According to his own account, William Williams of Ulster County, New York, came into British lines as an impoverished refugee after "being imprisoned and fined upwards of Eleven hundred pounds" by the revolutionary government "on a Charge for Sending Provisions into the City of New York."[35] Americans who traded with the British could also face punishment when the British Army pulled out of an area.[36] Thus, although it occurred on a large scale, trade had significant drawbacks and was hampered by a lack of trust on the part of British purchasers and the need for secrecy by many American traders.

When it could not trade for enough provisions, the military raided local rebel-held areas and appropriated produce and livestock for the use of the army and navy. Following the occupation of New York, British commanders pursued a series of campaigns in New Jersey in an attempt to secure provisions for the army stationed in the city. Although they met with mixed success, such endeavors continued throughout the war.[37] In Newport, parties of loyalist refugees took boats to raid the neighboring coasts of Rhode Island, Connecticut, and New York in search of food and other provisions. On one trip in May 1779, a party brought back, according to one witness, "upward of 1000 Sheep and 40 Cattle" for the use of the garrison.[38] Although controversial and potentially a violation of the rules of eighteenth-century warfare, these raids continued throughout the war, especially in areas where large bodies of armed loyalists served with the British Army. As late as April 1782, when for the most part the war had already been decided, the British commander of Charleston continued to send raiding parties out into the South Carolina countryside to confiscate provisions, allegedly in response to rebel seizures of loyalist property.[39] Such activities may have secured food for the British Army in the short term but did little to encourage Americans to continue to supply it, except at gunpoint.

Even supposedly friendly areas were not immune to plundering by soldiers, and British commanders proscribed such acts under penalty of death. Officers constantly published orders to prevent theft and plundering by soldiers in occupied territories, with General Howe going so far during the invasion of New York as to order that any solider found plundering "be Executed on the Spot" by his officers. In Philadelphia a year later, the General again ordered his officers to "Suppress such Unsoldierlike Behaviour so absolutely Repugnant to all Military Order & Discipline."[40] Still, soldiers and their families continued to illegally plunder in every territory the army controlled. In late September 1775, Winifred McCowan, a camp follower with the army in Boston, stole a valuable bull from the town common and had it butchered, for which a court-martial ordered her whipped and imprisoned for three months.[41] In occupied New York, British soldier Loftus Cliffe remarked to an acquaintance that, even had he wanted to engage in such theft, his encampment was "too close neighbors to the Hessians to find an Ox or Sheep in the Woods," continuing that in defiance of orders against "moroding [sic]," the German mercenaries "if they even meet a milch Cow take her aside and knock her in the head."[42] This behavior also occurred where the British Army hoped to conciliate, as in Georgia and South Carolina. Despite officers' attempts to present the army as liberators, between the conquest of Savannah in December 1778 and the fall of Charleston in May 1780, several Georgia planters complained that the army's agent for collecting provisions carried off their "Stock, Provisions & many Articles of Household Furniture . . . refusing to give receipts for what they carried away."[43] Plundering and theft, even when the British Army attempted to stop it, remained a fact of life in occupied and enemy territory alike.

In addition to plunder, the British Army intentionally destroyed food supplies in contested areas to deprive the Continental Army of succor. These tactics often hurt those loyal to the Crown as well. In January 1782, British soldiers destroyed the entire rice crop of Alexander Wright, a relative of the Georgia's governor whose plantation lay only a few miles from Savannah. According to documents later produced by Wright in an attempt to obtain compensation, the destroyed grain amounted to "Six Thousand Seven Hundred & twenty Bushels of Rough Rice."[44] Such destruction occurred not only in the South, where rebel guerillas lurked in the backcountry, but in the area around New York as well. William Tryon, the former governor of New York who during the war commanded a force of British and American troops guarding northern Manhattan, led several raids into Connecticut and New Jersey, burning farms, supply depots, and other sources of victuals that could be used by revolutionaries.[45] While these raids robbed the enemy of essential supplies, they also deprived the soldiers stationed in nearby cities of those same provisions and alienated the very farmers and herdsmen necessary to feed both the army and local civilians.

Supplies coming from Canada and Britain could be as unreliable as locally sourced provisions. Foodstuffs often spoiled en route. In the fall of 1775, out of a shipment of 6,995 barrels of flour to the British Army in Boston, over two-thirds was condemned as completely ruined. A year later, nearly three hundred thousand pounds of ships' biscuit intended for the army's use in New York were condemned.[46] Such deliveries could also be unreliable and were subject to petty corruption. In January 1779, General Richard Prescott, commander of the British garrison in Newport, complained that "the Butter promised us by the Naval Agent has fallen short, as also the supply of Oatmeal, which, I find, will not amount to more than Nine days of that kind of Bread."[47] Poor logistics both hindered the war effort and forced soldiers to rely more and more on local food supplies, which squeezed those civilians living behind the lines.

Poor equipment exacerbated these logistical dilemmas. In Savannah, although the army could procure rice in large quantities, a commanding general reported that "for the want of kettles [it] is generaly wasted," warning that "the Consequences may also be Fatal, as the Necessity of Regular Cooking & Dressing of Victuals is more obvious in this Country than any where Else."[48] Lieutenant General Earl Charles Cornwallis's force in North Carolina also suffered from supply shortages throughout the campaign that culminated in the Battle of Yorktown as he forced his troops to drop much of their heavy cooking supplies during forced marches through the Carolinas and Virginia. Ultimately, this shortage contributed to Cornwallis's defeat, as his underfed and overworked soldiers were weakened by hunger and disease by the time of his surrender at Yorktown.[49] While the British Army in America generally had enough food to function, the circumstances of the war and its often counterproductive policies ensured that gathering provisions was always, if not a crisis, at the very least a pressing concern for military leaders.

For civilians, the army's struggles meant a massive increase in price and decrease in availability of food. In New York, the wholesale price of a hundredweight (100–112 pounds) of brown bread—a basic staple—rose from fifteen shillings (New York currency) in September 1776 to seventy shillings in the beginning of 1782, and a barrel of flour rose from sixteen to eighty shillings over the same period. Pork, corn, and other essential foodstuffs underwent similar price increases.[50] Although reliable records of prices do not exist in other cities, shortages plagued occupation life everywhere, from the earliest instances of military rule until the end of the war. In Boston, during the summer of 1775, merchant George Brinley wrote to his brother, "It is now seven weeks since we have had a Joint of Fresh Provisions in our Family."[51] In January 1779, printer Solomon Southwick lamented of occupied Newport that "the distress of numerous poor Men, Women & Children from that Town, is truly Deplorable," adding that many people "can scarcely get a Single Mouthful of Bread for several Days together." The writer pleaded to an acquaintance in Boston for aid, asking "the Town of Boston to remember its own sufferings" under occupation and to help those facing similar deprivation.[52] Such scenes repeated themselves in New York, Philadelphia, Savannah, and Charleston throughout the war and forced even the most ardent supporters of the occupation regimes to undercut them to survive.

Because aggregated economic data on prices of food and shelter do not survive for most occupied cities, it is hard to know whether the dire shortages described by many witnesses and later historians were hyperbole or stark

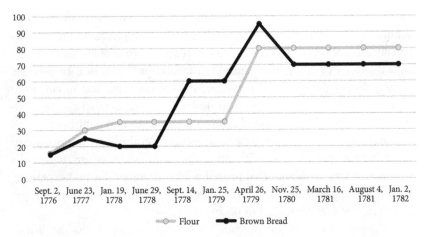

Figure 9. Flour and brown bread prices in occupied New York City (in shillings), September 1776 to January 1782. Prices are from Hugh Gaine's *New York Gazette and Weekly Mercury* (1776–1779) and James Rivington's *Royal Gazette* (1780–1782).

economic reality. The truth seems to lie somewhere in between. What data are available—mostly from New York City, whose newspapers recorded prices on an irregular basis throughout the seven-year occupation—suggest that prices did rise exponentially, though inflation of the various colonial currencies during the war again makes it hard to judge by exactly how much. Evidence on the number of buildings occupied by soldiers and sailors compared to the population estimates for the cities suggests that housing was also a pressing issue, though whether the shortage of living quarters led to as dramatic consequences as some witnesses attest cannot be known for certain. Still, the letters and journals of civilians, soldiers, and visitors to occupied cities reveal that nearly everyone felt the pinch and that the high price of food, shelter, and fuel, whether illusory or real, remained at the forefront of nearly everyone's mind for the duration of military rule.

In addition to food, acquiring enough fuel to serve both the military and civilian populations of occupied zones remained a consistent problem throughout the war, especially in the northern cities. The logistics of fuel for the soldiers proved to be an enormous challenge to army officers, with the occupying force in New York alone requiring around seventy thousand cords of wood per year to keep warm and cook what victuals could be found. Problems arose in finding sources for this supply, as occupied zones usually did not contain enough open forest acreage to provide for the army. This dilemma came up early and often in occupied America. In besieged Boston during the winter of 1775–1776, the British Army had to cut down every tree within their lines and tear down numerous derelict and unoccupied buildings, including the old North Church, to maintain heating and cooking fires. The situation grew so desperate that the army imported coal from Britain and Quebec, with three thousand caldrons arriving in the summer of 1775. Although coal proved wildly impracticable and expensive, British leadership sought again to import it to New York in 1777 and 1778 as a deficit of fuel continued to plague the army.[53]

Occupied Newport felt the fuel shortage most heavily, as the British garrison's situation on a heavily populated island combined with harsh New England winters to create logistical nightmares. By the end of the first year of occupation, one officer in the quartermaster's department recalled that he had been forced "to give orders for the Cutting Down of almost every Tree on [Aquidneck] Island for fuel."[54] Once the trees had been used up, British troops tore down fences and derelict buildings.[55] When these ran out, the garrison began sending ships to other islands in Narragansett Bay and even as far as Long Island to cut lumber for the post, exposing them to the dangers of bad weather and attack by privateers. Even with these extraordinary measures, the situation of the garrison on Rhode Island became desperate. During one particularly brutal winter storm in December 1778, several Hessian soldiers froze to death in their unheated guard houses. They were found, as a nineteenth-century antiquarian put it, "standing in their sentry boxes frozen to death; each with his musket standing by his side!"[56]

The army in New York also suffered from lack of fuel, although ready access to the forests of Long Island made the situation much less dire for that city's garrison. Still, harsh winters and transportation problems made getting enough wood to the city's garrison difficult. Baroness Fredericke Riedesel, who as wife of a general should have been well supplied by the commissary, recalled that during the winter of 1779–1780, her family's ration of firewood, issued on Monday, often ran out by the weekend, after which she had to borrow from other officers or purchase cords on the open market. In one instance, the baroness complained, "I have myself paid one piaster (which is a crown with us) for a single stick."[57] Riedesel was not alone in her privations. The winter of 1779–1780 marked a crisis over fuel in New York, brought on by deforestation of Manhattan Island and increased rebel raids on woodcutters and woodcutting vessels on Long Island. During that winter, the price of wood soared to above five pounds sterling per cord, making it easily the most expensive staple in an already distressed city. Even though increased protection for woodcutters and vessels eventually brought down the price, it remained costly, rarely dropping below four pounds sterling, and the garrison continued to suffer severe shortages for the remainder of the war.[58] Although the army needed less fuel during its campaigns in the more temperate southern colonies than it did in Newport or New York, fuel shortages and high prices persisted there as well.

As armies struggled to find essential supplies, civilians found themselves even more hard-pressed. Although many commanders sympathized with the plight of the civilian populations, provisioning the troops came first. During the winter of 1778–1779, the commander of Newport's garrison confided to General Clinton that, due to shortages of food and the army's rapid consumption of available provisions, "what the Inhabitants will do next Summer for Provisions . . . I cannot imagine."[59] A year earlier, the city's occupation regime had actually attempted to expel some twenty poor families from town so they would not become a drain on the garrison's store of provisions.[60] In December 1781, General Alexander Leslie, commander of British forces in South Carolina, wrote for additional food stores to distribute to Charleston's civilians, despairing that the "the number of Loyalists & helpless Refugees, with their Women & Children is very great," and warning that "unless the Inhabitants get some Supply they must all leave Town."[61] Where the inhabitants would go, since they likely faced legal retribution or even violence if they fled to areas controlled by revolutionaries, he did not say. Regardless of officers' intentions, however, civilians residing in occupied areas faced the same problems of provisioning as did the army with far fewer resources to combat it.

Shortages strained resources as people struggled to feed themselves and their families and heat their homes. In March 1777, only three short months after the British had invested Newport and the island on which it sat, an escaped prisoner reported that there was no fresh meat to be had in the market and that a loaf of bread, "which used to be six Coppers," now cost eight silver pennies, more than quadruple the previous price.[62] Often such high food prices bore a stark contrast to the low prices of other goods. In the same February 1781 in which he crowed about the rebuilding of Charleston, Lieutenant Governor William Bull lamented that, despite the economic revival, "the price of corn & common articles of provisions is nearly double what they were in our former happy Prosperity."[63] William Eddis, a customs collector who fled to New York in 1777, observed a similar phenomenon in that city, writing, "Though comparative plenty abounds in this garrison, yet almost every needful article bears so exorbitant a price."[64] Such shortages, which occurred almost everywhere, forced civilians to turn to other sources of food and fuel. Baroness Riedesel recalled that, during the cold New York winter of 1779–1780, "the poor were obliged to burn fat, in order to warm themselves and cook their meals."[65] High prices for the necessities of life made day-to-day survival difficult for everyone in occupied cities, but those less fortunate felt the pain most acutely.

Refugees, who often came without money or sufficient support networks in occupied cities, both exacerbated the problem and suffered the worst of these shortages. As British control of the southern borderlands crumbled during the summer of 1781, thousands of loyalists fled to Savannah and Charleston. In Savannah, the situation became so grave that Sir James Wright borrowed £2,652 on his personal account, with no guarantee of government reimbursement, to purchase "Rice, Flour & what Beef & Port could be got" to succor these unfortunates, "for they had not a Shilling in their Pockets & Could not be allowed to Perish."[66] When pressed about his generosity months later by Whitehall, Wright responded, "My Bills on the Lords of the Treasury Run high, but Loyal Refugees must not Perish with Hunger in our Streets."[67] Charleston faced a similar dilemma. In October 1781, the city's military commandant reported, "The Number of Refugees & Militia . . . will greatly contribute to exhaust our resources, especially of Provisions, as these poor People come to us in the possession of every want."[68] Still, the military government did allocate resources to feed and clothe the refugee population.[69] In the southern cities, at least, the restored royal government made some provision to deal with the influx of refugees caused by the brutal nature of war in the South.

Refugees elsewhere did not meet with such compassion. In New York, where the refugee crisis hit hardest, the city's commandant wrote to a colleague of "the Legions of women from the Jersey's" who had fled to Long Island, complaining, "I can consider them in no other Light than as a Swarm of Locusts" who would quickly consume the army's valuable supplies.[70] New York City attracted large numbers of refugees throughout the war, and commanding generals received hundreds of petitions for rations and alms.[71] For much of the war, relief was awarded on an ad hoc basis, with each new arrival making his or her individual case based on that individual's demonstrated loyalty and need. By the end of 1781, however, there were so many refugees that the occupation regime established guidelines as to how to distribute aid. The inspector of refugees was to divide people into four ranks "in some relation to their Stations in Life," with the first rank receiving rations and a dollar per day for sustenance, and the poorest receiving only rations. Further, the guidelines specified that "no able bodied single man used to Labor, or having a Trade" would be allowed to draw rations or support. Finally, the occupation regime claimed the right "to confine any Refugee, of suspected character or disorderly behavior."[72] Relief for refugees in New York was to be tightly limited and controlled, leaving most to fend for themselves, competing with locals and soldiers on the scarce marketplace for food, fuel, and shelter.

If treatment could be harsh, the petitions submitted by refugees to authorities in the later years of the war reveal the dire circumstances of many. Alice Armstrong, an eighty-four-year-old widow, came to Manhattan in 1780 after her home in Stoney Point, New York, was destroyed in the struggle waged by British and Continental forces over the forts of the lower Hudson River. In a petition to the inspector of refugees, Armstrong sought provisions for herself and several elderly family members, claiming that "the excessive high Price of Provision and every necessary of Life" and her "great Age" left the family "unable to support themselves."[73] Rachel Myers, a widow who had resided in Newport, "where she supported by her Industry a large Family," found herself exiled to New York with her nine children after the evacuation of Rhode Island in late 1779 because of her son's having taken up arms with other loyalists to plunder the neighboring coasts. Although she had subsisted for over a year by relying on "a few benevolent friends," by the spring of 1781 she had exhausted her resources and found "all her Industry is not now sufficient to attend [her children with] the Necessaries of Life."[74]

Despite the large numbers of petitioners, pleading for rations remained for many a last resort, to be taken only when all other options had been exhausted. Mary Tailer, another widow who had been a refugee inside British lines since the evacuation of Boston in 1776 but "being resolved never To become burthensoom [sic] while in her power to avoid it," waited five years to apply for aid. Her petition in the fall of 1781 asserted her impoverished circumstances, as she claimed that "from the high price of provisions

Rents & having herself two Children [and] a Servant To sup[p]ort[,] her finances are Exhausted," forcing her to turn to the army for relief.[75] By the later years of the war, as British positions collapsed or were evacuated, the influx of refugees became greater as longer-term exiles ran out of resources, creating a crisis and contributing to the skyrocketing food prices in occupied New York.[76]

Refugees escaping slavery came into occupied zones with far less than other migrants, making their situations even more precarious. The problem grew most pronounced in the South, where promises of freedom behind British lines brought tens of thousands of enslaved people to British garrisons at Savannah and Charleston. While occupation regimes paid close attention to these people and attempted to sort out who belonged to loyalists and who could legally claim their freedom, slaves crossing the lines in the South often had little or no familial support and became dependent on occupation regimes, leaving them vulnerable to the worst conditions of occupation society.[77] In cramped conditions, disease swept through these populations at a harrowing rate. James Simpson reported during the first month of the occupation of Charleston that "a malignant Fever hath broke out amongst the negroes who have loiterr'd in and about Charles Town since the surrender; which sweeps them away in great numbers." The self-emancipated people who sought salvation with the British Army had perhaps the most to gain from occupation, but also faced some of the worst conditions that military rule had to offer.[78]

In addition to supply shortages and the persistent refugee crisis, the need to house soldiers and their families further stretched the resources of those living in occupied cities. Throughout the war, the British Army tried to keep soldiers separate from civilian populations by encamping them just outside of town in tents or in barracks that could be sequestered from residential neighborhoods. However, officers kept quarters within the cities throughout the year, ordinary soldiers often had their winter quarters located inside the towns, and the exigencies of war often forced the army to quarter soldiers in town when they could not guarantee the safety of camps on the outskirts. Although the army tried to house troops in public buildings or houses abandoned by rebels, these buildings were always in short supply, and placing soldiers in already occupied private houses became a necessity. The imposition could be unpleasant. An escaped prisoner from Newport told the reverend Ezra Stiles that he "found 5 or 6 to Ten [soldiers] quartered in most of the Houses on the [roads]" on the island, and more in the town.[79] Despite the attempt to shield civilians from the burden of quartering soldiers, in actuality the burden fell on them at their most vulnerable point.

Soldiers often damaged the dwellings they inhabited, sometimes irreparably. In 1781, homeowner Sarah Gay complained that her house in Savannah had been occupied as a barracks and hospital with no rent paid and that soldiers had pulled down her shed and done so much damage as to render the dwelling "totally useless to her." Even worse, because the house lay near the fortifications of the city, it was "Lyable to be pulled down at any time when it may be thought necessary."[80] Such destruction occurred frequently, as engineers built defensive works and officers strove to create more secure positions. As the commanding general of Newport's garrison prepared for the winter of 1777–1778, he tore down several houses where troops had been quartered the year before to avoid false alarms that had plagued the garrison the previous winter.[81] Military commanders' standard preparations for defense of their position could prove devastating for the civilians within their lines.

With so many needing to be housed and a limited supply of adequate quarters available, officials in charge of billeting wielded a great deal of power. Some, such as General James Pattison, commandant of New York from 1779 to 1780, tried their best to shield civilians from the worst of quartering, spreading billets equally and exempting the poor and infirm. In denying one officer his preferred accommodation, Pattison reminded him, "I cannot but attend to the Ease of the Citizens (who are equally under my Protection)," advising him that the house he desired already had several officers quartered in it and ordering that he choose another.[82] Despite his feeling for those civilians under his protection, Pattison still had to make hard choices, and New York's civilian population suffered for it. In August 1779, the army took the home that a Mrs. Campbell had been living in for the use of troops, but the billeting officer saw to it she was given "a Billett of two good Rooms and the use of a Kitchen in a Respectable Family," which, he pointed out, "is a greater allowance than falls to the Lott of a Captain."[83] Even with this assurance, losing her home could not have improved Mrs. Campbell's lot in life, and many Americans living under military rule suffered the same fate, no matter how compassionate their rulers may have been.

While officers and soldiers were assigned billets by the army's bureaucracy, soldiers' families often simply took up residence wherever they could find space, with no permission from anyone. In March 1780, a Mr. Burton complained that "a number of Women belonging to the 37th Regt." had taken over his home in New York's Bowery Lane.[84] Although the commandant ordered them removed, both the military families and the officials charged with evicting them ignored his instructions. Burton's situation was typical. Vestry inspectors found that Daniel Deuscomb's house at 50 Wall Street was inhabited by soldiers' wives in March 1778, and the commandant again ordered the barrack master, a Mr. Page, to remove them. Nevertheless, three months later, the women remained, as "Mr. Page has never troubled himself about it."[85] Such problems existed because soldiers' wives, although they had always resided with the British Army, had little official standing and were expected to live in the same cramped barracks and quarters as their husbands, who often slept ten or twelve to a room. Crowded circumstances forced these women to seek alternative housing arrangements, especially when they had children to care for. Officers often turned a blind eye to their squatting for lack of a better solution to the problem. Still, in times of shortage, these military families could become very unwelcome in occupied society. At one point, the problem of housing and feeding soldiers' families became so cumbersome that the army began to encourage commanders to send those who could not be provided for to Ireland on returning provisioning ships.[86] When officers refused to intervene, civilians had to deal not only with the housing needs of soldiers themselves but also with their families and other camp followers.

Despite the inconveniences and drain on resources that housing military personnel caused, having officers quartered in one's home could have advantages. During the frigid winter of 1778–1779, Samuel Freebody, a distiller in Newport, confided to a relative that, despite having "had half the wood you shipt us taken away from us by the Barrack Master . . . by the kind assistance of an Hessian Officer Quartered upon me, we have as yet been Comfortable on Acct of Fuel." Freebody expected this generosity to continue as long as the German soldier lived in his home, "as there is the greatest harmony between us."[87] Officers also received a housing stipend from the army, and so paid rent, a perk that helped many in occupied cities scrape together enough income to cope with rising food prices. Despite fringe benefits for some, however, the burden of quartering the British Army fell heavily on residents with already-stretched resources.

Scarcity of resources, an increase in the poor and refugee populations, and the burden of quartering soldiers combined to force civilians to take increasingly desperate measures, undermining the authority of British military rule. In this struggle to survive, connections to friends, family, and acquaintances living elsewhere became crucial, as people tried to make up shortfalls. The wartime experiences of the Brinley family, which originated in Newport but extended to throughout New England, explicate how such links remained essential. During the siege of Boston in 1775–1776, Francis Brinley, a wealthy Newport merchant and farmer, supplied several friends and relatives with fresh provisions. In July 1775, Brinley's brother Thomas requested that he send up "two or three Dozen of well grown Chickens, and a Dozen of Ducks which are not to be procured here at any Rate."[88] A few weeks later, brother George also requested a few dozen birds, as well as "Two good Fatt Sheep or Shoals, and a little good Butter," warning him to mark the animals so that they would not be stolen, as a previous shipment had.[89] In the fall, Francis's cousin Mary Garrish also wrote to request "a little good Butter a Chese & some Eggs."[90] This request was followed a month later by a similar missive from Nathaniel Brinley, another brother.[91] Francis Brinley even went so far as to offer family members who wished to leave Boston sanctuary in Newport. Although the situation was grim, however, Thomas assured his brother that his family, at least, "at present do not think of quitting this unhappy Town."[92] Still, the members of the Brinley clan in Boston depended on Francis's generosity as conditions deteriorated and British supplies fell short.

Francis Brinley's kindness to his Boston relatives was reciprocated when British forces came to Newport at the end of the 1776. After fleeing Boston with the British evacuation, George Brinley followed the army to New York and managed to obtain a civilian position in the commissary department, which he used to support Francis in occupied Newport. In the spring of 1777, George sent his brother a quantity of wheat purchased on Long Island, though he lamented that there was "no Port wine to be had."[93] A few months later, perhaps to make up for the lack of port, George sent up several casks of Madeira via a British captain headed to Newport, although he confessed, "[I] can't think of sending you any Butter as what we have here is horrid."[94] In March 1778, George sent his brother something far more valuable: a letter of introduction to Newport's new commissary, who, he assured Francis, would help him "at any time you should be in want of Salt Provisions, Butter, or anything in his power."[95] George's generosity to his brother was not limited to food. In the fall of 1778, he sent Francis several trunks of warm clothing for the upcoming winter but had to wait for a safe vessel that he was sure would not be stopped and inspected by British warships.[96] Despite his attachment to New York's occupation regime, George Brinley proved willing to use his position and to take potentially illegal measures to support his brother in occupied Newport.

The family network that supported the Brinleys during the war persisted as the physical areas they occupied changed hands. Even as he relied on supplies from George in New York during the occupation of Newport, Francis continued to correspond with and support his brother Nathaniel, who had had remained in Boston and been placed under arrest by the revolutionary government as a suspected loyalist. In April 1779, Nathaniel wrote to request "a couple pieces of Linen suitable for Shirts," as the price of cloth in Boston had risen beyond his capacity.[97] Similarly, George kept up his correspondence with Francis even after the British had evacuated Newport. In October 1781, two years after Newport had reverted to revolutionary rule, George wrote that he had been unable to return to Newport one of Francis's slaves who had absconded to New York City, but he was able to send his brother twenty guineas, which would surely have been welcome in the economically depressed port.[98] George continued to write to Francis through the end of the war, after which he faced exile for his activities in service to the British Army.[99] Familial support transcended zones of control for the Brinley family, as its members attempted to aid each other regardless of which claimed sovereignty in a particular region.

The ties that residents of occupied cities maintained to rebel-controlled areas had the potential to subvert British authority. In addition to smuggling food and other necessities in and out of the lines, civilians living in occupied areas shipped money and other valuable assets to hide them from authorities. In addition to resuming correspondence with British merchants when the occupation began, Stephen Ayrault of Newport also wrote to business associates in Boston. In January 1777, he used his connections in Massachusetts to send 625 Continental, congressional, and Rhode Island paper dollars, "which cannot purchase anything here unless it be to very great Disadvantage" to the rebel-held zone, asking his acquaintance to "purchase some Land, or Interest me in some Manufacture of Iron." This money belonged not only to him but to several of his neighbors and likely represented an attempt to shield these assets, which had been issued by various rebel governments, from seizure by the returned British authorities. More important, the investments acted as a hedge against the potential failure of the occupation regime.[100]

Correspondence and movement outside of the lines of occupation could also turn a profit for the entrepreneurially inclined. John Adlum, a captured rebel soldier on parole in occupied New York City, unwittingly became part of his landlady's profiteering scheme when he volunteered to fetch produce at the market for the household, which included around a half dozen other Continental prisoners. Adlum had discovered that, as a Continental soldier, he could buy food from sympathetic vendors cheaper than his landlady, one Mrs. Carrow, who had a reputation as "a great favourite" of New York's then-commandant, General James Robertson. Once ensconced in Mrs. Carrow's finances, Adlum discovered that Carrow profited not only from renting her house to paroled Continental officers but also from their resources. As the young man recounted, Carrow would offer a silver dollar for four or five paper Continental dollars. Once she had collected "a considerable sum," she would obtain a pass to leave the city from her benefactor, General Robertson, to visit her husband in revolutionary-controlled New Jersey. At the same time, she also procured letters recommendation from her boarders "to General Washington, mentioning the service done to our officers in supplying them with hard money for their paper." Using this endorsement, she then sought and obtained permission to buy provisions in revolutionary-held Newark, where provisions were far more plentiful than in besieged New York, with her Continental money. In one instance, she returned with "two Sloop loads of flour beef & pork," which she sold to purveyors in New York City for below market price. Still, her proceeds were more than enough to turn a profit, considering that she had purchased the foodstuff with Continental money that she obtained at a fraction of its face value, yet reaped her proceeds in hard currency. While Adlum left New York in early 1777, his erstwhile landlady likely continued her lucrative practice of taking revolutionary-issued paper money outside the lines to purchase food throughout the war. Indeed, her profits likely grew larger in the war's later years, as food prices increased and the value of Continental money plummeted.[101]

Mrs. Carrow's scheme only scratches the surface of New York's position as a center of illicit commerce between zones of control throughout the Revolutionary War. According to records kept by the occupation administration, hundreds of people passed in and out of the lines on a weekly basis throughout the town's seven-year occupation. In the eight months between October 1, 1779, and May 30, 1780, alone, the commandant's office issued 434 passes to individuals passing into and out of the lines. Taking a conservative estimate of 50 passes a month during the 84 months of occupation, the occupation regime probably issued at least 4,200 passes during the war.[102] While heavily regulated, the army made passes available to those wishing to attend to urgent financial affairs, visit sick relatives, and reunite with family members. John Vanderhoven, for example, obtained a pass in March 1780 to visit his father in Elizabethtown, New Jersey, while a Mrs. Allison got a pass on to see her husband, a prisoner of war on parole on Long Island, on the condition that on her return she escort another woman to see her children in New Jersey.[103] Many more people passed through the military lines on vessels flying flags of truce, which regularly trafficked between New York and designated points in rebel-held New Jersey and Connecticut. Many used these conveyances to take manufactured goods and money out of New York and to bring food and other essentials back into the city, hiding these illicit items in their personal effects to avoid detection.[104] Unsurprisingly, a thriving black-market trade also emerged between the occupied zone and the neighboring rebel states, in which smugglers brought foodstuffs from hostile areas and took away rum, manufactured foods, and hard currency from the occupied city, in defiance of both British and revolutionary law.[105]

Smuggling also took place between occupied cities and places outside North America. Merchant vessels given permission to trade manufactured goods often diverted from their course to trade elsewhere. While managing New York's port during the winter of 1777–1778, superintendent Andrew Elliot worried that merchants applying for licenses to export goods outside of the thirteen colonies intended to "elude the Restrictions here and the laws of trade at those places." Had they been granted licenses, Elliot continued, these traders "would have pretended to have met with bad weather, drove off by Rebel Privateers."[106] When the city did begin to issue export licenses a year later in an attempt to alleviate the glut of manufactured goods in the city, Elliot's fear came to pass. The captain of the brigantine *Cato*, loaded with "225 packages of British manufacture and 179 Casks of Nails and Ironmongery" and issued a licensed to trade at the British island of Saint Christopher, diverted at the last moment to the Dutch port of Saint Eustatius. According to the testimony of a ship's boy, the cargo was then sold to American vessels on the island, and much of it ended up in revolutionary Philadelphia.[107] In the South, where legitimate trade with the West Indies had been restored, merchants still engaged in illegal practices with alarming frequency. Traders often absconded with refugee slaves, selling them to planters in Jamaica and other West Indian islands, often with the support of corrupt British soldiers or civilians in the army's employ.[108] Such practices ranged throughout occupied port towns, undermining the policies put in place by occupation regimes to regulate trade and weakening their authority.

The measures that the British Army took to prevent smuggling reveal the extent of the problem. In July 1779 alone, New York's occupation regime made three new regulations to curb boats coming into the city, ordering flags of truce to be stopped and searched at certain points, restricting market boats to daylight hours, and issuing rules for fishing craft and other small boats that frequented the harbor and rivers.[109] These measures evidently proved ineffective, as only two months later the commandant ordered even stricter rules, limiting the amount of baggage that civilians passing out of the city could carry "a bundle containing cloathing and necessaries" and subjecting that bundle to search on leaving and entering the lines.[110] In Newport, authorities periodically searched vessels flying flags of truce as they went back and forth from revolutionary Providence. One such inspection, conducted in July 1777, discovered among the 131 women and 85 children aboard large quantities of duck cloth and men's clothing.[111] Authorities also monitored ferries. In New York, the inspection of a ferry traveling between Manhattan and Brooklyn in the summer of 1780 yielded a box of women's shoes destined for New Jersey.[112] Despite the restrictions that military regimes imposed to stop inhabitants from smuggling goods and money in and out of the occupied zones, such activities persisted as city residents attempted to overcome shortages and help family members elsewhere.

People and goods traveled between zones of control with startling regularity. Thomas Hazard, a blacksmith living across the Narragansett Bay from Newport in Kingstown, Rhode Island, often traveled to and from the city on flag vessels during the occupation, at one point noting the death of a slave aboard during a trip in the summer of 1778.[113] Elizabeth Morris, a Newporter who joined her loyalist husband in New York a year after the British evacuation (presumably also using a flag vessel), felt comfortable enough after her arrival to write her sisters back in Rhode Island to request an "agreeable bedsted " and several other household items for her new life in New York, though she admitted that her writing had been hurried as "this Flag has been so often countermanded" by British vessels, that she had expected it to be stopped and diverted once more.[114] Such seizures were so commonplace as to be routine. In June 1781, a British warship stopped and seized the schooner *Endeavor*, a flag vessel headed from North Carolina to Charleston, which had on board "a quantity of tobacco for the use of the American prisoners there."[115] Still, no one batted an eye. Despite the risk, Americans living in British-occupied ports used flag vessels, private correspondence, and other means of communication to keep ties with those outside of the lines, exchange goods and money, and provide mutual support across zones of control.

Smuggling and trading between rebel-held territory and British occupied areas quietly subverted the reach of military rule, much as they did in other parts of the British Empire both before and after the Revolutionary War.[116] However, other tactics employed undermined British authority in more overt ways. In their struggle to survive, civilians stole from the army and from one another. Timothy Downing, a civilian employed in the commissary department in occupied New York, began embezzling stores from the army to sell for his own gain. Like George Brinley, Downing likely used the access to food that came with his position to help himself and his family. Unfortunately, Downing sold oats to the wrong soldier, and it cost him both his employment and his liberty.[117] Despite this danger, such acts, and even more brazen crimes, were commonplace in occupied society, as people took increasingly desperate measures to survive. In the summer of 1779, Richard Brown and Elijah Davis of Staten Island were accused of cutting timber on lands that did not belong to them.[118] On Long Island, three civilian men were tried by court-martial for stealing sheep along a country road, with one receiving a thousand lashes as punishment—likely a death sentence.[119] Such theft became so bad that on at least one occasion New York's commandant called out regular troops to patrol the area alongside the civilian city watch.[120] Although property crimes plagued cities prior to the imposition of military rule, desperation turned many who would not otherwise have committed such acts into criminals.

Whether they resorted to smuggling goods in and out of the lines, subverting positions in occupation regimes, or outright theft, people living under military rule were forced by scarcity to go around the structures imposed by the army and its civilian allies. For many, the necessity of these measures began to undermine faith in imperial authority. While long-held beliefs may have assured city dwellers that the king would provide for them in their times of need, the experience of living with the king's forces under military rule taught a different lessen. As a result, men and women living under occupation increasingly began to question their faith in royal authority and the benefits of a reunion with the empire. Even as support for Britain flagged, however, those living in cities under the royal army's control had to learn to obscure their true political beliefs. Staying alive in occupied America required complex political calculations, and those who inhabited port cities became adept at espousing different beliefs to different people at different times. Although the rot did not become apparent to most observers until after British military defeat in 1781, these shifting politics—which had their root in the unstable social experience and fraught economic and material environments of occupation—doomed British attempts to restore imperial authority both in occupied ports and elsewhere in North America.

CHAPTER 5

Ambiguous Allegiances

For people living under British military rule, political allegiance was fluid, contingent, and often contradictory. Men and women living in occupied zones chose sides for a variety of reasons, both personal and ideological, and often changed their loyalties as circumstances shifted. These shifts occurred in reaction to the harsh conditions and the new opportunities offered by occupation. In the course of their everyday lives, civilians made pragmatic, calculated decisions to ensure their own survival, protect loved ones, and safeguard property. These choices could tacitly or openly support either side without prejudice, and as a result the same individual could appear to one side a revolutionary while maintaining loyalist status on the other. Despite the fluidity of their loyalties, these people cannot be regarded as mere opportunists, although opportunism surely played into their calculations. Keeping one's loyalties ambiguous represented a deliberate and necessary strategy to survive the food shortages, cramped quarters, and often dangerous circumstances of occupation.

Nevertheless, flexible allegiances frustrated British officers and their loyalist allies, and attempts to pin down loyalties came to dominate occupation society. To cope with the uncertain political positions of citizens, officials and loyalists wrote polemics, issued proclamations, and developed legal policies to persuade people to side with the king. As these instruments evolved over the course of the war, a distinct vocabulary of loyalty developed in the print culture, court proceedings, and public life of occupied cities. Occupation regimes used this emerging loyalist lexicon to craft arguments intended to induce wavering Americans to openly declare their loyalty to the Crown, rewarding those who signed oaths of allegiance and punishing those who refused. As they did so, professions of loyalism came increasingly to define everyday life under military rule. Pledging allegiance to the king offered avenues for physical protection, social advancement, and economic opportunity. Oaths and petitions also ensured access to material support from the occupation authorities. By necessity, everyone living under British rule became fluent in both the vocabulary and customs of loyalism, and many people successfully used acts and public affirmations of their allegiance to procure relief from British authorities. While many—perhaps even most—of those who professed their loyalty in occupied cities indeed favored the king's cause, the effectiveness of professions of allegiance in securing aid and opening avenues for advancement could, and did, allow inveterate rebels to use it to their advantage.

Ironically, the transformation of loyalism into an organizing principle of occupation society undermined its effectiveness in achieving the restoration of royal rule in the colonies. As the possibilities for abuse became more and more apparent, those who had declared their allegiance early in the war came to distrust the larger numbers of refugees and newcomers who claimed these protections later on. As they observed overtly loyal American civilians continuing to hold social, commercial, and political ties to friends and relatives in rebel-held areas, British officers also became increasingly suspicious of affirmations of loyalty. Even as more and more civilians declared their allegiance as the war progressed, an atmosphere of suspicion permeated occupation societies, and trust frayed between occupation regimes and the civilians in their charge. The increasing cynicism this phenomenon engendered, even among the most vehement supporters of royal rule, undercut all of the work that army officers and their loyalist allies had done to bring about the restoration of British authority in the occupied territories, ultimately causing the king's cause to rot from the inside out.

The final year of military rule in Charleston, South Carolina, indicates not only the flexibility of loyalty in occupied cities but also how that flexibility hastened the collapse of imperial authority. Early on in its occupation, Charleston seemed to hold the brightest prospects for a full restoration of imperial authority in any major port. By the summer of 1781, almost two thousand men and women had signed oaths of allegiance to the Crown, and, according to the recollections of one witness, many more had come in to take advantage of the king's protection within the city.[1] Despite British ambivalence toward deploying loyalists in military campaigns, thousands more South Carolinians from across the state joined the royal standard during the early days of restored British rule, enlisting in militia and forming provincial regiments to fight against their rebellious countrymen.[2] Thousands of escaped slaves further strengthened the royal position by seeking the freedom afforded by fleeing revolutionary masters and declaring loyalty to the Crown.[3] Finally, mercantile business had resumed, and British specie and manufactured goods were quickly flooding into the city.[4] To many observers in mid-1781, the results of the first year of Charleston's occupation seemed a model of how to restore order and loyalty to the rebellious colonies. In April 1781, Lord George Germain expressed his hopes that the province would soon be "ripe for the enjoyment of Civil Government, and when their Constitution is restored [the population] will chearfully [sic] concur in the measures necessary for giving it permenancy [sic]."[5]

A year later, however, things looked markedly different, and not only because the battle of Yorktown had crushed hopes of a British military victory. Cornwallis's defeat in October 1781 deprived the Crown of nearly half of its forces in America, forced the ouster of Sir Henry Clinton as commander in chief in North America, and caused the military to cease offensive actions, ceding the countryside to the revolutionary army and fortifying New York, Charleston, and Savannah. Many observers, from the eighteenth century to the present day, have credited Britain's crushing military defeat as a primary factor in losing support among American civilians. However, Yorktown did not change hearts and minds on its own. Rather, it triggered a sea change in political identity that had long been simmering under the surface. Absent the prospect of military victory making permanent the social and material benefits that British military rulers promised in exchange for allegiance, the vocabulary of loyalism, already stretched thin by overuse, finally failed.

As a result, the occupation government of Charleston foundered and collapsed with amazing speed. In April 1782, a council of top military officers concluded that "the Inhabitants of Charles-Town (amounting to eight Thousand) are mostly of doubtful principles, many desirous by every means to make their peace with the country."[6] Around the same time, city residents ceased to utilize the board of police, and cases languished as witnesses and defendants refused to appear. William Bull Jr., who had become leader of the civil wing of the government after James Simpson's return to New York, complained that many who had previously espoused loyalty had begun to "withdraw . . . themselves from the reach of Justice, [and] hold such of their Creditors as remain within the Protection of the British Government at defiance."[7] Despite expanding from four original members to eight, the board saw fewer and fewer cases as 1782 wore on.[8] In October, it disbanded entirely.[9] A seemingly sudden decline in popular support had caused the occupation regime, once so full of promise, to fail completely. At the same time, similar scenes took place in Savannah and New York, Britain's last remaining occupied territories. These sudden failures astonished many of the officials who administrated military rule, but their seeds lay in nearly eight years of civilians navigating an increasingly treacherous world of loyalty and betrayal.

In this fraught environment, holding ambiguous loyalties prevented people from being categorized one way or another by either side, an activity which occurred with some frequency and which held considerable consequences. In 1777, Reverend Ezra Stiles recorded the loyalties of many of his former neighbors during the occupation of Newport, placing a number of stars next to their names to denote the level of their support for British rule. Stiles recorded no fewer than fifteen "four-star" loyalists, and dozens of others whose loyalty was aligned with the Crown less strongly.[10] However, out of 331 people Stiles listed, only 71 are classified as loyalists, and most of those were designated as "one-star," or lukewarm loyalists. Aside from about a dozen people Stiles classified as "Whigs," the remaining names defy classification. Expanding Stiles's analysis to the wartime population of Newport, which numbered between 2,300 and 5,530, it stands to reason that perhaps as many of three-fifths remained uncategorized.[11] This accounting does not imply that the majority of Newport's citizenry were somehow neutral in the conflict. Rather, their defiance of simple classification reveals the breadth of ambiguity among the populations of cities under military rule.

British occupation regimes faced the same troubles as the revolutionary-leaning Stiles. Ambrose Serle, Admiral Howe's private secretary, noticed that almost everywhere he went Americans wavered between support for the Crown and sympathies with the rebel camp. In one particularly flagrant example in New York, Serle observed that "a man of some Rank in this Town . . . has a Correspondent to the Southward among the Rebels," with whom he had arranged "to give the proper Intimation when it will be proper to leave the Rebels, & so *vice versa* . . . making Loyalty a sure Game!"[12] As occupations wore on, British officials and their American sympathizers developed increasingly sophisticated strategies to convince people living in occupied territories to openly declare their support for the British cause. In so doing, however, they inadvertently eroded the very concept of loyalism on which all their hopes depended.

Keeping flexible loyalties proved especially useful to the most vulnerable people living in occupied cities. These included women who supported families or lived under the thumb of male relatives. Such was the case with Hannah Lawrence, the New York teenager, poet, and critic of occupation who nevertheless married British officer Jacob Schieffelin. Despite her strong feelings against the British cause, Lawrence apparently felt few qualms about marrying into the occupying force. In a journal she kept during her courtship, her prospective husband's position came up only once, when Lawrence confessed, "To marry him while he continues in any way connected with the military will be certainly very disagreeable to me, but even that may have its advantages in traveling."[13] Still, even after the event she continued to harangue against military rule. In a farewell to the Hudson River, Hannah Schieffelin wrote, "On thy banks while dire oppression reigns / Thy beauties hasten to a general doom / No future spring renews thy faded plains / No more thy groves shall rise, or orchards bloom."[14] After this bitter farewell, the newly wed Schieffelins left New York for the safety of British Canada.

Hannah Lawrence Schieffelin's elastic loyalties mitigated the risks of occupation and allowed her greater freedom within military society. Given the dangers facing many women in occupied New York and the material hardships of garrison life, choosing a promising marriage represented perhaps Schieffelin's best chance to survive and thrive in precarious times. And, the union did allow her freedom of travel through British military lines and the opportunity to escape the dangers of occupied New York for more hospitable territories. Keeping her loyalties flexible allowed her to maintain connections with her revolutionary-leaning family, continuing to correspond with them while in Canada and even moving back to New York after the war. For Schieffelin, ambiguous allegiances proved essential to the successful navigation of the precarious circumstances of occupation. Nevertheless, people like her continued to frustrate occupation regimes, who sought overt support from their populations.

In developing strategies to encourage fence-sitters to openly declare for the Crown, occupation regimes drew on ideas of loyalism that had developed during the decade prior to the outbreak of open revolution. These concepts originated in the writings of defenders of the Stamp Act during the 1760s and came into use again during the crises of the early 1770s. Such rhetoric took on several guises. Many who otherwise agreed with the arguments of the protesters decried the emotionalism of the protest rhetoric against Great Britain, responding with their own, more measured arguments and urging a more conciliatory approach.[15] Other emerging loyalists feared the rising power of demagogues, inciting the masses with incendiary language to obtain dictatorial power.[16] Still more, mostly men trained in the law, took a constitutional tack, stressing the impossibility of protest outside of proper channels.[17] By the early 1770s, a rich literature of loyalism abounded in pamphlets and newspapers, as colonists debated the imperial crisis. Although these early loyalists never established a viable alternative to republicanism, pro-imperial essays nevertheless became ubiquitous in the public sphere.[18]

The proliferation of loyalist pamphlets and newspaper polemics only increased with the outset of war in 1775, taking on greater urgency as what had been an intellectual debate transformed into a desperate attempt to sway wayward countrymen to return their allegiance to the Crown. Twelve different loyalist newspapers appeared between 1776 and 1783, spanning the six occupied cities in the thirteen colonies as well as Saint Augustine in East Florida.[19] In occupied New York, printer James Rivington ran a newspaper entirely devoted to the royal cause, at some points even making up outright lies to encourage loyalty. In one particularly egregious attempt to rally spirits after the British loss at Saratoga, Rivington invented from scratch a newly signed Anglo-Russian alliance that would put thirty-six thousand additional troops at His Majesty's disposal.[20] Others employed logic in their criticisms of the republican regime. In Newport, Rhode Island, an anonymous loyalist delivered a step-by-step critique of the revolutionary position, beginning by lamenting, "The Miseries attendant upon even the most successful Revolution" and continuing to refute the "Doctrine of Anarchy and Confusion" that the revolutionary regime sought to "compensate for the Loss of British Liberty and Laws."[21] More polemicists drew on their own experiences. Levi Smith, a loyalist officer who had been imprisoned by revolutionary guerillas in the South Carolina backcountry, took to occupied South Carolina's *Royal Gazette* in 1781 to tell his story of torture and deprivation, making a powerful argument for the barbarity of the revolutionaries and the degeneration of those who rebelled against the natural order.[22]

Much as revolutionary governments relied on newspapers to create propaganda and rally support for the war effort against Great Britain, occupation regimes and their supporters knew well the value of the loyalist press, and often took advantage of these papers to forward the goals of their administrations.[23] During his travels throughout occupied America,

Ambrose Serle took a keen interest in encouraging loyalist newspapers, arranging with printer Hugh Gaine and former governor William Tryon to restart Gaine's paper at the outset of the occupation of New York. During the winter of 1777–1778, Serle even penned several pro-British polemics himself, using the pen name "Integer," which he shared with the loyalist and Anglican reverend Charles Inglis. Under both Serle and Inglis, the Integer letters focused on the benefits of reconnecting North America to the profitable trade of the British Empire.[24]

Early on in the occupation of Charleston, an anonymous essayist called Drusus—likely a pseudonym for the superintendent of police, James Simpson—prepared the way for restored royal rule in the state by denigrating both the revolutionary government and the former colonial system. Writing in June 1780, Drusus characterized the revolutionary government of South Carolina as "Anarchy," and thanked the British Army for "delivering the Country." However, the essayist lashed out at the antebellum colonial government as well. Drusus blamed the colonial executive for the rebellion, declaring that "the Governor, and part of the Council, DESERTED THE TRUST REPOSED IN THEM," in refusing to negotiate with the colonial legislature and provoking a political crisis in the province during the 1770s. While Drusus favored the royal government, he did not want a return to the prior colonial system. He even conceded that, when government failed, an individual had "to consult his own happiness." To appeal to former rebels, Drusus articulated his ideas in a language grounded in traditional royalist thought but influenced by revolutionary language.[25] Later in the occupation, Drusus returned to defend the military-civilian regimes fiscal policy, making explicit the link between the loyalist press and the occupation authorities.[26] In the thriving print culture of occupied cities, the language of loyalism evolved to meet wartime conditions and appeal to a wider audience.

While essayists developed variations of loyalist ideology and accompanying rhetoric in essays and polemics, British officers and civilian officials borrowed their language for proclamations, forms for oaths of loyalty, and ad hoc legal systems, bringing it into the center of everyday life for men and women living under military rule. Major proclamations designed to encourage Americans to return their loyalties to the Crown were issued at the commencements of the occupations of every territory the British came to control, and newspapers became their primary vector of distribution. Such proclamations began as early as General Thomas Gage's assumption

of command in Boston and continued throughout the war. These proclamations took the form of a much older instrument of communication
between the royal government and its subjects, informing the populace of
new policies, laws, restrictions, and privileges granted by the monarch. Such
usage, however, had fallen out of favor by the early 1700s, as colonial newspapers published more public debate and fewer official documents.[27] Proclamations during the Revolutionary War, mediated through agents of royal
authority, reflected this change, taking on a new status as rhetoric in addition to law; a persuasiveness that had been unnecessary before the outbreak
of the revolution.[28] Military commanders and civil officials leading occupation regimes carefully crafted their proclamations not just to lay down the
law but also to compete for the allegiance of civilians in territories they
conquered.

As the British Army fought for and conquered New York, the Howe
brothers issued three successive proclamations, each more enticing for
potential loyalists than the last. In the first, issued from Staten Island before
the attack on Long Island, the Howes informed the public of their intention
to restore "public Tranquility" to the region and offered protection to those
who "who are willing, by a speedy Return to their Duty, to reap the benefits
of the Royal Favor." Once in possession of Manhattan two months later,
the brothers again appealed to "his Majesty's well-affected Subjects," promising "a permanent Union with every Colony" and encouraged others to
"return to their Allegiance, accept the Blessings of Peace, and be secured in
a free Enjoyment of their *Liberty* and *Properties*, upon the true Principles of
the [British] Constitution."[29] In their attempts to sway New Yorkers to
pledge allegiance to the Crown, or at the very least not resist British forces,
the Howe brothers used much the same vocabulary as the loyalist press and
in doing so contributed to the propagation of a language of loyalism that
reached a wide audience.

Different commanders echoed this language in printed proclamations
issued when British forces entered Georgia and South Carolina. In January
1779, only a few weeks after the conquest of Savanah, Colonel Archibald
Campbell and Admiral Hyde Parker issued a proclamation, printed in
broadside and reproduced in newspapers, extending "the Blessings of
Peace, Freedom and Protection . . . to all His Majesty's faithful subjects of
the Southern Provinces," going so far as to offer former rebels the chance
to benefit from "a firm and perpetual Coalition with the Parent State," and
"ample Protection in their Persons, Families, and Effects, on Condition

they shall immediately return to the Class of peaceful Citizens."[30] While besieging Charleston in the spring of 1780, General Henry Clinton issued a proclamation similar to the one the Howes had issued from Staten Island four years earlier, appealing to the "natural loyalty" of those who had been "seduced by the arts of faction, or hurried away by the tumult and disorder of the times," and offering "a free and general pardon for all treasons" should they return their allegiance to the Crown.[31] Months later, with most of the province conquered, Clinton repeated his proclamation twice, though the second one required those seeking protection not only to sign a loyalty oath but to volunteer to defend the province against rebels. Many understood this change as a requirement of military service, though the commander in chief did not necessarily intend it as such.[32] Although residents of soon-to-be-occupied areas may have greeted these proclamations with skepticism, and indeed the revolutionary press mocked them as empty promises, for many people they nonetheless represented their first exposure to concepts of loyalism that they would have to utilize themselves to gain the favor of occupation authorities.[33]

Whereas large-scale political proclamations introduced thousands to the language of loyalism, more mundane printed proclamations reiterated this language and made it a part of everyday life. While such proclamations ran the gamut from regulating prices to inflicting punishments for looters and poachers, all drew on the language of loyalism and, in so doing, normalized it. Proclamations appearing in Newport and New York during the spring of 1777 offered "all His Majesty's liege Subjects" living in the occupied territories encouragement to bring in "a plentiful Supply of Vegetables, and of fresh Provisions of all Kinds" for the use of the troops and promised "a full Assurance of all Possible Protection in so doing."[34] A proclamation issued in Savannah in January 1781 dealt with the dangers of smuggling livestock in similar language, warning that "his Majesty's loyal subjects . . . may suffer for want of fresh provisions" should the practice continue and offering rewards to "peace officers, and others of his Majesty's liege subjects, to apprehend such of the felons above mentioned."[35] Proclamations dealing with such everyday matters became so common in occupation society that an exasperated Andrew Elliot complained to military authorities that "repeated Proclamations loose[n]s their effect" in encouraging compliance with military rule.[36] Still, their very ubiquity in occupied society, combined with their reliance on a very narrow vocabulary drawn from loyalist polemics and official language, exposed thousands to the language of loyalism.

If proclamations demonstrate how a distinct vernacular of loyalty could affect civilians in their everyday lives, loyalty oaths became the first and most important tangible way for civilians to tap into that language for their own benefit. Administered en masse during the outset of occupations in each city except Boston and signed in duplicate with British officials keeping one copy and their signer keeping the other, these oaths were simple documents by which Americans seeking the protection of the British military signed their names to signify their allegiance to the Crown. Like loyalist essays and the proclamations issued by British officials, loyalty oaths became increasingly sophisticated as the war stretched on and the language of loyalty evolved. In New York, the oath administered by former governor William Tryon to nearly three thousand people in and around the occupied city in late 1776 read, in its entirety:

> I . . . do promise and swear to bear faith, and true allegiance to His Majesty King George the Third, and to the utmost of my Power, to Defend His Sacred Person, Crown and Government against all Persons Whatsoever.[37]

While New York's oaths were relatively simple, those taken four years later by two thousand Charlestonians reflect the increasing sophistication of loyalist language:

> I . . . do hereby acknowledge and declare myself to be a true and faithful Subject of His Majesty, the King of Great-Britain, and that I will at all Times hereafter be obedient to his Government, and that whenever I shall be thereunto required, I will be ready to maintain and defend the same, against all persons whatever.[38]

The Charleston oaths contain vocabulary taken in large part from newspaper essays and proclamations developed between 1776 and 1780. Rather than merely "swear[ing] to bear fair, and true allegiance" to the king, now a loyalist swore, "[I] declare myself to be a true and faithful Subject." In addition, signers were now required to be "obedient to his Government," a provision found nowhere in the New York oath but which reflected Henry Clinton's proclamations at the outset of the occupation of Charleston. Similarly, the South Carolina oath implied, though did not actually impose, a duty to actively defend royal authority, rather than passively submit to it.

As the war stretched on and the language of loyalty developed further, so too did the forms and rituals used to signify that allegiance.

Unlike proclamations and essays, however, loyalty oaths took on different meanings for civilians who signed them and the regimes that issued them. Occupation regimes saw the expanding oath-books they kept as tangible evidence of the success of their policies to reinstill loyalty among those who had been disaffected with royal government. Further, officials used them to gain support for these policies in Whitehall. William Tryon, the former governor who took charge of collecting oaths from areas around occupied New York City, boasted in an early letter to Lord George Germain that "Large bodies of the People have already taken the benefit of the Grace therein offered them."[39] Printers later published the names of those who had subscribed in newspapers, making the act public and, by placing these columns next to loyalist essays and proclamations, tied the oaths to the larger language of loyalism.[40] For occupation regimes, loyalty oaths represented proof of their support among the local population.

For civilians, however, loyalty pledges became passports through which they could access the benefits of occupation society. Once civilians had signed their oaths, they obtained access not only to the protections offered under proclamations but to the entire social world of occupation regimes—one which offered dazzling opportunities for social freedom, wealth accumulation, and political advancement. Signing one's oath of allegiance to the Crown also brought with it access to the legal systems of occupation society. And, perhaps most importantly, signing the oath gave citizens standing to petition for aid from the government to assuage the harsh material conditions of military rule. More than just a declaration of political allegiance, a loyalty oath became an essential legal document for everyone living in the occupied zones.

In order to reap the advantages of their oaths, would-be loyalists had to declare their allegiance using concepts and vocabulary that would be recognizable to their rulers. These articulations most often took the form of written petitions and memorials to occupation officials. By petitioning military authorities, people living in occupied zones requested, and often obtained, relief from hardships suffered during the war. Many of these pleas came from refugees driven into cities by marauding armies or revolutionary governments. Often, these people had lost their homes, livelihoods, and family members in the war. Displaced people thus used their professions of loyalty as a tool to recoup losses or, more often, obtain the barest necessaries of survival. To do so they appealed to the humanity of British officers to grant them aid, and to conceptions of social class, gender, and race.[41] More important, however, was the language that these petitioners used, which employed the loyalist vocabulary developed in polemics, newspapers, proclamations, and oaths, and had become the lingua franca of survival in occupied America.

As the repeated appeals and professions of allegiance explicate, employing the vocabulary of loyalism became, for many, the only way to salvage shattered lives. Petitions from civilians to occupation officials followed a familiar, formulaic pattern which emphasized, above all else, their loyalty to the king—often using the same terms and phrases as loyalty oaths and proclamations. In document after document over the eight years of the war, memorialists and petitioners in each occupied city described their situation, attributed it to the consequences of remaining loyal to the British cause, and requested assistance or compensation. Often, petitioners attached written testimonies of their loyalty from friends and neighbors, or even from high-level loyalists in occupied cities.[42] The petition of Cornelius Luyster, for example, described the Duchess County, New York, farmer as "a Firm steady Loyalist" who "has been greviously Persicuted [sic] for his Loyalty." These persecutions, which included confinement in a Boston jail and destruction of his property, had "Rendered [Luyster] incapable of Supporting himself and Family," leading the petitioner to request "such Aid and Support as your Excellency [the commanding general] shall Judge to be Right & Just." Like many other petitioners, Luyster attached several endorsements from former neighbors and acquaintances which spoke of his loyalty to the empire.[43] Daniel and Henry Van Mater of New Jersey similarly claimed themselves "uniform Friends to Government" who had been forced to "quit their Homes, and Property in a Very Precipitate Manner."[44] Several petitioners even went so far as to claim not only their loyalism but their usefulness to the royal cause. William Williams of Ulster County, New York, claimed that he had been imprisoned, impoverished, and exiled by the revolutionary government on "a Charge for Sending Provisions into the City of New York" to succor British forces.[45] All used their loyalty to anchor their requests for aid.

The vernacular of loyalism also permeated social relationships. Notions of class intermingled with allegiance as petitioners attempted to appeal to occupation authorities. Sarah Morris, whose New York estate had been decimated by foraging British cavalry, not only stressed her loyalty in her petition to the garrison's commanding general for restitution but claimed that these conditions had reduced her "to a state of wretchedness which her former Rank and Station renders Her ill qualified to bear."[46] Elizabeth Rogers, who fled to Manhattan after the destruction of her home in Norwalk, Connecticut, stressed in her application for relief that her family had "lived in a genteel affluence" before their "affection to the British Interest" led to their persecution.[47] Isaac Touro, the erstwhile leader of Newport's Jewish community, complained that by "persecution and distress" at the hands of revolutionaries he "was reduced from a comfortable livelihood to necessity" in New York's harsh wartime economy.[48] For Touro, who had fallen from a high station in prerevolutionary Newport to poverty and squalor after the army pulled out of Rhode Island, the act of putting his tribulations to writing may have been his only remaining recourse, and reminding officials of his previous high standing almost certainly increased his chances of receiving compensation for his losses.[49] The vocabulary of loyalty borrowed in many cases from ideas of class and respectability to incite the sympathies of genteel British officers and to document the personal tragedies of elite refugees.

Combining notions of gender with the language of loyalism could also help petitioners achieve success. When Ann Cook petitioned for redress, for example, she stressed her widowed status, writing that, while her husband was alive his work as a pilot for the navy and "his Industry" had helped him to "Support his family comfortably," but his death had left her "without any relief or support, or any means for . . . her distressed & Fatherless Family."[50] Although Isabella Raymond's husband had died "after tedious illness," she too had found herself "in a very difficult situation . . . utterly incapable" of "support[ing] herself without the assistance of Government."[51] By representing themselves as helpless in every way, these petitioners played on the self-image British officers held of themselves as masculine protectors of endangered women. Others were more overt in this appeal, relating acts of violence done against them in the course of their sufferings. Jane Cadmus, a landowner whose home on Bergen Neck, New Jersey, had been overrun by displaced migrants, raged that not only had her land and livestock been "entirely ruined by the Refugees," but that she herself had been "severely beat by a white man and most severely threatened and abused by a negro."[52] Cadmus not only invoked gendered vocabulary in her petition for relief but racial prejudice as well.

That the language of loyalty employed by petitioners reflected class, gender, and racial beliefs should not diminish its power within occupation society but simply reveal different strategies used by civilians to claim it for themselves in their particular situations. While most of these petitions only survive in the records of the British War Office, with almost no background or recording of their outcome, the ordeal of Cadwallader Colden Jr. illuminates how many of these petitions came to be and in what circumstances they could meet with success. When Colden, son of a former New York royal official, arrived in New York City in the summer of 1778 after imprisonment and exile from his property further north on the Hudson River, he lodged with family already there in exile and "waited on Generall Clinton," commander in chief of British forces immediately. Still, although Clinton received him "as an Old Acquaintance," he "took no more notice" of Colden until January 1779, when the formerly wealthy loyalist "at length thought proper to present a Memorial to him," in which he laid out his sufferings at the hands of the revolutionary state of New York on account of his "loyalty and attachment to the British Constitution" and begged the general to "appoint him to some office," where he could "render that service he wishe[d] to King and Country, and obtain a support for the present time." Ultimately, Colden did receive a stipend of one dollar a day from the military regime, as well as a promise of consideration for the next available civil office.[53]

Colden's travails explain much about the way that conceptions of allegiance functioned within the loyalist society constructed by occupation authorities. Upon his arrival, Colden drew on the support of wealthy loyalist relatives and even pled his case with General Clinton in person. Still, despite his standing, the customs of occupied New York forced Colden to pen a written memorial to the military regime and to couch it in the by-then familiar language of hundreds of refugees who came before him, and hundreds who would come after. Despite his connections and well-known history of support for the Crown, written memorials had come to function as the mechanism by which refugees arriving in the city formally entered society, and so in order to obtain his relief and enter into that society fully Colden had to resort to the language on which that society was built.

Still, loyalist language had its limits, even for the wealthy and connected. In a series of petitions to three successive commandants of Newport, wealthy farmer John Malbone attested his loyalty in order to recoup losses caused by the military. Malbone complained of a number of injustices, from the decimation of his crops by British and Hessian troops to the destruction of his prized arbor, which was torn down for firewood. Like the New York refugees, Malbone insisted on his unquestioning loyalty, writing that he had always been "a well known Friend to Government."[54] The landowner further called on British officers' sense of class, warning that if they ignored his entreaties, "a well known Family accustomed to Affluence, will be scarcely able to live with Decency and Decorum."[55] Since Malbone drew on the rhetorical and class-based aspects of the language of loyalism, based on the examples of others, he should have expected to receive some relief. Unexpectedly, however, his case met not just with failure but with contempt. According to a note that Malbone affixed to one of these documents after a particularly unpleasant meeting, the commandant he had petitioned threw the memorial aside "after reading a few Lines . . . declaring the same too trivial at that conjuncture for his Attention."[56] Not all British officials, apparently, were sympathetic to the pleas of loyalists, despite their use of generally accepted arguments based on suffering for their allegiance.

Malbone's petitions expose how many Americans hedged their political positions, even when they espoused their ardent loyalism in writing. Although he went to great lengths to claim his loyalty to the British, and his brother-in-law and father were listed by Ezra Stiles as three-star and one-star loyalists, respectively, the reverend regarded John Malbone as a "Whig," or revolutionary sympathizer.[57] Although he supported the rebellion enough to merit notice by some of its principal adherents, Malbone nevertheless protested his loyalty again and again in attempts to gain redress from British commanders. These tactics proved increasingly common among Americans living in occupied cities, as they attempted to benefit from occupation society while mitigating its dangers. Whatever his true beliefs, Malbone likely held them deeply, but as the war continued it proved essential for him to keep them to himself.

Such ambiguities persisted even among those lower down on the social spectrum than the well-off Malbone, much to the surprise even of those who had experienced the trauma of revolutionary divisions. When he secretly visited his hometown in January 1777, Newport native and Continental sailor John Trevett found a much more complex situation than he had expected. Early in his sojourn, Trevett encountered one Mrs. Battey, an old acquaintance who "four or five months before, [he] took . . . for a Torrie." Despite her beliefs, which she gave no indication of rejecting, Battey surprised Trevett by aiding the rebel spy, offering him food and drink and expressing concern for her son in the revolutionary army. Even still, Battey admitted to her guest "that she was afraid her son and I [Trevett] would be hanged, for the British certainly would beat the Americans." Later, Trevett received aid and information from several different people whose actions during the occupation, which included willingly quartering soldiers, providing support to the British Army, and socializing with British soldiers and officers, could credibly classify them as loyalists. One even promised to care for his abandoned pet dog.[58] As Trevett discovered, many proclaimed loyalists proved willing and eager to maintain friendly ties with those in the rebel camp, even if they steadfastly maintained their commitment to the king.

Mary Almy, the keeper of a boardinghouse who remained in Newport while her husband volunteered for the Continental Army, also maintained her allegiance to both husband and king, despite their opposition to one another. During the summer of 1778, Almy's husband, Benjamin, was attached to an American army which besieged and almost captured the town of Newport. In spite of their relationship, Almy expressed ardent support for the British cause. In a series of never-sent letters to her husband during the siege, Almy made no secret of her thoughts on the matter, writing, "My dislike of the natives that you call your friends is the same as when you knew me," and "You will not be surprised at my warmth [anger] when you find how I suffered." Later, describing the destruction of much of the city in an artillery barrage, she turned her anger against the revolutionary army and its leader, exclaiming, "Cursed ought to be and will be the man who brought all this woe and desolation on a good people!" Still, Almy expressed affection for her husband and worried that, if the revolutionaries did seize the town, her husband would be resented in his own home, exclaiming, "after three years a wanderer and not to meet a welcome!"[59] Like other residents of occupied towns, Mary Almy's loyalties encompassed both support for the British cause and sympathy with friends and relatives engaged in rebellion. Although these may have seemed a contradiction to the leadership of both sides, for Almy they merely represented two facets of her life that had to be reconciled in her everyday experience.

If the language of loyalism granted access to the benefits of the British occupation regimes, maintaining ties to the rebel camp acted as a hedge in case those regimes failed. The experiences of Elizabeth Drinker and Grace Galloway in occupied Philadelphia demonstrate that keeping allegiances malleable could be absolutely essential for those with families to protect. In addition to opening her home to a British officer in exchange for his protection, Drinker allowed one of her family's vacant properties to be occupied by soldiers' wives, on the condition that the women desist from tearing down her fences for firewood. Later, Drinker used her connections to other British soldiers living in town to intimidate an officer who had seduced and abducted her servant. In confronting the man, Drinker claimed that she had been quiet about the matter up until that moment, but "if thee dont very soon pay me for my Servants time, as there is officers quarter[e]d among Numbers of my acquaintance, I will tell all I meet with" about his indiscretions.[60] Although she never carried through on the threat, her language suggests that Drinker moved freely within the social circles of British officers and their civilian hosts.

Nevertheless, Drinker kept ties to the rebels as well. In April 1778, she and several other Quaker women ventured to Valley Forge to meet with Continental Army officers about Congress's harsh treatment of a number of prominent members of the Quaker community, including her husband, Henry, who had been sent into exile in Virginia for refusing to sign oaths of loyalty to Pennsylvania's revolutionary government.[61] At the army camp, Drinker and her companions, other wives and family members of those in exile, enjoyed "an aligant [sic] dinner" with George and Martha Washington, along with several other generals and their families, and obtained the Washington's support in releasing their family members from internment, along with a pass to proceed to York to present their case before the Continental Congress.[62] At first glance it may seem incongruous that a woman like Drinker could leave her home after breakfasting with a British colonel and two days later dine with the commander in chief of the revolutionary army. But such contradictions were essential in keeping her family alive and eventually reunite them with her exiled husband.[63] And, when the British evacuated Philadelphia the Drinker family faced no real ill will from returning revolutionary authorities, despite having housed members of the occupying army.[64]

Others did not succeed at maintaining the delicate balance required to keep their allegiances undefinable. Grace Growdon Galloway, whose husband, Joseph, served as superintendent of police in occupied Philadelphia, found that her failure to cultivate ties with the revolutionaries during the period of military rule prevented her attempts to live peaceably in Philadelphia afterward. Despite having operated in the same social circles as Elizabeth Drinker, and even espousing ambivalence about the British military presence, Galloway had neglected to maintain her relationships with friends and family in the revolutionary camp. As a result, she underwent severe hardship when her husband left after the British evacuation. The returning

Continental Army seized much of her property based on Joseph's collaboration. In August 1778, only two short months after the end of the British occupation, she was turned out of her home by the restored revolutionary authorities, and she died impoverished four years later.[65] The distance between the success of Drinker, who thrived in postoccupation Philadelphia, and Galloway, who failed in it, underscores the absolute necessity of obscuring one's allegiances.[66]

That many Americans maintained flexible, contingent allegiances, even in the face of attempts to persuade them to declare openly for the Crown, did not go unnoticed by British authorities and their sympathizers. As the war progressed, these people's own faith in the concept of loyalty itself began to break down, dooming the efforts of occupation regimes to fully restore royal rule. In this, they proved many early loyalists—who had always distrusted latecomers to the cause—correct. As early as 1776, during the first months of the occupation of New York, longtime loyalists like the Reverend Charles Inglis, rector of Trinity Church, argued against offering loyalty oaths at all, fearing that they might allow the revolutionaries who aided in their oppression only a few months earlier to be rehabilitated without punishment. Even Lord George Germain at times distrusted professions of loyalty from those who had previously supported the rebellion, worrying that amnesties offered by occupation regimes could backfire and demoralize those who had supported the Crown from the start of the conflict.[67] Worse, despite the apparent successes of their policies to encourage allegiance—signed loyalty oaths—the occupiers and their superiors in London could still never be sure of their subjects' actual loyalties. The fear of inhabitants professing their loyalty in public and then acting to the contrary when it suited them proved a constant worry for British authorities charged both with keeping order and prosecuting the war. As William Smith Jr., a New York counselor before the war and an advisor to the occupation regime during it, lamented as early as the spring of 1780 that "the King's Interest is weaker *within* than *beyond* the Lines" of the city.[68] Smith himself had experience with this, as he had tried to avoid taking a side for the first several years of the war.[69] Even though thousands had signed loyalty oaths, benefited from occupation, and even volunteered in the king's service, urbanites and refugees continued to come under suspicion for harboring secret loyalties to the revolutionary side.

British officers and their civilian allies grew increasingly frustrated with Americans' ambiguous loyalties, and as the war stretched on tensions rose between city residents and occupying soldiers.[70] In one particularly striking incident during the summer of 1777, Captain John Cambel of the Royal Engineers beat his Newport landlord, Joseph Tweedy, over an altercation involving the captain's slave. The conflict hinged on Tweedy's contested status as a loyalist and his class position. Their altercation began when Tweedy "ducked" Captain Cambel's young black servant in the water near one of the local wharves. According to a witness, upon hearing of the affront, Cambel "came down the stairs cursing and swearing . . . said 'Damn you Mr. Tweedy' . . . [and] immediately fell to beating him." Tweedy, outraged, declared that "he was a Gentleman, and demanded satisfaction," eventually seeking help from an officer friend in the British navy to bring charges against the engineer. In his defense against the charge of unlawful assault, Cambel argued that Tweedy had abrogated his status as a gentleman by cooperating with Rhode Island's revolutionary government, calling witnesses to prove his actions before the occupation had been those of "a rascal and a scoundrel." In closing, the Captain called on the members of the court-martial to reconsider their "sense of this Man's conduct in the assumed Character of a gentleman." While the court found Cambel guilty and forced him to apologize for his behavior, the case nevertheless highlights British officers' growing suspicion of those who professed loyalty in occupied society, as well as the ways that the language of loyalty could operate in the official structures of British occupation rule.[71]

In other cases, British soldiers found hard evidence of Americans' flexible loyalties. Just before the battle of Camden, James Simpson recalled that "the minds of the inclaimable [sic] Rebels, we have in Charles Town, were big with some important event." Many suspected that those who had taken parole and signed their loyalty oaths were still secret rebels. Indeed, proof of their communication with the Continental Army came after the battle "from some papers, which were found in the Pockets of the Slain, it appeared a correspondence had been carried on, between the Town [Charleston], and the Rebel Army."[72] As a result of this discovery, Clinton authorized the commandant of Charleston to take whatever means he found necessary to quell this insurrection by military courts-martial promising to "immediately send execution warrants for such as the law pronounces against."[73] While ultimately the regime did not execute most Charlestonians found guilty of conspiracy with the rebel army, the British did send several dozen prominent citizens into exile in Saint Augustine, deeming their loyalties too questionable to safely remain in the city.[74]

As a result of the questionable loyalties of men and women in occupied cities, an atmosphere of suspicion came to permeate these towns. Newport resident Fleet Greene recalled that during its occupation the town teemed with secret informers ready to report on the loyalty of its inhabitants, and that "by their Reports the Jails and Prison ships were continuely [sic] Crowded with the Namable Inhabitants."[75] Occupation officials sought out any hint of sympathy with the rebel cause, both in Newport and elsewhere. James Hector St. John de Crèvecœur, a French immigrant and later author of the loyalist paean *Letters from an American Farmer*, found himself victim to one of these informers when he arrived in New York City in the summer of 1779.[76] Despite having been exiled from his rural New York community, and even bringing intelligence from the backcountry of rebel military strength and positions, authorities imprisoned the wealthy landowner on suspicion of holding revolutionary sympathies. As William Smith Jr. explained, the issue stemmed from a letter in which Crèvecœur expressed "anguished Emotions of Pity on the Prospect of Indian Irruptions" in back-country New York and Pennsylvania. As many of these Native Americans had allied themselves with the British, expressing discontent with their actions could be interpreted as disloyal to the king.[77] Crèvecœur's French descent also raised suspicion about his allegiances. While trying to get his friend out of prison, Smith heard rumors that after the revolutionaries signed an alliance with France, the farmer "talk'd favorably of the Issue of Rebellion and reconciled it to some who had been as averse from it as himself."[78] Although a bond posted by Smith and Cadwallader Colden Jr. eventually proved enough to get him out of jail, Crèvecœur's experiences in occupied New York demonstrate the extent of suspicion cast upon even the most loyal of subjects. The entire experience caused Smith to observe wryly in his journal, "At such times . . . the greatest Circumspection is necessary, and one should keep but little Company and of the best Sort."[79]

The suspicion that Crèvecœur came under as a latecomer from the countryside came largely from elite loyalists who had resided in the city for years. These longtime loyalists often became the fiercest persecutors of those they suspected of harboring rebel tendencies.[80] By 1779, William Franklin, the former governor of New Jersey and one of the most vocal loyalist civilians living in New York City, had begun to see the military's efforts to conciliate and persuade former rebels as an outright betrayal of the loyalist cause.[81] While William Smith Jr. continued to favor amnesty for those willing to sign oaths of loyalty, he seems to have been in the minority of long-standing, elite loyalists. In an October 1778 dinner party held by Tryon, at which several prominent loyalists assembled, Smith noted, "They act under the Spirit of Revenge . . . every mercy [toward civilians and former rebels] will be imputed to Fear until there is a Superiority in the Field and the Colonies are distressed." Such observations caused Smith and many other moderates to despair of a loyalist elite who mingled their desire for personal revenge with their efforts to restore a more general allegiance to royal rule.[82]

The jaundiced eye that loyalists like Smith began to take toward political allegiance undermined occupation regimes' attempts to secure the loyalty of their subject populations. The evacuations of Philadelphia and Newport in 1778 and 1779 reveal how this atmosphere of suspicion translated to weakened support for occupation regimes and the principled loyalism that undergirded them. When the British Army evacuated both cities, thousands of loyalists followed them to New York, forming a large refugee population. But thousands more remained, disillusioned with restored British rule. These included many who had previously benefited from loyalist society, such as Mary Almy, the loyalist boardinghouse keeper in Newport, and Tench Coxe, the audacious young Philadelphia merchant. While Almy's reasons for staying in Newport after the British evacuated remain a mystery, Coxe left no doubt as to why he rejected British rule.[83] Throughout the occupation, the young merchant became increasingly remained frustrated by the suspicion placed on even the most prominent loyalists in occupied Philadelphia. Because of suspected smuggling, in the spring of 1778 the army placed restrictions on commerce with the Europe, the British Caribbean, and even occupied New York. These new policies largely prevented Coxe from obtaining the special trading licenses on which his business depended.[84] Customs officials also seized goods imported at his warehouse, and soldiers harassed his employees, once even imprisoning one of his ships' captains over a minor misunderstanding.[85] Despite Coxe's initially warm relationships with occupation officials, this series of small slights, transgressions, and misunderstandings alienated him from the military government, which seemed to in turn increasingly suspect him of disloyalty. By the time the British left the city, Coxe wrote to a friend that "the British Army have used me in such a way that I must not trust myself to speak of their Conduct on paper." Like thousands of other Americans, he decided not to follow the British Army back to New York in the summer of 1778 but to become, as he wrote, "a perfect American" within the new state.[86]

Many other men and women in Philadelphia and Newport shared Coxe's disillusionment with the army and the occupation regime. Although a few thousand became refugees after the evacuations, the majority of the populations of both cities remained and reconciled themselves to revolutionary rule.[87]

The same factors led to the weakening of loyalist societies in Charleston and New York. In Charleston, the catalyst proved to be the trial of Colonel Isaac Hayne, whose summary execution for violating parole and serving in a rebel militia caused an uproar among both refugees and longtime city residents. Hayne, a colonel in the South Carolina militia, had signed an oath of allegiance and been paroled to his nearby plantation after Charleston's capture, but in the summer of 1781 British forces captured again him in arms against the Crown. Later that month, a council of army officers met, and, without consulting the loyalist board of police, ordered Hayne executed. For the officers Hayne's fate was simple: the colonel had violated his parole and deserved death under the Articles of War.[88] For loyalists in the city, however, the affair violated the due process they expected from a restored royal regime. In a vain attempt to defend Hayne, attorney John Colcock argued against the execution order on the basis that "neither the Members or Witnesses were sworn," further stating that "no Enemy is liable to suffer Death by the Articles of War or any other Military rule or law which have ever had cognizance without [formal] Trial."[89] Like the harassment of Tench Coxe in Philadelphia, the abrogation of Hayne's right to trial by Charleston's military governors proved that British suspicions of Americans' loyalties could not be overcome even with reasoned arguments by irreproachable loyalists. It is no coincidence that Charleston's occupation effectively ceased to function around the same time as Isaac Hayne's execution on August 4, 1781—two months before the news of Yorktown reached the city.

Even New York's sophisticated occupation regime, which touched the lives of thousands, ceased to have much practical authority as the dangerous political atmosphere inside the city combusted after the battle of Yorktown made British defeat all but inevitable. As the prospect of peace loomed, New Yorkers abandoned in droves the institutions that had benefited them under the occupation. In the spring of 1783, New York merchant Evert Bancker Jr. found that, despite having obtained orders from the Office of Police threatening imprisonment, his debtors refused to pay him. Eventually, the situation forced the ever-loyal Bancker to flee to Long Island rather than face his own creditors, who persisted in their demands.[90] Land-lord James DeLancey, who had already escaped to England, also found that, despite appeals to various British officials, he could not recoup lost rents or evict delinquent tenants.[91] In both of these situations, British authorities proved powerless to enforce their edicts when the population refused to go along. Just as occurred in Charleston, where the occupation regime ceased to benefit them or lacked the power to compel them, New Yorkers refused to cooperate with it. As tenants living in New York, these people had to have signed loyalty oaths, and likely took advantage of the services and benefits offered by the occupation regime. Despite their former professions of loyalty, these people readily abandoned a regime that had held them in suspicion even as it granted them protection and opportunity. Military defeat did not suddenly cause these people to change their principles, but rather provided a catalyst for the bursting of a language of loyalty that had long been frayed by British suspicion and ill use of locals. In the end, the philosophy of loyalism failed even its truest adherents in hastening the res-toration of royal rule.

Those who suffered most from this failure were not Americans like Hannah Lawrence, Tench Coxe, and John Malbone, who kept their allegiances malleable, but rather those who had bought into the loyalist regimes wholeheartedly and cut off social and economic ties with those in revolutionary-held areas. At least seventy-five thousand people, including fifteen thousand slaves and free blacks, went into exile after 1783 because of their attachment to the British Army and the occupation regimes.[92] These included not only wealthy loyalists such as Andrew Elliot and William Smith Jr., who went on to relatively comfortable retirements in England and Canada, but also those on the lower rungs of society, such as the ex-slave Boston King.[93] King, who like thousands of other ex-slaves faced the bleak prospects of a return to bondage or an uncertain future elsewhere in the British Empire, chose the latter, resettling first in Nova Scotia, then in London, then finally in Britain's short-lived refuge for black loyalists in Sierra Leone.[94] For these people, British officials' refusal to trust civilian loyalists tragically altered what had been promising futures under the brief restored royal rule in the thirteen colonies.

Thousands of other Americans, disillusioned with imperial authority by the experience of occupation, remained in the new republic even after the war. If, as seems likely, about half a million Americans took loyalist actions, spoke loyalist words, or wrote loyalist declarations during the war, the seventy-five thousand who left constitutes only about 15 percent of the total.[95] Many of these people, like Tench Coxe and Mary Almy, had most likely once been true-hearted loyalists, but the day-to-day experience of occupation over the course of the war had soured them on the empire. Because of the British Army's increasing distrust and the need to keep loyalties flexible in the face of wartime conditions, royal authority weakened to a breaking point in the eyes of many of its subjects. Although it did not collapse fully until military defeat at Yorktown and its aftermath, the experience of shifting loyalties under occupation, combined with disruptions of the social hierarchy and the material privations of military rule, nonetheless doomed the attempt to restore imperial authority in British North America.

CHAPTER 6

Making Peace

In the twilight of the Revolutionary War, occupied cities became sites where ordinary people made their own personal settlements in the face of a quickly approaching peace between Great Britain and the fledgling United States. Although civil-military regimes had lost their effectiveness as early as the summer of 1781, occupied cities still served as prime spaces for peacemaking on the ground level. As diplomats representing the belligerent nations met in Paris through 1782 and 1783 seeking negotiated settlements for the difficult problems of loyalty, property, and territory, ordinary people on both sides of the Atlantic found their own solutions, often well before the preliminary articles of peace were agreed to in April 1783. Inhabitants, refugees, and exiles used British-occupied ports as staging grounds to reach out to family members, friends, and even government officials in rebel-held areas and other parts of the empire, making accommodations and negotiating the terms under which they would or would not take up new lives under the emerging American republic. Families long estranged by war and politics made amends with one another, men and women of the market reconnected with old trading partners, and self-emancipated people and runaway servants negotiated with their former masters. In the process, occupied territories took on a new importance as sites of transition and reunion.

That occupied cities became centers of reconciliation between local populations and the revolutionary governments underscored the failure of the attempt to restore royal rule. As exiles returned, refugees negotiated with their former oppressors to salvage property and social position, and slave owners sought to recover their human property, occupation administrations stood by helplessly—and, in some cases, actually abetted the process by helping to facilitate the transition of power. Indeed, by late 1781 the British Army could offer its most loyal subjects only the prospect of resettlement in different parts of the empire; a prospect not relished by many with deep connections to the thirteen newly independent states. As a result, British soldiers and their most stalwart loyalist allies watched helplessly as the occupation societies that had held so much promise for the resuscitation of imperial authority crumbled around them. Worse still, they themselves were forced to take part in the dismantling of these once-hopeful societies. By the end of this process, any veneer of hope for a restored British Empire in the United States had vanished.

Even as that hope vanished, however, the lessons of the occupation experience lived on and continued to prove useful to Americans caught in precarious positions. Carefully honed techniques to manage risk and reward in the midst of constantly changing wartime social dynamics gave men and women who had lived through them the skills to manage the shifts that occurred with the oncoming peace. Methods of alleviating shortages and protecting property—especially maintaining connections with those in areas under revolutionary control—also proved critical in achieving successful personal settlements after the fighting stopped. Most important, carefully cultivated positions of allegiance that were intentionally murky left room for residents of occupied cities and others who followed their examples to negotiate the best possible terms for their lives in either the new republic or the remnants of the empire. Even though the project of occupation failed, then, the day-to-day experience of it nevertheless continued to shape the lives of those who had endured it.

The Reverend Henry Addison's experience demonstrates the role of occupied cities in these delicate personal negotiations, as well as just how futile British attempts at retaining control had become by the end of the war. A Maryland-born minister in the Church of England, Addison traveled to New York City in late 1781 after a desultory six-year exile in England. The reverend sought an opportunity to return to his property in the Chesapeake and to live in peace in the soon-to-be independent state of Maryland. Part of his motive stemmed from an ideological conversion to independence, if not republicanism, just before Yorktown. As he wrote a friend in the summer of 1780, "I am a true convert to the opinion, *that . . . undertaking Divorce is best for both Countries.*"[1] Having broken with his British patrons in the Church, Addison saw in the prospect of peace a way to reconnect with American relations and regain his property in Maryland.

Still, his name had been attached to acts confiscating his property and he remained skeptical of the republican form of government in the revolutionary United States. Even after his voyage, the poor reverend contemplated immigrating to Italy or giving up his possessions to live with the Moravians in Pennsylvania, writing, "To see the Ruin of my Country, & of my Family, [would] imbitter [sic] my Life."[2] Nevertheless, sometime shortly after the battle of Yorktown, Addison arrived in New York and attempted to resume his interrupted life in America.

Once in New York, Addison's earnest efforts met with mixed success. He first wrote to Governor Thomas Lee of Maryland for permission to visit his family in the state, promising "to be very peaceable, & to give no Offense." The reverend also begged George Washington for permission to travel through military lines, wrote to the governors of New Jersey and Delaware for similar permission, and sent a plaintive missive his nephew, George Plater, a former member of the Continental Congress and member of the Maryland state senate. Although Plater promised "to promote [Addison's] Return with all his Strength" and Washington agreed to allow him through Continental lines so long as he received permission from civil authorities, people in Maryland and elsewhere conspired against Addison's homecoming. His former enemies in the state, along with the clergyman who had taken over his parish, began to circulate a petition "to convince the People that I was a very dangerous Man," and, if allowed to return, would promote pro-British politics and sow dissent among the population. Still, the reverend received hopeful intimations from officials in Delaware that he would be allowed to return safely to estates he owned in that state, but still he feared, if he attempted to travel through New Jersey to get to those estates, "At the first Step I had taken in the Jersies, Bonds, Imprisonment, & the Tribunal of [Governor William] Livingston w[oul]d have await me." So, even though family members and friends continued to push his cause in Maryland and elsewhere, Addison continued to languish in British New York through the end of 1782 and well into 1783.[3]

As he negotiated with contacts in Maryland, Delaware, and New Jersey to return in peace to the new United States, however, Addison made sure to maintain his ties to the British and loyalist establishment in New York, which could also compensate him for his losses in the rebelled colonies—especially if his attempts to reconcile in Maryland failed. Before embarking for revolutionary territory, the reverend wrote to the commander in chief of British forces, "request[ing] to know if by going to Delaware for a time, he is likely to forfeit his claims on Government for compensation for his losses." General Sir Guy Carleton—who had succeeded Henry Clinton after Yorktown—answered that he was free to go, although if he succeeded in reclaiming his property in Maryland he would forfeit any entitlement to protection from the king's government.[4] As his negotiations dragged on through 1783 and the British evacuation of New York approached, Addison also used his ecclesiastical connections to obtain a chaplaincy aboard the warship HMS *Mercury*, which was to be permanently stationed in North America after the war. The position, which did not require the reverend to actually travel aboard the ship, provided an income which would allow him to remain in New York and later Halifax as he finalized the terms of his return to Maryland.[5] Even as he attempted to return to the revolutionary state he had fled years earlier, Addison hedged his bets by maintaining connections to the British government he was attempting to abandon.

While Addison eventually succeeded in returning to Maryland with the help of his son-in-law, his late-war travails nevertheless explicate many of the complexities of personal negotiations at the end of the war.[6] Well supplied with connections on both sides of the lines, Addison expertly used occupied New York City to gauge his prospects in revolutionary America while maintaining what advantage he could from the British government as a refugee and a clergyman. The reverend was not exceptional. Between 1781 and 1783, New York became a clearing house for those seeking to negotiate similar arrangements. As Addison himself observed in March 1782, "Every Body who can is deserting this Place," and half of the population would receive Washington's army "with open arms" should they enter the city."[7] Similar scenes played out in Savannah and Charleston, as Americans sought to use occupied space to get the best deal they could in the coming peace.

A month after Henry Addison journeyed to New York, diplomats began meeting in Paris to negotiate a formal end to the war. Whitehall, now operating under joint government by Lords Rockingham and Shelburne after the disaster at Yorktown had forced out Lords North and Germain, sought to use its remaining North American positions of New York, Charleston, and Savannah as bargaining chips to improve the British position at the peace table. Many of Britain's top diplomats wanted to keep New York City, which remained secure with twenty thousand troops and perhaps as many as thirty-five thousand residents and refugees, as a permanent trading entrepôt and naval base—a sort of Gibraltar or Hong Kong in

North America. Failing this outcome, the British representatives hoped to at the very least leverage the territory to insist on repayment for the losses of loyalists in revolutionary-controlled areas, and to secure more favorable borders between the new United States and Canada. As for the Americans, represented by Benjamin Franklin, John Adams, and John Jay, nothing but a complete cession of all three ports would suffice, with no provision made for loyalists whatsoever—Franklin, whose son, William, had sided with the Crown, particularly insisted upon this last point. For much of the summer and fall of 1782, the two sides remained at an impasse. As they dickered in Paris over the fate of British-occupied America, ordinary people like Henry Addison took matters into their own hands.[8]

Although negotiations for individual settlements became more urgent after British defeat at Yorktown, Americans had navigated the treacherous terrain of peacemaking before. When the British Army evacuated Boston in 1776, Philadelphia in 1778, and Newport in 1779, it took many loyalists and their families with them. As many as one thousand loyalists left Boston with the British Army, an additional three thousand people abandoned Philadelphia when the British left, and several hundred members of Newport's most prominent families left the city when troops pulled out. However, in all three cities, many more people stayed behind—if the best estimates hold that around thirty-five hundred civilians, mostly loyalists, lived in Boston during the siege, then the thousand who left represents only a third of the total civilian population. In Philadelphia, the disparity between those who stayed and those who left was similar—the three thousand loyalists represented around one in six of the approximately twenty thousand citizens who endured the occupation.[9] Many remained behind at the express urging of the departing Howe brothers, who advised loyalists in the city to make the best terms they could with the rebels to protect their property and families.[10] In Newport estimates are less reliable, but sources indicate that around five hundred people left out of an occupation population of between three and four thousand; again, roughly one in six or seven.[11] Those who left certainly represented a sizable proportion of townspeople and likely included many who had been most vehement in their loyalism or who had the most to lose under restored revolutionary control. Almost certainly, elite families were overrepresented in the diasporas, while those who remained were disproportionately poor. Nevertheless, in each case the majority of the civilian population—even those who had the chance to leave with the army—remained behind.

Those who stayed did so for a variety of reasons. Some—like Tench Coxe in Philadelphia—had become disillusioned with the British cause over the course of military rule. Others—the Newport innkeeper Mary Almy, for one—refused to abandon property or lacked the resources to support their families as refugees. Regardless, civilians who remained behind had to bargain with revolutionary officials and rely upon connections on the other sides for their protection, their continued enjoyment of their property, and the safety of their family members. Not all were successful. In Boston, several reputed loyalists were imprisoned after the evacuation, and others were stripped of their property or exiled.[12] In Philadelphia, two men who had served as civilian officers of the city watch under the British regime were hanged, and others forced to go before a judge to account for their actions under occupation. Grace Galloway, wife of Philadelphia superintendent of police Joseph Galloway, was dragged out of her home by vengeful revolutionary authorities and died a pauper in a friend's home in 1782.[13] In Newport, Ezra Stiles recounted that, shortly after the end of the occupation the revolutionaries had "about 40 Tories imprisoned," and the city's inhabitants continued under suspicion of loyalism for the rest of the war, even as French troops occupied the town in 1780.[14] Still, these cases represent a minority: although difficult while the passions of war raged, most civilians were able to find a place in postoccupation society. How they did so would become a template for those who wished to make their own personal settlements after Yorktown.

The British evacuation of Boston had a chilling effect on loyalists, although many remained peacefully in the city. The Reverend Mather Byles, a Congregationalist minister famous for his suspicion of the revolution, refused to leave when the British withdrew. Likely because of his age and respected position as Minister of the Hollis Street meeting, Byles was spared retribution, briefly being placed under house arrest but living in Boston until his death in 1788.[15] Others faced more difficult paths to rehabilitation. Nathaniel Brinley, whose brother Thomas had fled with the British, lived in fear during the first weeks after the British left. In mid-April 1776, he lamented: "10 or 12 Persons were carried for examination some of which I am inform'd are Committed to Gaol and how soon it may come to my turn is uncertain."[16] By the end of the summer, Brinley had been sent to labor for a tanner in the nearby town of Framingham, pending a decision on his case for remaining in Boston. Although he laid in grim expectations of "something very disagreeable to take place," by 1779 Nathaniel had apparently regained his rights in the city. Although exactly how he obtained his liberty is unclear, likely Nathaniel used the same familial and friendly connections to make his way from prisoner to citizen that he had used to survive in occupied Boston. In an early letter he mentions a "Mr. Hutchinson who has greatly assisted me and been Friendly beyond measure" in his various trials before the Massachusetts revolutionary regime.[17] Likely, this Hutchinson, or other friends of the Brinley family, had aided Nathaniel to mitigate his circumstances, just as they had during Boston's occupation in 1775–1776.

The methods by which ex-loyalists made their private peace settlements in the wake of occupation become clearer in the more well-documented case of Tench Coxe, the Philadelphia merchant who had made a fortune through deft manipulation of the city's occupation regime. Coxe had become thoroughly disillusioned with the British cause by the end of the occupation, but avoiding recriminations for his erstwhile loyalism required deliberate action. By any stretch of the imagination, helping to supply the garrison made him guilty of aiding and abetting British forces, a crime punishable under the laws of revolutionary Pennsylvania by seizure of property, exile, or even death. A month before the British evacuated, Coxe's name was placed on a proclamation issued by Pennsylvania's executive council against those "adjudged guilty of High Treason."[18] A few days later, Coxe snuck out of occupied Philadelphia to sign of an oath of allegiance to the revolutionary state of Pennsylvania, although he claimed to have no inkling of the planned British evacuation.[19] While not releasing him entirely from suspicion, the oath would at least allow him to claim loyalty to the revolutionary state and would entitle him to the protections of its laws. In his frantic preparations in the weeks leading up to the evacuation, Coxe attempted to cut his business ties to the New York loyalists as well, working furiously to send back all unsold goods he had accepted on consignment and to close out unsettled debts so that the connections would not linger to fuel potential enemies.

In addition to swearing allegiance to the state of Pennsylvania and ending his business associations with the New York loyalists, in the weeks leading up to the British evacuation the young merchant also eliminated written evidence of his complicity in British rule. In writing to a New York friend about his decision to remain in Philadelphia, he urged his acquaintances, "Destroy all my letters, that I may not suffer from their being seen by either side," worrying that "both might perhaps blame me."[20] In addition to instructing his correspondents to eliminate evidence of his collaboration, Coxe also made alterations in his mercantile letterbook, cutting out sections of letters sent to others to hide his actions. The entrepreneur excised names of ships he owned shares in, people he dealt with, and some of the methods by which he obtained his licenses to trade, as well as other aspects of his activities now completely lost. In one particularly egregious instance, Coxe ripped out almost all of a letter regarding a voyage to the Caribbean whose legality was dubious under both British and Pennsylvania law.[21] While the letterbook survives, likely because it also contained potentially valuable records of the firm Coxe operated with his father before and after the war, little else from the occupation years exists in an otherwise well-stocked family archive of correspondence and business ephemera. By altering and destroying the physical records of his actions, Coxe erased evidence of his complicity in British military rule forces and cleared a path for a new start under the republican regime.

Tench Coxe's selective redaction of his records likely aided in obtaining an acquittal from the charge of high treason, as did his family connections and class position. Coxe's father, who had remained outside of town during the occupation and made his reputation as a supporter of the revolutionaries, intervened on behalf of his son with Judge Thomas McKean, a family friend who had been put in charge of hearing the cases of accused collaborators. While he still had to go through a preliminary hearing, the charges were soon dismissed due to lack of written evidence of wrongdoing, or credible witnesses willing to testify against him. Coxe's social status almost certainly played a role in this dismissal. After his initial interview with McKean, he described the judge as "friendly" and "genteel," and granted the accused bail, a privilege that might have been denied to those of the lower classes accused of treason.[22] Although his loyalist background hung with him through the end of the war, causing difficulty with his business and harassment to his person, by the end of the war Coxe's politics had been almost completely rehabilitated.

Although made extraordinary by his rise to prominence as a political economist in the 1790s, Coxe's experience was not unusual in postoccupation Philadelphia. Although two men were hanged for their participation in Philadelphia's occupation regime, most others were spared, and negotiated reconciliation took precedence over recriminations. Out of 638 people accused of treason in the entire state of Pennsylvania between the British evacuation and the end of 1781, only 43 ever made it to trial. Of these, only

7 resulted in executions, including the 2 watchmen, a convicted burglar, and another man put to death by the army for espionage.[23] Such a small number of trials and convictions seems remarkable, but is a testament to the ability of those who survived occupation to use their positions and connections to make peace. Even the women who had participated in the Meschianza, the symbol of Philadelphia's occupied culture, achieved redemption, though not without a degree of public chastisement. During a July 4 celebration in 1778, revolutionary supporters made up a slave woman in a fine gown and an "Extravagant high head Dress" meant to evoke those worn by the Ladies of the Burning Mountain and Blended Rose, and paraded her through town heaping insults upon, as one account put it, "the Mistresses & Wh[ore]s of the British officers." Although humiliating, however, the ritual allowed the people of Philadelphia to reclaim the space from the British without any actual violence against the women themselves. Rebecca Moore Smith, one of the women likely involved in the Meschianza, even participated in the street performance from afar.[24] Through public shaming of a symbol, rather than individuals, Philadelphia's loyalist women could be reintegrated into postoccupation society.

Those who remained behind in Newport faced similar challenges and found similar solutions. Mary Almy, the boardinghouse keeper who had sided against her Continental Army officer husband to remain in Newport during the occupation, entirely escaped suspicion for her politics. She continued to live in Newport, and to operate her large boardinghouse on Thames Street (which, ironically, had been confiscated from another loyalist in 1776 and awarded to her husband, Benjamin, while a member of the council of the revolutionary state).[25] Likely her connection with her husband, who, as a Continental Army captain and civil officer in Rhode Island's government had unassailable republican bona fides, facilitated this smooth transition to civilian life. Almy's rehabilitation went so far that, when he visited the town in 1790, George Washington boarded at the Almys' residence. The visit was so remarkable that the family saved the blanket he had slept in for decades after the fact.[26] When she died in 1808, Almy's loyalism had been so long forgotten that her husband, from whom she had been violently estranged during the war, was according to her obituary "overwhelmed with sorrow" at "being deprived in an advanced age of so valuable an associate."[27]

Despite the protection of her husband's position and her postwar rise to social prominence, Almy did have to take measures to obfuscate her wartime actions. After the occupation ended, she concealed her diary of the Battle of Rhode Island, written as a series of never-delivered letters to her husband, which revealed her loyalist sentiments and railed against the revolutionary army besieging the town. While not destroying them, she gave the letters to a trusted friend and stipulated that it be sealed away. She was so successful that the bundle of pages was not discovered by family members until nearly fifty years after her death.[28] Had this epistolary journal been discovered, one wonders whether Washington would have deigned to stay at Almy's home, or whether her husband, who likely never read the document, would have forgiven her for breaking with him during the war. Like Tench Coxe, for Almy moving on with family protection and social prominence was not enough to move past the experience of occupation: rather, evidence of wartime complicity with the British Army had to be expunged, for fear that it could reemerge in the future and plunge her back into the confusion and anarchy of military rule.

The severity of the occupation in Newport may also have aided those former loyalists who remained. One survivor recalled to a historian in the 1830s that "about 480 buildings of various classes were wholly destroyed," likely representing a large proportion of the town's homes, barns, and outbuildings.[29] The British occupation also stifled trade, as many previously prosperous merchants left the town as the British arrived. The merchant Aaron Lopez, once the wealthiest man in the colony, left for Massachusetts when the British arrived, losing much of his property and fortune and ultimately dying in 1782 before ever returning to Rhode Island.[30] Finally, only eight months after the British left, in July 1780 the comte de Rochambeau arrived, along with seven thousand French troops, matching the size of the British occupation force and further straining the city's resources.[31] Conditions were so dire in Newport after the occupation that, in October 1781— the same month that Rochambeau's troops contributed to the allied victory at Yorktown—Newport's town council petitioned the government of Rhode Island for relief from the state's tax levies, pleading that it could not raise tax money from most citizens and that "by reasons of the town being for a long time in the hands of the enemy and since that time it hath been found extremely difficult to collect money enough to satisfy the requisitions of the public."[32] The British occupation, followed closely by the French army's landing, had devastated the finances of the once-wealthy port city to a point where its government could not even collect the barest taxes from its impoverished citizens.

Given these financial woes, it is perhaps little wonder that prominent merchants and landowners who had participated in the British occupation, such as Stephen Aryault and Francis Brinley, remained unmolested in Newport after the occupation ended. Both had been designated by Ezra Stiles at "three-star" loyalists, and Brinley even merited inclusion on the reverend's list of "Principal and Active Tories." However, in the absence of patriot merchants like Lopez, wealthy former loyalists willing to accede to the revolutionary governments could provide a valuable source of tax revenue and potentially reinvigorate the city's economy.[33] It was in this context that Ayrault, who had eagerly cultivated relationships with British captains to allow his goods to be transshipped from New York, remained one of the most prominent merchants in Rhode Island, even receiving encouragement from the revolutionary government he once scorned. In November 1780, just a year after the end of the British occupation and in the midst of the French, the state government returned to Ayrault the rent from a farm in nearby Tiverton, Rhode Island, that it had seized and leased out to another tenant.[34] Not only was Ayrault allowed to remain, but he also regained his rights as a prominent citizen of the state.

Francis Brinley, who had used his brother George's position in the British Army's commissary department to feed his family and enrich himself during the occupation, also thrived, even as he maintained connections to family members who remained with the British Army. In the fateful month of October 1781, Francis received news from occupied New York that his son, Ned, who had joined a loyalist regiment, had survived the march to Yorktown with General Cornwallis's army.[35] Yet despite his continued correspondence with family members in the king's army, Brinley also received financial encouragement from the revolutionary government to remain. In early 1783, he received part of the confiscated estates of Colonel Joseph Wanton's family after Wanton had fled with the British Army.[36] Although Rhode Island's government remained openly hostile to loyalists after the occupation, in practice it encouraged at least a few prominent supporters of the king to keep their assets in the state.

These economic incentives for allowing ex-collaborators to remain foreshadowed later arguments made by revolutionaries such as John Jay and Alexander Hamilton for the reintegration of loyalists after the war. In early 1783, as he observed countless loyalists preparing to leave New York City, Hamilton dreaded that each wealthy supporter of royal government "may carry away eight or ten thousands guineas" that could have been used to strengthen the young republic's finances and spur its flagging economy. Fellow New Yorker John Jay agreed, worrying that the loss of these loyalists' productivity would weaken the new state of New York and strengthen the British colonies in Canada. In early 1783, he wrote to Hamilton, "I would rather see the sweat of their brows fertilizing our fields . . . than those of our neighbours."[37] Like the Rhode Island government had after the evacuation, both revolutionary leaders recognized the need for loyalist capital and labor in building a new state in the wake of the destructive war.

Although Philadelphia and Newport provided instructive examples for both survivors of occupation and revolutionaries who sought to reincorporate them into society, these debates did not begin in earnest until after the Battle of Yorktown. Loyalist exiles in England and the West Indies recognized early on what Yorktown meant and began the scramble to return to North America on their own terms. For these people, territory became highly politicized and had to be navigated carefully. Just as often as occupied cities could be used as grounds for negotiation, they could be used against returnees by enemies in their former homes. Such was the case with William Rawle, the romantically frustrated young refugee who had railed against British officers' courtships of eligible American women. Frustrated by the limits of his legal education in occupied New York, Rawle had immigrated to London in 1781 to continue his studies. However, further alienated in the imperial capital, Rawle determined early in 1782 to return to his native land, writing his mother, "I doubt not you will approve my intention of returning to Philadelphia and submitting to that authority which is there established" on New Year's Day, 1782.[38] However, the young man quickly learned that returning via New York was a complicated proposition. While residing in London, Rawle's name had been placed on a list of loyalists proposed to be banned from the revolutionary state of Pennsylvania. Should the list pass the Pennsylvania assembly with Rawle's name on it, his mother and sisters would stand to lose all of their substantial property in the state. Unlike Addison, then, the young law student had to act decisively and quickly—as he wrote his mother later in March, he intended to "as soon as possible embrace [his] sisters whose unexpected situation requires a father in a brother." Still, Rawle understood the dangers of his situation and trod carefully. He knew that if he went to New York he "should expect to be brought to trial for an enemy &c on arriving at Philadelphia." Arriving from British-held territory would prove his enemies right and see him branded forever as a loyalist. Instead, Rawle decided, "The most eligible route I can think of is that of the port L'Orient," and he thus set sail for France three months later and thence directly to Philadelphia to plead his case before the revolutionary government.[39] Ultimately, the young man succeeded, not only reclaiming his status as a citizen of the state but also passing the bar in Pennsylvania by year's end and setting up a prosperous law practice in Philadelphia. Like Coxe three years earlier, Rawle's youth, and his family's wide array of well-placed friends in the city, had much to do with his rehabilitation. Still, by carefully choosing his route home, Rawle used politicized space to his advantage and end his wartime experience on his own terms.

David Greene, a merchant who spent much of the war on the British West Indian island of Antigua, also angled for a return to his native Boston around the period of Yorktown, and also faced prosecution for treason if he did so. Greene had been one of the thousand who fled with the British Army when it evacuated the city in 1776, and in five years of exile had made a life for himself in the Caribbean, trading sugar and other goods in a vibrant wartime economy. Greene even married in Antigua, wedding the daughter of his landlord and business partner James Russell.[40] Still, sometime in 1779 or 1780, Greene decided to attempt a return to mainland North America, perhaps motivated by a slowdown in business opportunities in the wake of successive hurricanes or, as he wrote to a business partner, because of "the Critical Situation of Property, & the disagreeable Alarms to which we are often subject" from the French fleet.[41] In November 1781, just a few weeks after Yorktown, Greene saw his opportunity. He and his wife made the move from Antigua to Norwich, Connecticut, likely through the neutral Dutch Island of Saint Eustatius. Still barred on pain of imprisonment from stepping foot in Massachusetts, however, for the next two years the Greenes lived and continued their mercantile business less than a hundred miles away in revolutionary Connecticut, all the while attempting to negotiate to a legal return to Boston.

Like Rawle, Greene had avoided occupied territory in his homecoming, but he still had to engage in delicate negotiations to effect his return to Boston. Like Henry Addison, Greene leveraged his connections across the war-torn Atlantic to his own political advantage in attempting this feat. Because of his British connections, Continental Colonel Thomas Fitch of Connecticut asked Greene to write a letter on his behalf to the commissary of British prisoners of war in the West Indies, asking for the parole of his son and several others who had been captured during privateering voyages in the Caribbean.[42] Greene succeeded in receiving lenient treatment for these men, likely through his father-in-law, who had become physician to the prisoners of war held at Antigua.[43] Greene also continued to correspond with his bankers in London, via intermediaries in Amsterdam, and even planned to use his wartime connections for future profit after the peace, writing to a friend, "As Peace is an Event not totally improbable, it may not be amiss to ask you whether . . . a Ship might not be kept going between Boston, St. Kitts, & London advantageously?"[44] Although he did not regain readmission to his native city until early August 1784, by exploiting his connections and moving at the right time from Antigua to Connecticut, Greene had set himself up for a prosperous postwar situation.

While exiles like Henry Addison, William Rawle, and David Greene had the luxury of choosing the time and place of their return, those living in occupied cities had fewer choices in the months after Yorktown. Although many New York loyalists believed that the war effort would go on, the abrupt evacuation of Savannah, Georgia, in July 1782 sent gave many a start. Early in June, General Sir Guy Carleton sent a fleet of transports to Charleston harbor with secret orders to evacuate the garrison of Savannah, along with any loyalists who wished to join them. Despite the protests of Governor Sir James Wright, who castigated the British military establishment as having "give[n] *the matter up* . . . ever Since the Unfortunate affair of Lord C[ornwallis]," the British Army left Savannah on July 11, carrying with it between 2,500 and 3,100 white loyalists and 3,500 to 5,000 enslaved blacks.[45]

Savannah's evacuees had many reasons for leaving, and all who could selected their destinations carefully. Charleston and New York became popular with those anticipating either a continued struggle against the revolutionaries or a reconciliation with the republic, but others chose exile. For many poor loyalists and free blacks, Nova Scotia, where the British government had begun to offer land to its supporters, became a sanctuary, especially for who had been stripped of their property in America or who faced the prospect of reenslavement if they remained.[46] Anticipating peace, the British government designated East Florida as another haven for well-off slaveholding loyalists, offering new plantations on cheap rent in order to populate the sparsely settled province. For many white slaveholders, it represented a place where they could begin anew while maintaining their slave property, and growing the same crops. However, such dreams died in 1783, when the final peace settlement turned the colony over to Spain, and most British refugees were forced to uproot themselves once again 1785.[47]

Jamaica, a more established colony, proved a popular destination among better-off slaveowners. The island had been a hub of illicit trade in human beings from North America for much of the war—between 1775 and 1785, over sixty-five thousand slaves were imported to Kingston at a time when the African slave trade stood at a virtual standstill. Most came from occupied territories on the mainland. Further, the island's the new governor, Archibald Campbell—the conqueror of Savannah in 1778—knew many of the new immigrants from his time in Georgia, and offered generous terms to those who chose to resettle there.[48] Even free blacks found a haven in Jamaica—George Lisle, a former slave and Baptist preacher, arrived with his family in a flotilla from Savannah in August 1782, finding a community of about ten thousand free blacks already settled on the island, with more loyalists arriving every day.[49] Still, even with all of these refuges to choose from, the suddenness of Savannah's evacuation proved traumatic for many, and thus began the great scramble among city dwellers, refugees, ex-slaves, and others to find a new place in the rapidly approaching postwar world.

For formerly enslaved black people, the evacuation of Savannah presented the first instance where newly gained freedom could be taken away. David George, an ex-slave butcher and lay preacher who by the time of the evacuation had been living in the city for two years, actively responded to this threat. As rumors of the British withdrawal circulated in the countryside, revolutionary forces swept in to reclaim as much of their lost property as possible, often launching raids to abduct slaves from farms and plantations on the outskirts of the city. George, fearing for his family's safety, arranged to purchase passage to Charleston through his familial networks —his brother-in-law, who likely lived outside of town in the backcountry, as George describes him as "half an Indian by his mother[']s side, and half a Negro," sent him a steer, which the preacher sold and "designed to pay our passage and set off for Charlestown" with the ensuing profits. However, after being robbed, George turned to the local black community who listened to his sermons. As he wrote years later, "I borrowed money from some of the Black people to buy hogs, and soon repaid them, and agreed on a passage to Charlestown."[50] Likely, many of these people also lived outside the lines, as the suppliers of George's meat almost certainly did.

After safely reaching Charleston, George and his family set out on a vessel bound for Nova Scotia, where they settled with other black loyalists before ultimately leaving again for Sierra Leone. As many others in Savannah had, George leveraged his connections to the countryside and to family and friends outside the lines to make the best of a bad situation.

Savannah's evacuation fleet carried not only white loyalists, slaves, and free blacks but also several hundred Native Americans who had sided with the British and who faced an uncertain future in the postwar world. Although the British position had weakened after Yorktown, many bands of Creeks, Chocktaws, and Cherokees, especially in Georgia, remained loyal to their old allies, continuing to battle revolutionary militias in the back-country even as republican representatives sought to make peace. Indeed, in May 1782 a group of 150 Creek warriors set off to help defend the belea-guered city of Savannah, ignorant of its impending evacuation. After a series of running battles with Continental and militia forces, the Creeks reached the Georgia capital on June 24, only two weeks before the evacua-tion fleet departed. When the British left, then, they took these warriors with them, along with around 250 other Creeks, and another 200 Choctaws, with then to East Florida, where they assisted the British government there in defending the colony against Spanish attack and continued to harass revolutionary forces in southern Georgia. Although both sides continued to urge bands of Creeks and the Chocktaws to put down their arms, fighting continued sporadically through 1782 and 1783, only ceasing with peace negotiations with the American and Spanish governments in 1783 and 1784, well after the Treaty of Paris had brought the conflict to a final close. While the evacuation of Savannah marked the end of the war for many of the loyalists, slaves, and free blacks who accompanied the fleet, for the Creeks and Choctaws it was a chance to continue their war to preserve their lands and, ultimately, to obtain peace on more favorable terms for their tribes.[51]

Despite the evacuation, many loyalists and other survivors of British military rule remained in Savannah after the British left. As in Philadelphia and Newport, these people made their peace with the new revolutionary government. Still, since the evacuees likely comprised between 15 and 33 percent of Georgia's prewar population, those who remained faced a bleak situation, as independent revolutionary and loyalist militias continued the armed struggle throughout the state for most of 1782, despite efforts by the Continental Army and Georgia's revolutionary government to stop the violence.[52] Many of these partisans ended up fleeing to the backcountry or even further west into Creek and Cherokee territory. By 1788 almost six hundred white people and more than eight hundred blacks had settled the area around modern-day Mobile, Alabama—likely refugees on both sides from the continuing violence in backcountry Georgia.[53] Still, eventually the spirit of reconciliation that had pervaded in Philadelphia and Newport won out in Savannah, at least for some. Such was the case for Donald McLeod, a physician who had lived in Savannah during the occupation and tended to prisoners of war aboard the British prison ships. Although denied citizenship when he first applied in 1783 due to accusations of abuses against Continental prisoners of war, McLeod was eventually granted liberty to live in the state in 1785, and by 1794 had much of his seized property returned to him.[54] Still, Georgia's evacuation and its violent aftermath marked the beginning of the end for many who had made their lives in the British-occupied territories, forcing all to reconsider their positions and their relationships to the authorities who had vied for their support.

As men and women in America and across the British Empire rethought their positions and began making moves to end their own personal wars in the aftermath of Savannah's evacuation, diplomats had only just begun meeting in Paris to consider the geopolitical settlement of the war. During these delicate negotiations, loyalists, slaves, and those residing in occupied territories became some of the most contentious issues. Although Parliament demanded in February 1782 that the government cease offensive operations and open negotiations with the Continental Congress and its French allies, British officials were still not willing to give up all the empire's territory in America. Even as Parliament voted on the matter, the retiring Lord George Germain recommended to the ministry that all efforts be made to hold onto New York, Charleston, and Savannah, citing "the very profitable and extensive commerce we carry on" in those ports, which "is universally felt, by our merchants and manufacturers and has greatly served to keep them in employment."[55] Germain, and many others in Britain, wanted to see at least the port cities remain in the king's power in order to facilitate future trade with the soon-to-be-independent colonies, and serve as naval bases to use in the event of a future conflict.

After Germain and his patron, Lord North, resigned in March, the new British administration under Lord Shelburne hoped to use occupied territory as a bargaining chip to maintain postwar presence in America or to force Congress's representatives to make allowances for refugees. In instructions to Henry Strachey, one of his chief negotiators, Shelburne expressed hopes to leverage the cities "to obtain some compensation for the Refugees, either by a direct cession of Territory in their favour, or by engaging the Half, or some proportion, of what the back Lands may produce when Sold, or a Sum mortgaged on those Lands, or at least a favorable Boundary of Nova Scotia."[56] To further this negotiating point, Shelburne had a state of the ports' defenses drawn up, noting that "Several Redoubts and other Field Works have been thrown up on the Continent opposite the upper End of York Island to defend the Pass into the Island at King's Bridge," and "at Charles Town South Carolina the Fortifications are in a complete state, and in a Condition to stand a formal Siege."[57] Retention of the remaining occupied zones clearly crossed the new prime minister's mind. Despite their bluster, however, Shelburne and his subordinates were unwilling to risk further war with the Americans to win their points, and it soon became apparent that the American representatives would not be placated on the issue of loyalists. As negotiator Richard Oswald wrote his superior, Congress's negotiators "would not in point of Conference think themselves justified in pardoning and providing for those who had burnt their Towns, & murthered their Women and Children."[58] In the end, concessions for loyalists, refugees, and those who remained in formerly occupied territories would be left to the states, rather than decided in Paris. Although the British government continued to press for aid and some in the military facilitated negotiations for those in occupied territories, residents of occupied cities were most often left to their own devices.

This fact began to dawn on many during the summer of 1782, as details of the peace negotiations began to trickle into New York and Charleston. When rumors broke out that Britain would recognize the independence of its rebellious colonies, residents and refugees in those cities began a frenzy of activity, attempting to get their affairs in order and either make peace with revolutionary authorities or settle with debtors and creditors to fund new lives elsewhere. The immediate effect of the news on loyalist and refugee communities within the cities was abject terror. In New York, loyalists petitioned General Carleton, expressing their fears that the British government intended to abandon them and begging that some consideration be made for their property in the now inevitable peace treaty.[59] William Smith Jr. observed in his diary that "the town is thrown into the most painful anxiety" upon hearing confirmation of the news, but "console[d] myself with the Hope that the King's Instruction to his Commissaries is a State Artifice," rather than a true recognition of the United States.[60] So ardent was his support for the Crown that Smith remained in denial of the British defeat until nearly the very last, only leaving with the final evacuation fleet in November 1783.

Like Smith, many of the most prominent loyalists in the city continued to believe that the war was winnable, or at the very least that they could improve their conditions. William Franklin left New York to lobby in London on behalf of loyalists, only to find his patron, Germain, no longer in office and many tenets of the final peace treaty already agreed upon. Others in the city continued to agitate for the restoration of civil government, seeing the removal of military role as a way to mitigate the hardships of the population and to deal with the republican government on a more equal footing.[61] Even as late as April 1783, loyalists kept up this façade, and as Governor James Robertson departed he appointed Andrew Elliot, his lieutenant, to act in his stead, promising him half his salary and his claim to the emoluments of the position, despite his own admission that "little will be left to assist you in preserving Order and protecting the distressed good subjects, but the name of Governor."[62] For the elite loyalists and ex-royal officials in the city, defeat was simply not an option many were ready to consider, and most of these people, including Elliot, ended up leaving the country into exile in England after the conclusion of the war.[63]

In Charleston, civil officials also agitated for the restoration of civil rule long after the defeat at Yorktown, even as the civilian board of police in that city began to lose effectiveness after April 1782.[64] As it became clear that the British intended to evacuate the city that summer, some diehard loyalists even concocted a plan to defend the port with a force of white loyalists and armed ex-slaves—a scheme that Continental Army officer John Laurens remarked "resembles the desperate unavailing efforts of a drowning man." Instead of acting on this plan, which, if Shelburne's assessment that the town could be defended with two thousand men, might actually have had a chance of succeeding for a time, General Alexander Leslie began to make preparations to withdraw the troops, announcing the evacuation on August 7 and dispatching the first convoy of troops and refugees to East Florida on October 10.[65]

The two-month withdrawal from Charleston saw different factions of city residents, enslaved people, free blacks, and British soldiers jostling to settle their affairs in the most advantageous way possible. By the time orders came to evacuate, perhaps eight thousand white civilians and another ten to fifteen thousand slaves lived inside the lines of the city, along with the force of around six thousand soldiers. Feeding this combined population proved impossible. The Continental Army prevented foraging expeditions and refused to allow local farmers to sell provisions to the British Army, as the Continental general Nathanael Greene hoped that allowing Charleston to starve would speed the army's evacuation and force civilians into the hands of the revolutionaries.[66] As a result, Leslie launched a series of raids against plantations and other settlements simply to secure enough food for the garrison, but he still did not believe that he could support the civilian population under his care. Late into the fall of 1782, Leslie complained to his superiors in New York of the "monstrous expense" of feeding, clothing, and supplying "the Numbers that may expect to be brought off" with the army. To limit these costs, the general sought to negotiate with the rebels, offering to allow some of them to come in and reclaim their slave property in exchange for provisions. Leslie also sought a truce with the rebels in the countryside, and the cessation of confiscation of loyalist property. In October, Leslie agreed with revolutionary officials to compensate rebels for slaves who had claimed freedom with the British Army and to return those who either had no claim to freedom or wished to return. In exchange, the republican state granted a cessation of violence and gave the British safe passage to buy food from revolutionary-controlled areas. Unfortunately, the accord soon collapsed, as representatives of the revolutionary government found that army officers and loyalists continued to take enslaved people out of the town, and South Carolina's governor abrogated the agreement only a week after having negotiated it.[67]

Even without the participation of the revolutionary representatives, a board of military officers and loyalists sat to hear the claims of ex-slaves and the representations of their former masters in the closing months of 1782. These officers largely sided in favor of the enslaved and granted most passes out of the city. While the board allowed ex-slaves to make their own choices, and the majority chose freedom in exile over a return to servitude, several masters did persuade their formerly enslaved men and women to return, promising better treatment and even eventual emancipation for children and family members still held in bondage. Although a return to slavery was certainly a bleak fate, the prospect of permanent separation from family members and an uncertain future in Nova Scotia or West Africa may have seemed even worse for many.[68] Some thousands of ex-slaves likely remained to face their fate in revolutionary South Carolina. The majority of the black population in Charleston at the end of 1782, however, left with the army. Most departed either as the enslaved property of loyalists headed to East Florida and the West Indies, or, like David George, as free blacks headed for New York and Nova Scotia. Others were kidnapped and smuggled out by British officers, many of whom made large profits by sending slaves to the West Indies for resale. Still more were con- scripted into further military service, which proved controversial even to loyalists. After Major James Moncrief drafted "about 260 able men" to help fortify the British position in Saint Lucia, the civilian members of the board ostensibly charged with deciding their fate resigned in protest, leaving the authority entirely in the hands of military officers. In all, the state of South Carolina lost around twenty-five thousand enslaved people—likely one- third of the pre-war population—in some form or another during the last months of the occupation of Charleston.[69]

As Leslie and other British officials sought to solve the problem of what to do with the enslaved population of the city, residents looked to their own devices to settle their affairs. In a council of war in April of 1782, Leslie observed to his colleagues that, despite the military ardor of some, the majority of Charlestonians would happily "make their peace with the country" upon an evacuation by the troops.[70] South Carolina's revolution- ary governor, John Rutledge, agreed, remarking that, if offered the choice, "99 in 100" Charleston residents "would come out if they thought they would be received" by the state government.[71] In order to assure these peo- ple of their safety, Rutledge offered amnesty to those who left and signed on to serve in the Continental Army or the South Carolina militia, causing many, especially poorer whites, to leave before the British evacuation began.[72] However, Rutledge's proclamation excepted those who had taken overt actions in support of the Crown. As Lieutenant Governor Bull com- plained to Germain in early 1782, "Mr. Rutledge the Rebel Governor is issuing Proclamations to call in all the Inhabitants to join him, & while he holds forth Pardon in one hand his other contains exceptions out of it."[73] Bull had a point; even with continued assurances, violence against loyalists outside Charleston continued for much of 1782 and into 1783—like Georgia, a rash of score-settling and vigilante justice prevailed before the spirit of reconciliation could take hold. Even after seeing the chaos that ensued in the evacuation of Savannah, however, many Charleston residents—white and black—remained when the British left. Alexander Garden, a veteran of the Continental Army, later recalled that when General Greene entered the city on the evening of December 14, "the persons found in the garrison were chiefly British merchants, who remained with permission to dispose of their goods, or Americans who had submitted" to republican rule.[74]

Civilians were not the only ones attempting to make their own peace settlements at the end of 1782. Loyalist soldiers and German mercenaries both began deserting at higher rates as peace approached. In early 1782, General Leslie complained that "some of the leading people in our militia" had defected, "persuading others to follow them." Low morale and offers of amnesty from Rutledge likely persuaded these soldiers to abandon their war and seek reconciliation with their former neighbors, despite the violence enacted against former loyalists in the countryside.[75] After the withdrawal from Savannah, many more followed, and even more once Leslie published his order to evacuate on August 7. As one observer remarked, "a prodigious number of refugees" departed in the days following, including militiamen "of all ranks and denominations" seeking "to make their peace with the State." In one instance, a Continental lieutenant on a routine patrol was flummoxed when three hundred loyalist deserters approached his post seeking amnesty. For many who had served the British cause in arms, the time had come to settle with the revolutionary government that they had fought for so long.[76]

German soldiers also deserted in large numbers, driven by connections forged within the lines and the prospect of going back to what remained one of the most impoverished and unfree regions in Europe. Leslie lamented the German soldiers' "connexion . . . with the Inhabitants of the town, their having been so long stationed in it, and the alarming instances of desertion from them."[77] Later in 1782, it became necessary to prevent desertion by force. In the fall, forty-six Hessian troops deserted the lines of Charleston in a single month. To counter this growing threat, the British Army deployed a force of ex-slave cavalrymen, called the Black Dragoons, to patrol the lines and intercept deserters. On October 31, the Dragoons killed two Germans attempting to make their escape from the encampment, and their ferocity in hunting escapees, for which they were paid a bounty of two guineas each, largely put a stop to such desertion in the final months of British occupation.[78] The irony of using ex-slaves to catch deserters was apparently lost on the British Army, though those on the revolutionary side saw the Dragoons and their ilk as yet another in a series of British atrocities against the system of race-based slavery—indeed, revolutionary governments in both South Carolina and Georgia continued to fear armed blacks, and the memory of them, throughout the 1780s and 1790s.[79]

After the British Army left Savannah and Charleston, New York became
the most important center for negotiations for individual peace settlements.
Already overwhelmed with refugees, more and people of all stripes came into
the city as the war wound down. Between July and November 1782, some
2,165 civilians, along with 3,340 enslaved people belonging to them, arrived
from the southern cities.[80] Revolutionaries also came into the city, seeking to
reclaim old property, seize that of their enemies, or make profit at the expense
of fleeing loyalists and refugees. Many who had determined to leave began
selling off their property to finance their new lives elsewhere in the British
Empire. New York's newspapers teemed with advertisements for all sorts of
nonportable, valuable items, to be sold cheaply at auction. Some of these
items proved good investments for those planning to remain. Rebecca Shoemaker, William Rawle's mother, bought some of Joseph Galloway's law books
for her son's future practice. Others bought stores, houses, and even enslaved
people from departing refugees, as many scrambled to depart as soon as
possible before the final terms of the peace came in.[81] Still more New Yorkers,
however, remained to await whatever outcome that peace brought.

Against this backdrop, word reached North America in March 1783 that
the British government and representatives of the Continental Congress,
bypassing the four-party Paris negotiations, had reached preliminary articles of peace in November 1782.[82] The preliminary bilateral treaty guaranteed American independence, granted the new United States almost all of
the territory still occupied by the British Army, and, most troubling for
those still living under military rule, contained only weak protections for
loyalists. Shelburne had had to abandon his hopes for loyalist compensation, as the American negotiators had insisted that they had only the power
to negotiate general terms on behalf of Congress; compensation and civil
forfeiture was a matter for the states to decide. While British diplomats had
held firm throughout the summer, an American threat to resume the war
finally brought them to heel, exchanging a strong plank in favor of full
compensation for a weak article allowing loyalists to return and attempt to
regain their fortunes, and Congress's promise to encourage the states to
allow for some compensation for lost property. In exchange, Britain
retained fishing rights in Nova Scotia and Newfoundland, free access up
and down the Mississippi River and a stable border for its Canadian provinces. Most importantly, Britain achieved leverage over France and Spain,
who, without the threat of a renewed land war in North America, made
much more generous bargains with Shelburne later that year.[83]

Although the terms of the peace confirmed the worst fears of those like William Smith Jr., who still hoped for a continuation of British rule, most residents had already begun to prepare either for exile or to remain in the city after its cession to the United States. The influx of people from the revolutionary side of the lines could be a benefit for those hoping to remain. William Walton, a prominent loyalist in the city, sought the protection of his aunt, Cornelia, who had fled in 1776 for rebel territory and had familial connections with the powerful Beekman clan. Writing to Cornelia in April 1783, just after news of the preliminary articles broke, Walton expressed his wishes for a happy reunion with his aunt, who owned the mansion house he had been living in and much of the property he had enjoyed in occupied New York. Although William had ignored her for much of the war, and still owed her rent on the house, Cornelia nevertheless embraced the opportunity for a reconciliation, leveraging her connections to protect her nephew from prosecution for his loyalism and even acquiring property in other parts of the state that had been confiscated from her nephew. In exchange, she demanded that William pay his back rent and act as her agent in New York, collecting debts from tenants in the city who had similarly ignored her pleas during the flush of the war. In this way, William Walton remained in New York, protected by his aunt's family, despite his high-profile support for the Crown.[84]

Although familial affection may have played a role in her decision, Cornelia Walton likely did not protect William purely out of the goodness of her heart. Having an effective agent to collect rent and protect property from speculators could prove invaluable in preserving property and wealth in the last days of British occupation in New York. James De Lancey, who had fled to London and depended on acquaintances, rather than family, in occupied New York to collect his rents, soon found that his tenants refused to pay him, having received better offers from those coming in from revolutionary territory. As one of De Lancey's agents reluctantly informed him in May 1783, "The Lines being now Open . . . your Tenants in Genl tells me Webers & Shourt [a landholding partnership in revolutionary New York that had purchased DeLancey's confiscated property at auction] desired them not to Comply with my demands and many have refused" to pay their rents.[85] Such difficulties proved vexing on both sides—as a young lawyer in the years just after the revolution, Alexander Hamilton made a fortune representing exiles and loyalists suing for back rents, confiscations, and other legal abuses that occurred during the scramble after the announcement of peace.[86] And while the wealthy DeLancey family could afford such setbacks, others found themselves financially ruined by such refusals. So, for Cornelia Walton, having a family member in place to collect these back rents may have proved as valuable as having an aunt with influential connections did for William.

Many used the same strategies to choose sides in the peace that they had used to obscure their loyalties during when the war was in full flush.[87] Although Walton had not been ambiguous about his support for the king, in the waning days of the war he nevertheless used his familial and business connections, in and out of the lines, to secure himself a reasonable settlement after the war. So too was the case with the unfortunate merchant and landlord Evert Bancker Jr., even if his efforts were less successful. Bancker, while a "model loyalist" within the city, had a brother in the Continental Army and continued to communicate with the rest of his vast New York family through his mother, Maria Ogden. He even collected rent for a cousin who lived in revolutionary territory.[88] Likewise, Cadwallader Colden Jr., who still had connections in New York's revolutionary government, took the opportunity in the spring of 1783 to write to Governor George Clinton arguing for leniency toward loyalists. Despite the threats of reprisal from the state government, Colden claimed that those who remained in New York would "be better and more faithful subjects to the States than thousands you now have among you."[89] As they had during the height of military rule, residents of occupied New York proved flexible, using their familial, political, and business connections to their best advantage as circumstances changed.

As in the southern cities, the process of achieving personal settlements proved most difficult for New York's black population, who even before the evacuation had faced danger to their persons in occupied New York. As preparations for evacuation proceeded, Sir Guy Carleton took measures to guarantee the safety of formerly enslaved people who had fought for the king, registering almost three thousand such ex-slaves in what came to be known as the "Book of the Negroes," a register of those who left with the British flotillas for resettlement in Nova Scotia.[90] These included Boston King and his wife, who had lived in New York by that point for two years after escaping slavery in South Carolina. Still, rumors of an impending betrayal abounded in the black community. According to King, "A report prevailed at New-York, that all the slaves, in number 2000, were to be delivered up to their masters, altho' some of them had been three or four years among the English."[91] Perhaps as a result of such reports, New York's newspapers registered the highest number of runaway-slave advertisements for the entire war in the months leading up to the evacuation—fully half of the slave runaways advertised during the occupation years happened in 1782 and 1783.[92]

Although the British Army honored its promises to some newly freed people like King, New York City was rife with bounty hunters, speculators seeking to purchase human property, and former owners searching for their lost enslaved people. Some of these had official sanction. In late April 1783, General George Washington wrote to Daniel Parker, a civil official who supervised many of the embarkations during the spring and summer of 1783, urging him to "prevent if possible, their carrying off any Negroes or other property of the Inhabitants of the United States," and enclosing "a List and description of Negroes which has been sent to me by Govr. Harrison of Virginia" for Parker's edification. In addition to those of his neighbors in Virginia, Washington hoped to recover his own enslaved property, many of whom had fled Mount Vernon either in 1776, when Lord Dunmore had offered freedom to blacks from his refuge on the nearby James River, or in the spring of 1781, when the frigate HMS *Savage* visited Mount Vernon on a cruise up the Potomac River. Suspecting the whereabouts of his missing property, Washington wrote in a letter to Parker, "Some of my own slaves (and those of Mr. Lund Washington who lives at My Ho[use]) may probably be in N[ew] York. . . . If by chance you should come at the knowledge of any of them, I will be obliged by your securing them."[93] Not stopping at this simple request, which Parker duly ignored, Washington also sent private slave catchers into the city. Washington had reason to make all possible attempts to retrieve his human property—later that summer the general's enslaved former groom, Harry Washington, escaped on the British transport *L'Abondance*, barely a step ahead of the agents Washington and other slaveholders had sent into the city to reclaim their human property.[94]

Others were not so fortunate, with their attempts at escape tied up in the convoluted legal system of occupied New York. A man called Tom was reenslaved by his former master with the approbation of a British court because he had been captured by a loyalist militia unit, rather than coming in on his own.[95] Frank Griffin, a freed slave who had been living in New York since 1776, was abducted by his former owner, Jacob Duyree, after a failed attempt to persuade the man to return to bondage. Duyree, who fled in a small boat in the summer of 1783, nearly escaped with Frank but for the intervention of another free black man and a boatful of soldiers who brought the matter before a British military court. During the trial, Duyree argued that Griffin had never been free because he willingly remained behind in New York to look after his master's property, rather than coming into the lines on his own, and thus made himself ineligible for the freedom offered by the British. Further, according to Duyree, Griffin had agreed previously to return with him to Poughkeepsie and continue in his service. Luckily for Frank Griffin, the British judge found that the extralegal way his former master had attempted to remove him proved the falsehood of his claims, and expelled Duyree from New York after forcing him to pay a fine for the benefit of "Poor and sick Negroes" in the city.[96] Although Griffin narrowly escaped a return to bondage, free blacks and ex-slaves alike lived in fear of abduction and reenslavement in the final months of occupation in New York.

Finally, after months of preparation, dispatching refugee ships, and subtle negotiations, on November 25, 1783, the last British soldiers left New York City, marking the end of British military rule in revolutionary America. As General Washington and the victorious Continental Army entered the town soon after, they found among the cheering throngs that welcomed them many of those who moved in prominent loyalist circles and who even served in the occupation regimes. William Seton, a Scottish immigrant who had held a variety of clerical posts in New York's occupation regime and who, during the war, counted the prominent loyalists William Smith Jr. and James Hector St. John de Crèvecœur as his friends, remained after the occupation ended, eventually becoming a cashier at the Bank of New York.[97] Jonathan Simpson, a refugee in New York in 1778 who later took a position in the British commissary department in Charleston, also stayed to see Washington's entrance into the city, living in the town until his death in 1802.[98] Evert Bancker, the loyalist merchant, remained as well, eventually becoming surveyor general of the city.[99] Even James Rivington, the loyalist printer who published and even penned loyalist propaganda throughout the war, was able to remain, continuing to operate his press—albeit without much success—and dying in New York City in 1802.[100] Like wartime residents of other occupied cities, these people made use of all resources available to them, along with a forgiving government, to negotiate the end of the war and were able to forge their own personal peace settlements.

Others returned home after relatively brief exiles. Hannah Lawrence Schieffelin, the young poet who left New York with her British officer husband, eventually returned to the city a decade after the war ended. Her husband became a successful druggist, she continued to write poetry, and neither faced repercussions for their loyalism.[101] Samuel Shoemaker, the former loyalist mayor, returned to his wife and stepson in Philadelphia in 1786, after a three-year exile in England, with little ill effect.[102] Often, return-ees had the patronage of powerful people within the new republic. When Peter Van Schaak, a prominent New Yorker who had sided with the king during the war, returned from exile in 1785, he was embraced on his landing at the wharf by his overjoyed friend John Jay, one of the American peace commissioners who had sealed the final political settlement of the war. Jay, along with Alexander Hamilton and several other prominent revolutionar-ies, strongly supported the reintegration of former loyalists, believing them to be of great benefit to the new republic.[103]

Despite the successes of these returnees, not everyone could negotiate their way to a satisfactory solution. Most of those who had been instrumen-tal in the British occupation regimes never returned to their former homes. Sir James Wright died only two years after the war in London, tirelessly lobbying the government for aid to American exiles. Andrew Elliot, whose daughter had married a British lord in New York in 1779, retired to a small estate in Scotland, living in comfortable obscurity until his death in 1797.[104] Joseph Galloway lived the modest life of an English country gentleman on a small pension from the British government until his death in 1803.[105] William Smith Jr. went on to England before taking an appointment as chief justice of Canada, where he died in 1793.[106] Even George Brinley, whose only involvement in the British administration had been a minor commissary post which he had used to aid his brother Francis in Newport, had to leave for Nova Scotia, writing his brother in a final letter from New York that he "must suppose Nova Scotia abounds with good things," and requesting that his relatives in Rhode Island send provisions and "an assort-ment of seed for a Kitchen Garden" in his future home.[107]

Others did not achieve such genteel retirements. Between 1781 and 1783, seventy-five thousand to one hundred thousand mostly impoverished loyal-ists left North America, spreading across the British Empire.[108] Many relied upon Whitehall for their support, receiving land in Nova Scotia, Ontario, and Sierra Leone and attempting to build new lives after having lost every-thing in America. Their fate has been rightfully deemed a tragedy. Still, the hard-won successes of people like Henry Addison, Tench Coxe, Mary Almy, William Walton, and Hannah Schieffelin demonstrate that these exiles may have been the exception rather than the rule. The exiles represent at most one-fifth of the half a million potential loyalists who could have been barred by the peace treaty from living in the United States; a figure, strikingly, in line with those who accompanied the British Army in its evacuations of Boston, Philadelphia, and Newport earlier in the war.[109]

These late-war negotiations affected not only the peace but also the shape of the postwar world. The survivors of occupation who remained in the new United States did not forget their experiences, nor the relationships they had forged in wartime with people across the Atlantic. All continued to correspond with acquaintances in the empire throughout their lives in the new republic. The story of peacemaking was not just one of separating the United States from the British Empire, but also of continuing personal relationships and networks that connected men and women living in the two nations long after the Treaty of Paris ostensibly divided them. In this way, the legacy of British occupation survived despite the failure of its architects to achieve reconciliation between Britain and its colonies.

Forgetting Occupation

In late 1783 or 1784, David Ramsay—a physician, Continental Congressman, and former state legislator from South Carolina—began research on a history of the American Revolution. Ramsay's two-volume *History of the Revolution of South Carolina*, published in 1785, drew on the records of the Congress, state documents, eyewitness accounts, and Ramsay's own experiences as a surgeon for the South Carolina militia. Four years later, after his first foray into history, Ramsay published a wider-ranging *History of the American Revolution*, based largely on records of both the Continental Congress and the Continental Army, along with other documents Ramsay had access to as a congressman, veteran, and member of the South Carolina elite.[1]

Although wide-ranging and perceptive, Ramsay's histories are nearly silent on the experience of British occupation. This omission bears examination. Ramsay himself surely recalled the ambiguities of life in occupied Charleston from his stint in the militia. He must have witnessed his neighbors, both revolutionary sympathizers and those who sided with the king, signing loyalty oaths, bringing cases before the board of police, and suffering the hardships of occupied life. From his acquaintances in Congress during the 1780s, Ramsay would have heard similar stories about the occupations elsewhere. His father-in-law, Henry Laurens, had been president of the revolutionary Congress when Philadelphia fell into British hands, and Tench Coxe, who had witnessed firsthand that city's occupation, served alongside Ramsay in Congress. Other acquaintances may have included William Rawle, who operated a bustling law practice in 1780s' Philadelphia, and Samuel Shoemaker, Rawle's father-in-law and a former civil official in both occupied Philadelphia and New York. All could have related tales of

the fraught allegiances, harsh material conditions, and shifting circumstances of occupied America. And, given Ramsay's nuanced treatment of
the causes and political processes of the revolution, the subject of military
rule might have received a characteristically rigorous analysis.

Yet Ramsay's discussion of occupation, and the circumstances surrounding it, is rather simplistic. In his earlier history of the revolution in South
Carolina, the physician credited the mass signing of loyalty oaths in occupied
Charleston to "fear and interest," which "had brought many of their new
subjects to the British standard." Further, Ramsay speculated that "their subsequent conduct made it probable that this was done, in many cases, with a
secret reservation of breaking the compulsory tie when a proper opportunity
should present itself."[2] Revising this thesis in his more general history of the
revolution, Ramsay maintained that most Americans had remained true to
the revolutionary cause even in the flush of occupation, writing, "Though the
inhabitants, from motives of fear or convenience, had generally submitted,
the greatest part of them retained an affection for their American brethren."[3]
The varied and complicated motives that most Charleston residents had for
submitting to British authority find no place in either of Ramsay's histories.
Rather, aside from a few treacherous loyalists "who cloaked the most consummate villainy under the specious name of loyalty," most South Carolinians, and others residing in occupied territory, simply awaited an opportunity
to throw off the shackles of British rule.[4]

Throughout his works, Ramsay minimized the complexities of the experience of revolution, preferring instead to recount the crimes conducted by
the British Army and its loyalist allies. During the occupation of Charleston,
Ramsay recounted the tale of "two young ladies, of most amiable characters
and respectable connexions" who were thrown into the provost jail, where
they were "crowded together with the sick, labouring under contagious
diseases, with negroes, deserters, and women of infamous characters."[5] British officials in Charleston "were generally more intent on amassing fortunes
by plunder and rapine, than on promoting a reunion of the dissevered
members of the empire."[6] The same occurred in other occupied zones.
During the occupation of Boston, according to Ramsay, "a licentious plundering took place; much was carried off, and more was wantonly
destroyed."[7] In New York, the historian castigated the refugee militias raised
by William Franklin and William Tryon, remarking that "the depredations
they committed would fill a volume, and would answer little purpose but
to excite compassion and horror."[8] Perhaps most surprising for a South

Carolinian, Ramsay made barely any mention of the slave insurrection in the revolutionary South, writing obliquely of "the mischievous effects of slavery, in facilitating the conquest of the country" by the British but that "as the slaves had no interest at stake, the subjugation of the State was a matter of no consequence to them. Instead of aiding in its defence, they by a variety of means threw the weight of their little influence into the opposite scale."[9] Thus was one of the most significant slave rebellions marginalized into nonexistence in the hands of the revolution's first historian. In all, Ramsay concluded that "the pride of conquerors" led the British Army to abuses of power that, in the long run, "contributed not a little to the utter ruin of their cause."[10]

Ramsay's narrative contributed to a larger reframing of the revolution that occurred after 1783 that was sympathetic to those trying to move past their lives under British military rule. In this context, Ramsay was not alone in largely omitting the occupation experience and its importance to the outcome of the American Revolution. Other early historians—Mercy Otis Warren, Jedidiah Morse, Carlo Botta, Samuel Wilson, and Alexander Garden—also left out the nuances of occupation and the wartime experience. From the 1780s until the revolutionary generation passed on, historians, politicians, clergymen, novelists, and others created narratives of the event that would be useful in building a new nation. They crafted polemic, nationalistic narratives of the war to which Americans seeking to reinvent their wartime experiences could cling. In many of these new works, ambiguities and contradictions inherent in the revolutionary experience were elided, ignored, or replaced with fabricated narratives more in keeping with the political ambitions of the authors. Such reenvisioning proved acceptable to a larger American society willing, in the interests of renewed economic prosperity and the maintenance of a fragile new social order, to overlook the offenses of all but the worst of those who, through actions or words, had sided with the British Army at one time or another during the war. So long as survivors of occupation could forget their past and embrace the new narratives provided by patriot historians, they could claim their place in revolutionary history alongside those who had fought against the Crown from the beginning. In so doing, they participated in both the consolidation of a new nation and the emerging vision of American empire distinct from the British one that so many had supported.

This remarkable turnabout resulted from a much wider change in the public memory of the American Revolution that took place in the years following 1783. Beginning during the war and continuing for decades after its end, Americans developed commemorative rituals, ceremonies, and myths designed to promote unity in the new nation. Politicians and civic leaders harnessed celebration and commemoration to unite diverse classes and races and create a sense of nationalism definite enough to cohere but vague enough that many different groups could claim it. While rhetoric against loyalism and symbolic punishment against loyalists played an important role in these fetes, their architects worked hard to restrain the fury of the crowds and incorporate those former loyalists willing to resign themselves to the revolutionary cause.[11] These celebrations combined with other aspects of the emerging nationalist culture, including material culture, music, art, and countless other manifestations, to change public memories of the revolution.[12] As historian Alfred Young demonstrates in his landmark study of Boston Tea Party participant George Robert Twelves Hewes, individual memories of specific events changed significantly in response to this commemorative culture. In the case of Hewes, many of the complexities and contradictions of his revolutionary experience had been smoothed over by the time he told his life story to biographers in the 1830s, and certain events had changed completely in nature in the intervening years.[13] For Hewes, as for thousands of Americans in the decades after the war, events reshaped themselves to conform to a revised public memory.

A similar process worked in the public and private memories of military occupation, in which public memory shifted to eliminate much of the ambiguity and compromise that living under military rule entailed. The lived experience of occupation—the upending of racial and gender norms, the advantages given to many who cooperated, the privations that forced many more to take desperate measures, and above all the inscrutable allegiances necessitated by the fraught political landscape—did not match the new national founding myth. As a result, the memory of occupation had to be modified to fit a new public imagination that transformed the Revolutionary War from a struggle in which hundreds of thousands of ordinary people gradually turned against the British Empire into an antiseptic War for Independence in which an already alienated population unilaterally rejected royal authority in a purely military struggle. In this retelling, military rule lost much of its nuance, and a new narrative, one of oppression under a brutal and inhuman British Army, emerged—ironically because of the very contradictions caused by the British Army's most humane policies, such as the liberation of enslaved people and providing of aid and comfort to poor and disenfranchised Americans. In this new version of events, the vast majority of those who endured occupation had been revolutionaries to begin with, had not compromised their republican values, and had actively resisted the brutality of British rule. Most of those who signed loyalty oaths never intended to cooperate but did so because they feared for their lives and fortunes. Those who deliberately collaborated with the British Army comprised hated former officials and backcountry ne'er-do-wells, vastly outnumbered by patriotic sufferers. As the opportunities, compromises, and ambiguities that marked the experience of military rule disappeared from public memory, so too did the new possibilities for social betterment that occupation society had briefly opened for many city residents. But, by reshaping their memories to fit into this new public narrative, survivors and their countrymen who spent the war outside the lines could live alongside one another largely without the cycles of blame, recrimination, and violence that have marked the aftermath of many other historical instances of military occupation.

Occupation's treatment in early published histories of the revolution helped to shape this shift in public memory. In the decades after the end of the war, many historians penned major works attempting to make sense of the event. Those who did so in America, or in sympathy with the republican cause, engaged in a deliberate nation-building project in tandem with the efforts of elites in the cultural sphere. They were typically either politicians, jurists, or intellectuals, and all were concerned with promoting American nationalism and establishing a rational, enlightened, and historical basis for the emerging patriotic consensus.[14] Their histories focused on political events preceding the revolution, state-formation and diplomacy, and the military campaigns, rarely touching on British occupation. Where they did describe military rule, however, these historical interpretations reveal how larger American society was coming to terms with the issues raised by military rule, and they begin to sketch a narrative that wiped the history of much of its nuance and may even have contradicted the authors' own personal experiences.[15]

The early histories almost universally emphasized the brutality and oppression of British forces in occupied zones, using accounts of abuses and atrocities to underscore the oppression of military rule. Accounts of plunder far exceeding even the most liberal postwar estimates of losses became common in these historical accounts, wherever the British Army

traveled. Mercy Otis Warren, another historian who endured the occupation of Boston at the beginning of the war—and, through her wide-ranging
social connections, likely had friends and acquaintances who experienced
military rule elsewhere—confidently related in her 1805 history that, after
the conquest of New York, the British Army engaged in "the most wanton
instances of rapine and bloodshed" during foraging expeditions to New
Jersey, and "the licentiousness of their officers spread rape, misery, and
despair, indiscriminately through every village."[16] Ramsay described a similar situation later in the war in New Jersey, writing that, as troops moved
back and forth across the no-man's-land between British and American
zones, "a war of plunder in which the feelings of humanity were often
suspended . . . was carried on in this shameful manner, from the double
excitements of profit and revenge."[17] Neither author described the extent
of plundering in areas they actually lived in but rather relied on generalizations and secondhand accounts of such activities.

Historians who never saw the inside of an occupied town relished the
plunder of the British Army more than those who had. In his *Annals of the
American Revolution*, the reverend Jedidiah Morse lambasted the British
treatment of a young Continental officer captured and executed on occupied Long Island, calling the British commander "as great a savage as ever
disgraced humanity."[18] Historian and veteran of the southern campaign
Alexander Garden claimed that the British Army plundered the people of
Charleston indiscriminately, simply labeling those from whom it stole as
revolutionaries: "the term *Rebel*, gave licence to plunder with impunity."[19]
In his brief 1826 history intended for school children, Samuel Wilson wrote
that during the southern campaign of 1779, "Negroes were seduced or
forced from their masters; furniture and [silver] plate were seized without
decency or authority; and the most infamous violations of every law of
honour and honesty were openly perpetrated."[20] Even the Italian scholar
Carlo Botta, who wrote his history largely based on documentary and anec-
dotal evidence, stressed the inhumanity of the British in their plundering,
writing hyperbolically of these crimes that "it was exclaimed every where,
that the English government had revived in the new world the fury of the
Goths, and the barbarity of the northern Hordes."[21] These descriptions
served a purpose beyond demonizing the British Army. Rather, in the
hands of these early historians, plundering became not just a facet of life
under military rule but its defining factor, and one that established the
British Army as an oppressive force to be resisted by patriotic Americans.

In addition to highlighting abuses committed by the troops, the historians piled vitriol on the British officers who commanded them. Warren, who had lived near occupied Boston, excoriated General Thomas Gage for at first denying passports for revolutionary sympathizers to leave the city, and then for forcing them to give up their goods and "depart naked from the capital, to seek an asylum from the hospitality of their friends in the countryside."[22] Early historians accused General Richard Prescott, the general who commanded Newport's garrison until he was kidnapped by Rhode Island militia in 1777, of rakishness and credited his capture by revolutionary forces to his sleeping at the home of his mistress, several miles away from his troops.[23] In the southern occupations, accusations became more dire. Cornwallis received heavy criticism for his harsh administration of the occupation of Charleston and other posts in South Carolina. Samuel Wilson related that, after his victory at Camden, South Carolina, Cornwallis's rule was "marked by peculiarly harsh and barbarous measures, and they were now prosecuted with greater severity."[24] Reports of executions, exiles, and other crimes also loomed throughout these histories. General Augustine Prevost, who took charge the occupation of Georgia, was represented as a notorious plunderer and abuser of rights in these histories, and Banastre Tarleton, who led a corps of provincial cavalry in the southern campaigns, became infamous for atrocities against civilian populations in South and North Carolina.[25] Sir Henry Clinton, the commander in chief of British forces for much of the war, drew surprisingly little criticism for atrocities but nonetheless was derided as an incompetent leader, whose pompous decrees, especially in the South, turned people against the British and whose naive support of loyalist refugees in New York led to unchecked plundering and banditry.[26] In the emerging new vision of the war, the British officers in charge of military rule were as oppressive as their rampaging troops.

The early historians lauded a few military leaders who escaped criticism as the exceptions that proved the rule of barbarity among the occupiers. Sir Guy Carleton, the general in charge of Canada and the last commander of British forces in New York, received accolades for his generosity in administration. Ramsay conceded that Carleton "conducted towards the American prisoners with a degree of humanity that reflected the greatest honour on his character" in Canada and during the final days of the occupation of New York.[27] Garden took his praise of Carleton further, arguing that "had the politic and generous *Carleton* been the victor, and possessed the power of directing the measures of government" in South Carolina, "the difficulties to

America in establishing her Independence, would have been increased beyond calculation."[28] Colonel Archibald Campbell, the officer who captured Savannah and restored it to the king's peace at the end of 1778, also received praise from the early historians. Botta wrote that, after the conquest of the city, "not only was the town of Savannah preserved from pillage, but such was the excellent discipline observed," and that this protection stemmed directly from "the fruit of the excellent dispositions of colonel Campbell." Garden agreed, writing, "Oppression was foreign to his nature, and incompatible with his practice." Both Botta and Garden also remarked how unusual this humanity was, especially as Campbell had been confined as a prisoner himself in harsh conditions in revolutionary Boston.[29] Still, presenting these officers, and a few others, as exceptions to the norm only served to highlight the barbarity of the rest of the British Army, which was hammered home again and again in the early patriotic histories.

One particular narrative most of these historians took up was the brutality British forces showed toward women, especially those of the upper classes. Warren decried that, while plundering in New Jersey, "the [British] army spared neither age or sex, youth, beauty, or innocence."[30] Ramsay narrated that, during a raid on Fairfield, Connecticut, by former New York governor William Tryon, "a suckling infant was plundered of part of its cloathing, [sic] while the bayonet was presented to the breast of its mother."[31] In writing about another incident on the Connecticut coast, Botta included an anecdote in which a woman was murdered by "a furious soldier . . . a Hessian, as it is said," who "took aim at this unfortunate mother, and pierced her breast with an instantly mortal shot; her blood gushed upon all her tender orphans."[32] He probably picked up the tale from Warren, who credited the act to "a British barbarian" who "instantly shot her threw [sic] her lungs."[33] The story clearly resonated in the new interpretation of the revolution and reverberated well beyond the first generation of revolutionaries; it also inspired a short novella published during the 1840s, in which a Hessian soldier in the outskirts of Philadelphia attempts to murder a virtuous young American woman by shooting through her window, only to be struck by lightning as his musket misfires.[34] In the new narrative that these historians were crafting, violence against upper-class women became further proof of the inhumanity of the British Army.

Racial and ethnic narratives also came into play in the public memory of the revolution. Historians saw the British alliance with escaped slaves as further proof of the atrocities of the British Army. Most historians attempted to ignore the issue entirely. While Ramsay minimized slavery's role in the war, evidence of black participation on the British side presented by other authors often stressed the army's abrogation of the racial hierarchy. In one story published by Garden decades after the occupation of Charleston, a Mrs. Elliot was engaged in a debate with a British officer over the United States' alliance with France when "a *Negro*, trigged out in full *British* uniform, happened to pass." The sharp-witted Elliot turned to the man and remarked, "See, Major . . . one of *your allies*—bow with gratitude for the service received from such honourable associat[ion]."[35] Botta also castigated the British for their alliance with freed slaves, writing that, although the revolutionaries engaged in retaliatory plunder, "the Americans should abhor to imitate their adversaries, or the allies they had subsidized, whether Germans, blacks, or savages."[36] Warren repeatedly criticized the British Army for using Native American auxiliaries, relating that as early as 1776 the "irruptions of the natives in various parts" of the country had proved devastating for civilians. These "irruptions" were variously "stimulated by their native fierceness, wrought up higher by British influence, and headed up by some American desparadoes [*sic*] in the service of Britain."[37] The violation of racial hierarchies, like atrocities committed against women, demonized the British forces in their conduct of military rule.[38]

Early historians' invocation of plundering, abuse against women, and abrogation of racial hierarchies served not only to cast the British troops as oppressors but also to erase the positive opportunities these groups realized under occupation. In making plunder and violence, rather than restructuring of the civil order, the main feature of life under military rule, the historians attempted to eliminate from memory the real opportunities that occupation regimes offered previously disenfranchised citizens. By emphasizing brutality against women, these narratives elided the memories, likely still active in many minds, of the greater social freedoms that women had exercised under military rule. Similarly, focusing on the outrage many whites felt at the British Army's offers of freedom for slaves and use of Native Americans as allies attempted to erase the memory of slave insurrection and disruption of the racial hierarchy. In doing so, they created a new narrative, unencumbered by the potentially positive aspects of the occupation experience.

To further suppress the potential danger to social order implied by the occupation experience, they cast upper-class women not as independent actors but virtuous symbols of resistance. The ladies of Charleston received particular acclamation from revolutionary historians. Garden claimed that "invitations to engage in scenes of gaiety and dissipation [were] indignantly rejected" by the ladies of the town, and that "the dungeons of the Provost, the crowded holds of the prison-ships, were anxiously sought."[39] Ramsay made similar assertions, writing that "the ladies in a great measure retired from the public eye, wept over the distresses of their country, and gave every proof of the warmest attachment to its suffering cause."[40] While Ramsay kept his observations general, Garden elaborated on the bravery of these women, recounting in one instance the "contrivances adopted by the ladies, to carry from the British Garrison supplies to the gallant defenders of their country." The veteran claimed to personally recall "a horseman's helmet concealed by a well arranged head-dress, and epaulettes delivered from the folds of the simple cap of a matron."[41] As with many other aspects of the revisionist narrative, the trope was picked up beyond those with personal experience of the war. Botta asserted of Charleston's women that "far from being offended at the name of rebel ladies, they esteemed it a title of distinction and glory."[42] Forgotten were the romances between British soldiers and civilian women, the accommodations women made, and, above all, the social freedom they exercised under military rule. In their place these historians applied a much safer postrevolutionary narrative of resistance and patriotism.

Having established the heroes and villains of the story, historians of the revolution went on to excuse the vast majority of civilians who had participated in military rule. This apologia came out particularly keenly in representations of Charleston, where the fact that thousands had signed loyalty oaths and submitted to the Crown could not be ignored. Still, the actions of survivors who cooperated and declared their loyalty to the British could be excused by their claiming to have sided with the British out of fear, or having been coerced because of threats to their families. Garden stressed that "the liberty of working for the support of their starving families, was denied to all who refused to solicit protection" of the British Army in Charleston, and that, worse, "suits against them were encouraged" in the occupation regimes' courts, "but against their pleas, the doors of Justice, as well as of Mercy, were closed."[43] Given these dangers, Americans could be forgiven for signing loyalty oaths. As Ramsay concluded in his earliest history of the war, "fear and interest," rather than ideology, had caused these desertions.[44] Stressing the brutality of the British Army and their total victory in South Carolina, these historians could begin to forgive and potentially rehabilitate those who had, by necessity, renounced the revolution.

These new stories allowed many loyalists to elide draconian laws passed in the later years of the war to prevent those who sided with the Crown from reclaiming their property and reintegrating into society. Spurred by desire for vengeance, many states passed laws specifically to punish loyalists. Even while Charleston and New York City remained occupied, South Carolina and New York both passed statutes making vengeance against loyalists state-sanctioned. In New York, a forfeiture law passed by the state assembly in late 1779 stripped fifty-nine prominent New Yorkers of their property for having acted as "enemies of the state" and created a legal process to convict others. In doing so, the legislature took control of and standardized a process previously carried out by ad hoc local committees and militias. In South Carolina, a similar confiscation act named 232 individuals as enemies, stripping them of their property and liberty within the state, although many had already fled North America. While strict, however, both laws, and those passed by several other states, left room for most loyalists to remake their lives. Aside from what was actually listed in statutes, discretion to prosecute was left with those in power—and if remaining or returning loyalists could make good cases for their rehabilitation, they could escape retributive justice in many places.[45] The stories provided by the early historians gave many the ammunition they needed to slip past these punitive laws.

Once desperate civilians had been forgiven for seeking British protection, the historians crafted a conversion narrative by which these people moved from loyalists of necessity to stalwart patriots. Much of this had to do with Clinton's and later Cornwallis's efforts to force Americans to serve in royal militias. According to Warren, these efforts caused many who had sought British protection to return to their arms: "On the first opportunity, many persons exchanged their paroles for certificates of their being good subjects, and immediately returned to the country, or to the neighboring state, and stimulated their friends to resistance."[46] The return of the Continental Army to South Carolina in 1781 also played a role in rehabilitating erstwhile loyalists. As Ramsay described, "When general [Nathanael] Greene returned to South-Carolina, in the spring of 1781, every thing was reversed," as people flocked back to the revolutionary cause.[47] The case of Colonel Isaac Hayne became a symbol of this and is mentioned in virtually all of the postrevolutionary histories that deal in depth with the occupation of Charleston. For Ramsay and others afterward, Hayne, the militia colonel

who signed a loyalty oath and was subsequently captured in arms and executed, became not only a martyr but also a stand-in for thousands of others
who acted—or may have acted—in similar ways.[48]

In the end, narratives such as Hayne's could exonerate those who took
British protection during the occupation but remained behind when British
troops left. In describing the aftermath of the British evacuation of Charleston (which, as a member of the southern division of the Continental Army,
he likely witnessed), Garden recalled that the population mostly comprised
"Americans who had submitted, and who, though rejoiced at heart, might
have considered it as indecorous to have shown external manifestation of
it."[49] Although chagrined, these people's sincere regret, combined with the
necessity of their submission in the face of a brutal and superior enemy,
could lend them forgiveness. And, once established in one place, this concept could be extended beyond Charleston and into other occupied towns:
Botta claimed that, after witnessing the plundering that followed the conquest of New York, "the few remaining friends that England had, became
enemies" to their cause.[50]

The tendency toward a narrative of mitigation and forgiveness of collaborators in postrevolutionary histories even extended to some ideological
loyalists, especially if that loyalism had stemmed from circumstance rather
than malice. This model worked especially well for women, whose politics
were often assumed subordinate to their husbands'. In his reminiscences
decades after the conflict, Garden recounted the tale of a Charleston woman
who, though she had been "led, from the political creed of her friends and
family, to favour the British interests," nonetheless remained "an honour
and ornament to her country." To bolster this woman's character, Garden
recalled that, "if she engaged in scenes of gaity [sic]" during the occupation,
"it was evident . . . that it was more from necessity than choice" and that
"every act of oppression was abhorrent to her nature." This virtuous
woman also joined the petition against the treatment of Colonel Hayne and
reportedly "wept his fate as she would have done that of a martyr."[51] While
women could most easily claim honorable conduct to excuse collaboration,
even those who had fought with the British could be saved through evidence of honorable conduct. Later in his reminiscences, Garden wrote,
"Many of the officers of the Provincial Corps, were pure in character, and
are to be named with respect," especially those that refrained from plundering and attempted to reign in the excesses of the military regime. These
men, according to the veteran soldier, "forgot not *that they were men*" and

thus could be reintegrated into postrevolutionary society.[52] Despite having kept their honor intact, however, Garden refused to name either these respectable loyalist soldiers or his honorable loyalist woman, citing, in the latter case "circumstances of particular delicacy" should her name be revealed.

As the account of Garden's anonymous Charleston woman suggests, the smear of loyalism still cast a pall over survivors of occupation. And, indeed, early historians of the revolution reserved their bitterest rhetoric for those who sided with the British Army for ideological reasons. Ramsay dismissed those who came to serve the British Army in Georgia as "a plundering banditti, more solicitous for booty, than for the honour and interest of their royal master," and denigrated those who aided the British cause in the southern backcountry as men "who cloaked the most consummate villainy under the specious name of loyalty."[53] Alternately, the victorious revolutionaries saw these loyalists as schemers, feeding lies into the ears of British officers in order to punish their erstwhile neighbors. While critical of General William Howe, Warren noted that "he often found himself deceived by the misrepresentations of the loyalists," especially during the Philadelphia campaign.[54] While depictions of loyalist overoptimism sync with more modern analyses of the war, the early historians took great pains to depict loyalists as not just misguided but actively treacherous.[55] In his history of South Carolina, Ramsay described with great emotion "a desperate band of [T]ories [who] adopted the infernal scheme of taking their last revenge" and proceeded to "plunder, burn, and murder" defenseless settlements in the Carolina up-country. Samuel Wilson, in a later history, picked up on these tropes, writing of loyalists "committing great devastations and cruelties on their way" to join the British forces.[56] Given these harsh descriptions, it might be hard to see how former loyalists could find a strain to hold on to within the public memory these histories were quickly creating.

Still, the revolutionary historians attempted to mitigate this stigma and facilitate rehabilitation by declining to name many of the loyalists they described, instead resorting to generalizations about "the king's friends" or "[T]ories" in their narratives. In doing so, they followed a practice of avoiding mentioning the names of patriots as well, for fear of being seen as venturing into politics.[57] While identifying prominent loyalists did not have the same drawback, publishing their names would prevent those people from laying claim to the sympathetic narrative the historians were laying out. As a result, when loyalists were named in these works, they were those safely resettled in England or elsewhere. Ramsay lamented the thousands betraying the revolution and "daily flocking to the royal army" after it took New York, but he only named Joseph Galloway and the Allen family as examples of "the leading men in New-Jersey and Pennsylvania [who] adopted the same expedient."[58] Warren castigated the "desparadoes" [sic] who joined the British but only named a few Bostonians in her history as actual loyalists.[59] Even some of those named were forgiven, or at the very least historians refrained from passing judgment. In describing the occupation of Charleston, Garden named the members of the board of police but directed his sharpest criticism toward Sir Egerton Leigh, who served on the board during the last year of the occupation. Remarking that "the character of Sir E. Leigh, is so well known in Carolina, that it is sufficient to establish the infamy of a Court, to say that he presided at it," Garden went on to relate an anecdote in which two parties competed to bribe Leigh in favor of their case, using the instance to prove the corruption of the loyalist regime. Board members Thomas Phelpe and Joseph Gordon also received rebukes, but Garden noted, "I would not be supposed to implicate Lieutenant Governor Bull, Colonel Innes, Mr. James Simpson, and other members of the iniquitous decrees of these men," making distinctions even among the disgraced exiles.[60] Those farther removed from the occupation experience, such as Carlo Botta, Samuel Wilson, and Jedidiah Morse, named virtually no individual loyalists in their accounts.[61] Because of their anonymity in these histories, any survivors who had not fled into exile, and even some who had, could potentially conform to the conversion narrative presented there and, in so doing, obtain forgiveness and escape repercussions for their complicity in occupation.

Taken as a whole, the early historians' rhetorical depiction of military rule, and the wider reinterpretation of the revolutionary experience of which it was a part, provided an opening for those who had participated in occupation to rehabilitate themselves by rewriting the history of their own lives to conform to the new narrative. A brief return to the postwar experiences of the Philadelphia merchant and early republican politician Tench Coxe demonstrates how one survivor, at least, retroactively molded his occupation experiences to escape potential consequences of his acts. Throughout his political career, Coxe's opponents periodically brought up his former loyalism to discredit his ambitions. In defense against these critiques, Coxe's arguments tracked remarkably well to the narrative set forth by Ramsay and the other historians. In one early instance, brought on by

Coxe's potential appointment to Congress in 1788, the merchant-turned-politician cast his collaborator past as "one youthful indiscretion" and explained his loyalism as circumstantial. Coxe had rather been "*driven* by the violence and threats of a body of armed men, when a boy to the British army"—that is to say, life under occupation had not been his choice—and while living in occupied Philadelphia had "in many instances [been] kind to the friends of the American cause." Finally, Coxe and his supporters appealed to "the necessity of moderation and conciliation" in the postwar era, in a ploy perfectly adapted to the sentiments of many in American society after the end of the war.[62] By adopting this carefully developed narrative in 1788 and again and again throughout his life, Coxe successfully defended himself against accusations of collaboration and rehabilitated himself in early republican society, where he became a congressman and eventually Assistant Secretary of the United States Treasury. Although Coxe's case is particularly well documented due to his eventual high standing, thousands of others followed more obscure routes to acceptance in the new republic.

By first decade of the nineteenth century, then, American society proved ready and even eager to forget the ambiguities, compromises, and messiness of the revolutionary experience, and to accept a much more clear-cut version of its memory. This public forgetting was not only deliberate on the part of historians and nation builders but also vital to the survival of thousands of Americans who lived under military rule and whose experiences shaped the course of the event. But it came at a steep cost, and one that remains with us today. Because of this selective narrative that allowed for the forgiveness of occupation survivors, much of the complexity of the revolutionary experience has been washed from our memory of the event. In its place, popular memory from Ramsay's time to the present largely clings to a static, simplistic narrative populated by virtuous patriots fighting against misguided loyalists and oppressive British soldiers. Only by recounting the experiences of the war on their own terms can we begin to understand the complex experiences, dynamic processes, and lost opportunities of the American Revolution.

NOTES

Introduction

1. For accounts of the political transformations of revolutionary America, see classic works such as Bernard Bailyn, *The Ideological Origins of the American Revolution* (Cambridge, MA: Harvard University Press, 1967); Gordon S. Wood, *The Radicalism of the American Revolution* (New York: Random House, 1992); and Pauline Maier, *From Resistance to Revolution: Colonial Radicals and the Development of American Opposition to Great Britain* (New York: Alfred A. Knopf, 1973). See also more recent works such as Woody Holton, *Forced Founders: Debtors, Slaves, and the Making of the American Revolution in Virginia* (Chapel Hill: University of North Carolina Press, 1999); Brendan McConnville, *The King's Three Faces: The Rise and Fall of Royal America, 1688–1776* (Chapel Hill: University of North Carolina Press, 2006); T. H. Breen, *American Insurgents, American Patriots: The Revolution of the People* (New York: Hill and Wang, 2010); and Patrick Griffin, *America's Revolution* (New York: Oxford University Press, 2013).

2. John Adams to Thomas Jefferson, August 24, 1815, in *The Works of John Adams*, ed. Charles Francis Adams (Boston: Little Brown, 1856), 10:172.

3. "Memorial from the Quakers of Rhode Island, January 2, 177[6]," vol. 20, folder 4, Henry Clinton Papers, William L. Clements Library, University of Michigan, Ann Arbor. The address and Quaker neutrality during the occupation are also described in Benjamin Carp, *Rebels Rising: Cities and the American Revolution* (New York: Oxford University Press, 2007), 131.

4. William Tillinghast, "Physician's Book, 1777–1785," p. 21, Newport Historical Society, Newport, RI; Ambrose Serle, *The American Journal of Ambrose Serle: Secretary to Lord Howe, 1776–1778*, ed. Edward H. Tatum (San Marino, CA: Huntington Library, 1940), 227.

5. Tillinghast, "Physician's Book," pp. 1, 3, 5, 7, 34–36, 62.

6. Tillinghast, "Physician's Book," pp. 4, 58; John Peebles, *John Peebles' American War: 1776–1782*, ed. Ira Gruber (Mechanicsburg, PA: Stackpole Books, 1998), 75; for more on Sally Allan and other affairs between soldiers and civilians in occupied Newport, see Lauren Duval, " 'she was very fond of soldiers': Laboring and Enslaved Women in the Occupied City" (seminar paper, McNeil Center for Early American Studies, University of Pennsylvania, Philadelphia, February 2, 2018), 25–26, cited with permission of the author.

7. Tillinghast, "Physician's Book," pp. 34–36, 112; Wayne Tillinghast, *The Tillinghasts in America: The First Four Generations* (Newport, RI: Rhode Island Genealogical Society, 2006), 408; Fleet Greene, diary entry, October 11, 1777, Newport Historical Society, Newport, RI; "A list of Persons Taken from the Town of Newport (by the influence of the Tories) and put on

board the Lord Sandwich British Prison Ship, in October 1777," Newport Historical Society; Christian M. McBurney, "British Treatment of Prisoners During the Occupation of Newport, 1776–1779: Disease, Starvation, and Death Stalk the Prison Ships," *Newport History* 79, no. 263 (Fall 2010): 1–42, esp. 8.

8. See, for a few recent examples, Alan Taylor, *American Revolutions: A Continental History* (New York: W. W. Norton, 2016); Griffin, *America's Revolution*; and Robert Middlekauf, *The Glorious Cause: The American Revolution, 1763–1789* (New York: Oxford University Press, 2005). For a few notable exceptions that do comingle the war and revolutionary change, see Charles Royster, *A Revolutionary People at War: The Continental Army and American Character, 1775–1783* (Chapel Hill: University of North Carolina Press, 1979); Sylvia R. Frey, *Water from the Rock: Black Resistance in a Revolutionary Age* (Princeton, NJ: Princeton University Press, 1991); Harry Ward, *The War for Independence and the Transformations of American Society* (London: University College London Press, 1999); David Hendrickson, *Peace Pact: The Lost World of the American Founding* (Lawrence: University of Kansas Press, 2003); Benjamin Irvin, *Clothed in the Robes of Sovereignty: The Continental Congress and the People out of Doors* (New York: Oxford University Press, 2011); Eliga Gould, *Among the Powers of the Earth: The American Revolution and the Making of a New World Empire* (Cambridge, MA: Harvard University Press, 2012); and Kathleen DuVal, *Independence Lost: Lives on the Edge of the American Revolution* (New York: Random House, 2016). For a particular focus on the war, see John Shy, *A People Numerous and Armed: Reflections on the Military Struggle for American Independence*, rev. ed. (Ann Arbor: University of Michigan Press, 1990; first published in 1976 by Oxford University Press); Shy's collection of essays considers the war as a revolutionary struggle in its own right. For one of the most recent assessments of this historiography, see T. H. Breen, "What Time Was the American Revolution? Reflections on a Familiar Narrative," in *Experiencing Empire: Power, People, and Revolution in Early America*, ed. Patrick Griffin (Charlottesville: University of Virginia Press, 2017), 233–245.

9. See, for two excellent accounts, David Underdown, *Revel, Riot, and Rebellion: Popular Politics in England, 1603–1660* (New York: Oxford University Press, 1987), and Christopher Hill, *Change and Continuity in Seventeenth-Century England*, rev. ed. (New Haven, CT: Yale University Press, 1991). For a study that traces many of the same phenomena to an even earlier period in English history, see Ethan Shagan, *Popular Politics and the English Reformation* (New York: Cambridge University Press, 2002).

10. Elena Schneider, *The Occupation of Havana: War, Trade, and Slavery in the Atlantic World* (Chapel Hill: University of North Carolina Press, 2018).

11. For perhaps the most best iterations of how individual experience shaped the events of the French Revolution, see Timothy Tackett, *The Coming of the Terror in the French Revolution* (Cambridge, MA: Belknap Press of Harvard University Press, 2015), and Colin Jones, "The Overthrow of Maximilien Robespierre and the 'Indifference' of the People," *American Historical Review* 119, no. 3 (2014): 689–713. See also Peter McPhee, *Living the French Revolution, 1789–1799* (New York: Palgrave-Macmillan, 2006); Susan Desan, *The Family on Trial in Revolutionary France* (Oakland: University of California Press, 2004); James Livesay, *Making Democracy in the French Revolution* (Cambridge, MA: Harvard University Press, 2001); and others. For the importance of events and contingency in the French Revolution from a more theoretical perspective, see William Sewell, *The Logics of History: Social Theory and Social Transformation* (Chicago: University of Chicago Press, 2005), esp. chap. 8, "Historical Events as Transformations of Structures: Inventing Revolution at the Bastille."

12. For the American Civil War, see Gregory Downs, *After Appomattox: Military Occupation and the Ends of War* (Cambridge, MA: Harvard University Press, 2015); for its resonance through the twenty-first century, see David Blight, *Race and Reunion: The Civil War in American Memory* (Cambridge, MA: Belknap Press of Harvard University Press, 2001). For the best scholarship on World War II–era occupations, see Philippe Burrin, *France Under the Germans: Collaboration and Compromise*, trans. Janet Lloyd (New York: New Press, 1996), 4. For more on European occupations under the Nazis, see Mark Mazower, *Inside Hitler's Greece: The Experience of Occupation, 1941–44* (New Haven, CT: Yale University Press, 1993); Karel C. Berkoff, *Harvest of Despair: Life and Death in Ukraine Under Nazi Rule* (Cambridge, MA: Harvard University Press, 2004); Laura Hein, "Revisiting America's Occupation of Japan," *Cold War History* 11, no. 4 (2011), 579–599; and Ronald C. Rosbottom, *When Paris Went Dark: The City of Light Under German Occupation, 1940–1944* (New York: Little, Brown, and Company, 2014).

13. Early works questioning the stability of loyalism and patriotism during the 1760s and 1770s include Alexander Frick, *Loyalism in New York During the American Revolution* (New York: Columbia University Press, 1901); William A. Benton, *Whig Loyalism: An Aspect of Political Ideology in the American Revolutionary Era* (Cranbury, NJ: Associated University Press, 1969); Bernard Bailyn, *The Ordeal of Thomas Hutchinson* (New York: Belknap Press of Harvard University Press, 1974); Leopold Launnitz-Schürer, *Loyal Whigs and Revolutionaries: The Making of the Revolution in New York, 1765–1776* (New York: New York University Press, 1980); and Philip Ramlet, *The New York Loyalists* (Knoxville: University of Tennessee Press, 1986). Perhaps the best recent iterations of this trend are the excellent chapters on the American Revolution as a civil war by Michael A. McDonnell, Travis Glasson, Kimberly Nath, and Aaron Sullivan in Patrick Spero and Michael Zuckerman, eds., *The American Revolution Reborn* (Philadelphia: University of Pennsylvania Press, 2016). Recent monographs addressing the same themes include Judith Van Buskirk, *Generous Enemies: Patriots and Loyalists in Revolutionary New York* (Philadelphia: University of Pennsylvania Press, 2002); Jim Piecuch, *Three Peoples, One King: Loyalists, Indians, and Slaves in the Revolutionary South, 1775–1782* (Columbia: University of South Carolina Press, 2008); Joseph Tiedemann, Eugene Fingerhut, and Robert Venables, eds., *The Other Loyalists: Ordinary People, Royalism and the Revolution in the Middle Colonies, 1763–1787* (Albany: State University of New York Press, 2009); Robert Calhoon, *Political Moderation in America's First Two Centuries* (New York: Cambridge University Press, 2009); Irvin, *Clothed in the Robes of Sovereignty*; Maya Jasanoff, *Liberty's Exiles: American Loyalists in the Revolutionary World* (New York: Alfred A. Knopf, 2011); Ruma Chopra, *Unnatural Rebellion: Loyalists in New York City During the Revolution* (Charlottesville: University of Virginia Press, 2011); Frank Mann, "The British Occupation of Southern New York During the American Revolution and the Failure to Restore Civilian Government" (PhD diss., Syracuse University, 2013); John Roche " 'America May be Conquered with More Ease than Governed:' The Evolution of British Occupation Policy During the American Revolution" (PhD diss., University of North Carolina at Chapel Hill, 2015); and Robert G. Parkinson, *The Common Cause: Creating Race and Nation in the American Revolution* (Chapel Hill: University of North Carolina Press, 2016).

14. For the most recent and best conceptualization of the category of "disaffected," see Aaron Sullivan, *The Disaffected: Britain's Occupation of Philadelphia During the American Revolution* (Philadelphia: University of Pennsylvania Press, 2019). Other works that address neutrality and disaffectedness during the war include Adrian C. Lieby, *The Revolutionary War in*

the Hackensack Valley: The Jersey Dutch and the Neutral Ground, 1775–1783 (New Brunswick, NJ: Rutgers University Press, 1962); Ronald Hoffman, "The 'Disaffected' in the Revolutionary South," in *The American Revolution: Explorations in the History of American Radicalism*, ed. Alfred F. Young (Dekalb: Northern Illinois University Press, 1976), 273–318; Joseph S. Tiedemann, "A Revolution Foiled: Queen's County, New York, 1775–1776," *Journal of American History* 75, no. 2 (1988): 417–444; Sun Bok Kim, "The Limits of Politicization: The Experience of Westchester County, New York" *Journal of American History* 80, no 3 (1993): 868–889; Judith Van Buskirk, "They Didn't Join the Band: Disaffected Women in Revolutionary Philadelphia," *Pennsylvania History* 62, no. 3 (1995): 306–329; Michael McDonnell, *The Politics of War: Race, Class, and Conflict in Revolutionary America* (Chapel Hill: University of North Carolina Press, 2007); and Parkinson, *Common Cause.*

15. See, for example, Alan Taylor, *The Internal Enemy: Slavery and War in Virginia, 1772–1832* (New York: Hill and Wang, 2013); Alan Taylor, *The Divided Ground: Indians, Settlers, and the Northern Borderlands of the American Revolution* (New York: Alfred A. Knopf, 2006); Frey, *Water from the Rock*; Colin Calloway, *The American Revolution in Indian Country: Crisis and Diversity in Native American Communities* (New York: Cambridge University Press, 1995); Colin Calloway, *The Indian World of George Washington: The First President, the First Americans, and the Birth of the Nation* (New York: Oxford University Press, 2018); Gary Nash, *The Forgotten Fifth: African Americans in the Age of Revolution* (Cambridge, MA: Harvard University Press, 2006); Cassandra Pybus, *Epic Journeys of Freedom: Runaway Slaves of the American Revolution and Their Global Quest for Liberty* (Boston: Beacon Press, 2006); DuVal, *Independence Lost*; and Parkinson, *The Common Cause.*

16. For John Shy's original exploration of this area, see Shy, "The Conflict Considered as a Revolutionary War," in *A People Numerous and Armed*, 213–244. For the most prominent recent exploration of violence during the war, see Holger Hoock, *Scars of Independence: America's Violent Birth* (New York: Crown, 2017). For other influential explorations of the role of violence in the American Revolution, see T. Cole Jones, *Captives of Liberty: Prisoners of War and the Politics of Vengeance in the American Revolution* (Philadelphia: University of Pennsylvania Press, 2019); T. Cole Jones, "'The rage of tory-hunting': Loyalist Prisoners, Civil War, and the Violence of American Independence," *Journal of Military History* 81, no. 3 (2017): 719–746; Calloway, *Indian World of George Washington*; Patrick Spero, *Frontier Rebels: The Fight for Independence in the American West, 1765–1776* (New York: W. W. Norton, 2018); Matthew Spooner, "Origins of the Old South: Revolution, Slavery, and Changes in Southern Society, 1776–1800" (PhD diss., Columbia University, 2015); and Peter Silver, *Our Savage Neighbors: How Indian War Transformed Early America* (New York: W. W. Norton, 2007). For good overviews of earlier scholarship on violence and its effects on the war, see the chapters by Allan Kulikoff, Jane Merritt, Gary B. Nash, and Sarah Pearsall in Edward Gray and Jane Kamensky, eds., *The Oxford Handbook of the American Revolution* (New York: Oxford University Press, 2013).

17. In this vein, see Carl Bridenbaugh, *Cities in Revolt: Urban Life in America, 1743–1776* (New York: Oxford University Press, 1955); Elaine Foreman Crane, *A Dependent People: Newport, Rhode Island in the Revolutionary Era* (New York: Fordham University Press, 1985); Gary B. Nash, *The Urban Crucible: Northern Seaports and the Origins of the American Revolution* (Cambridge, MA: Harvard University Press, 1986); Peter Thompson, *Rum Punch and Revolution: Tavern-Going and Public Life in Eighteenth-Century Philadelphia* (Philadelphia: University of Pennsylvania Press, 1998); Carp, *Rebels Rising*; Emma Hart, *Building Charleston: Town*

and Society in the Eighteenth-Century British Atlantic (Charlottesville: University of Virginia Press, 2009); Ellen Hartigan-O'Connor, *The Ties That Buy: Women and Commerce in Revolutionary America* (Philadelphia: University of Pennsylvania Press, 2009); Jessica Roney, *Governed by a Spirit of Opposition: The Origins of American Political Practice in Colonial Philadelphia* (Baltimore: Johns Hopkins University Press, 2014); and Mark Peterson, *The City-State of Boston: The Rise and Fall of an Atlantic Power, 1630–1865* (Princeton, NJ: Princeton University Press, 2019).

18. See Kenneth Coleman, "Restored Colonial Georgia, 1779–1782," *Georgia Historical Quarterly* 20, no. 1 (1956): 1–20; Frederick Bernays Wiener, "The Military Occupation of Philadelphia in 1777–1778," *Proceedings of the American Philosophical Society* 111, no. 5 (1967): 310–313; Frederick Bernays Wiener, *Civilians Under Military Justice: The British Practice Since 1689, Especially in North America* (Chicago: University of Chicago Press, 1967); George McCowen Jr., *The British Occupation of Charleston, 1780–1782* (Columbia: University of South Carolina Press, 1972); John Jackson, *With the British Army in Philadelphia, 1777–1778* (New York: Presidio, 1979); Kim, "Limits of Politicization"; Van Buskirk, *Generous Enemies*; and Chopra, *Unnatural Rebellion*.

19. See Sullivan, *Disaffected*, and Lauren Duval, "Mastering Charleston: Property and Patriarchy in British-Occupied Charleston, 1780–82," *William and Mary Quarterly* 75 no. 4 (2018): 589–622.

20. For deeper explorations of Drinker, see Sullivan, *Disaffected*; David Waldstreicher, *In the Midst of Perpetual Fetes: The Making of American Nationalism, 1776–1820* (Chapel Hill: University of North Carolina Press, 1997). For King, see Edward Larkin, "Loyalism," in Edward G. Gray and Jane Kamensky, eds. *The Oxford Handbook of the American Revolution* (New York: Oxford University Press, 2013): 291–310. Frey, *Water from the Rock*. For Smith, see Chopra, *Unnatural Rebellion*. For Wright, see Greg Brooking, " 'My Zeal for the Real Happiness of Both Great Britain and the Colonies': The Conflicting Imperial Career of Sir James Wright" (PhD diss., Georgia State University, 2013); Kenneth Coleman, *The American Revolution in Georgia, 1763–1789* (Athens: University of Georgia Press, 1958).

21. For the definitive biography of Coxe, see Jacob E. Cooke, *Tench Coxe and the Early Republic* (Chapel Hill: University of North Carolina Press, 1978). For Galloway, see John Ferling, *The Loyalist Mind: Joseph Galloway and the American Revolution* (University Park: Pennsylvania State University Press, 1991); John Coleman, "Joseph Galloway and the British Occupation of Philadelphia," *Pennsylvania History* 30, no. 3 (1976): 272–300.

22. For accounts of Elliot, see Robert Ernst, "Andrew Elliot, Forgotten Loyalist of Occupied New York," *New York History* 57, no. 3 (1976): 284–320; Chopra, *Unnatural Rebellion*. For Simpson, see Donald Johnson, "The Failure of Restored British Rule in Revolutionary Charleston, South Carolina," *Journal of Commonwealth and Imperial History* 41, no. 1 (2013): 22–40; Piecuch, *Three Peoples*.

23. For population estimates for the "big five" colonial cities (Philadelphia, New York, Boston, Charleston, and Newport), see Carp, *Rebels Rising*, 225. Savannah, though of lesser scale and smaller than other "secondary" colonial ports such as New Haven, Baltimore, and Norfolk, had nevertheless by 1776 developed into a prosperous trading center and, after Charleston, was the second-most important port for the shipment of rice, indigo, and timber to the West Indies, in addition to serving as a conduit for commerce with southeastern Native Americans and Spanish colonies in the greater Caribbean basin (Bridenbaugh, *Cities in Revolt*, 217, 262).

24. Bridenbaugh, *Cities in Revolt*, 216.

25. For a detailed description of the war's various campaigns, see Middlekauf, *Glorious Cause*, 340–578.

26. For a quick exploration of the economic development and importance of revolutionary cities, see Mark Peterson, "The War in the Cities," in Gray and Kamensky, *Oxford Handbook of the American Revolution*, 194–211. For deeper analyses of individual port cities, see Hartigan-O'Connor, *Ties That Buy*; Hart, *Building Charleston*; Serena Zabin, *Dangerous Economies: Status and Commerce in Imperial New York* (Philadelphia: University of Pennsylvania Press, 2009); Cathy Matson, *Merchants and Empire: Trading in Colonial New York* (Baltimore: Johns Hopkins University Press, 2003); Carp, *Rebels Rising*; Thomas Doerflinger, *A Vigorous Spirit of Enterprise: Merchants and Economic Development in Revolutionary Philadelphia* (Chapel Hill: University of North Carolina Press, 1986); and Bridenbaugh, *Cities in Revolt*.

27. For the political development of urban areas in late colonial America, see Bridenbaugh, *Cities in Revolt*; Nash, *Urban Crucible*; Carp, *Rebels Rising*; and Roney, *Governed by a Spirit of Opposition*.

28. For a brief overview of the differences between the port cities, see Peterson, "War in the Cities," 195–197. For the demographics and culture of each city, see Carp, *Rebels Rising*; Nash, *Urban Crucible*; Bridenbaugh, *Cities in Revolt*; Hart, *Building Charleston*; Roney, *Governed by a Spirit of Opposition*; and Coleman, *American Revolution in Georgia*. For politics, see Breen, *American Insurgents*; Spero, *Frontier Rebels*.

Chapter 1

1. For the most recent and thorough analysis of these community-level revolutionary organizations, see T. H. Breen, *American Insurgents, American Patriots: The Revolution of the People* (New York: Hill and Wang, 2010), esp. chaps. 6–8.

2. On the strategies of the early committees and councils of safety, see Breen, *American Insurgents*, esp. 160–164, 275–288, and Aaron Sullivan, *The Disaffected: Britain's Occupation of Philadelphia During the American Revolution* (Philadelphia: University of Pennsylvania Press, 2019), esp. 19–49. For the importance of old imperial symbols, see Benjamin Irvin, *Clothed in the Robes of Sovereignty: The Continental Congress and the People out of Doors* (New York: Oxford University Press, 2011), esp. chaps. 1–2.

3. Henry Preston, "Narrative of January 25, 1776," MS 634, Georgia Historical Society, Savannah, GA.

4. For the organization of the Boston Sons of Liberty, see Pauline Maier, *From Resistance to Revolution: Colonial Radicals and the Development of American Opposition to Great Britain* (New York: Alfred A. Knopf, 1973), 78–86. For the destruction of Hutchinson's home and the intimidation of royal officials, see Robert Middlekauf, *The Glorious Cause: The American Revolution, 1763–1789* (New York: Oxford University Press, 2005), 94–97. For accounts of the *Liberty* riots, see Maier, *From Resistance to Revolution*, 124–125, and Benjamin Carp, *Rebels Rising: Cities and the American Revolution* (New York: Oxford University Press, 2007), 45–49.

5. For the aftermath of the *Liberty* Riot, see Carp, *Rebels Rising*, 52–53; for more on this early occupation of Boston, see Richard Archer, *As If in Enemy's Country: The British Occupation of Boston and the Origins of Revolution* (New York: Oxford University Press, 2010), esp. chap. 7–8. For the definitive account of the Boston Massacre, see Eric Hinderaker, *Boston's Massacre* (Cambridge, MA: Belknap Press of Harvard University Press, 2017). For the destruction of the tea and its consequences, see Middlekauf, *Glorious Cause*, 231–238, and Benjamin

Carp, *Defiance of the Patriots: The Boston Tea Party and the Making of America* (New Haven, CT: Yale University Press, 2010).

6. Peter Oliver, *Peter Oliver's Origin and Progress of the American Rebellion: A Tory View*, ed. Douglass Adair and John A. Schutz (Stanford, CA: Stanford University Press, 1961), 115–116. For Gage's actions as commander in chief and governor of Boston before the outbreak of war, see John Shy, *A People Numerous and Armed: Reflections on the Military Struggle for American Independence*, rev. ed. (Ann Arbor: University of Michigan Press, 1990; first published in 1976 by Oxford University Press), 104–110.

7. Richard Frothingham, *History of the Siege of Boston* (Boston: Little, Brown, 1849), 113–115; see also Nathaniel Philbrick, *Bunker Hill: A City, A Siege, A Revolution* (New York: Viking, 2013), 189–191.

8. Philbrick, *Bunker Hill*, 172–174, 183–187.

9. Philbrick, 168–169; Benjamin Carp, *Rebels Rising*, 225.

10. Oliver, *Origin and Progress*, 123–124.

11. Sarah Winslow Deming, Journal of Sarah Winslow Deming, MS, c. July 1775, Massachusetts Historical Society, Boston.

12. Acts 1:19 (Authorized King James Version).

13. For the definitive account of the battle, see Philbrick, *Bunker Hill*, 188–230.

14. Peter Edes, Diary of Peter Edes, August 31, 1775, MS, Massachusetts Historical Society, Boston.

15. Edes, Diary, August 19, 1775.

16. Edes, Diary, August 20, 1775.

17. For an account of the army's disciplinary practices, see Sylvia Frey, *The British Soldier in America: A Social History of Military Life in the Revolutionary Period* (Austin: University of Texas Press, 1981), 71–93.

18. For an account of Washington's command of the siege and the British evacuation of Boston, see Middlekauf, *Glorious Cause*, 307–309, 314–317.

19. For accounts of events in Newport during the 1760s, see Middlekauf, *Glorious Cause*, 104–110; Elaine Forman Crane, *A Dependent People: Newport, Rhode Island in the Revolutionary Era* (New York: Fordham University Press, 1985), 112–116; Edmund Morgan and Helen Morgan, *The Stamp Act Crisis: Prologue to Revolution* (Chapel Hill: University of North Carolina Press, 1995), 151–154. For the tradition of resistance to naval impressment in the city, see Denver Brunsman, *The Evil Necessity: British Naval Impressment in the Eighteenth-Century Atlantic World* (Charlottesville: University of Virginia Press, 2013), 128–129.

20. Crane, *Dependent People*, 116; Middlekauf, *Glorious Cause*, 219–220.

21. Carp, *Rebels Rising*, 120–129.

22. Daniel Beck, *The War Before Independence: Igniting the American Revolution* (Naperville, IL: Sourcebooks, 2015), 230–231; see also Crane, *Dependent People*, 121–123.

23. Nicholas Cooke to Newport Town Council, October 21, 1775, folder 22, Newport Town Records, Rhode Island Historical Society, Providence, RI; see also Crane, *Dependent People*, 122–123.

24. Newport Town Council to Nicholas Cooke, December 1, 1775, folder 23, Newport Town Records.

25. Charles Dudley to Catherine Dudley, n.d., c. November 1775, Charles Dudley Papers, Newport Historical Society, Newport, RI.

26. Catherine Dudley to Charles Dudley, n.d., c. late 1775 or early 1776, Dudley Papers. A vendue was an eighteenth-century auction typically carried out on the waterfront.

27. Catherine Dudley to Charles Dudley, n.d., c. early 1776, Dudley Papers.

28. Various letters between Charles and Catherine Dudley, c. late 1775 to early 1776, Dudley Papers.

29. Charles Dudley to Catherine Dudley, March 1776, Dudley Papers.

30. For estimated troop levels in the initial invasion, see Charles Neimeyer, "The British Occupation of Newport, Rhode Island, 1776–1779," *Army History* 74 (2010): 30–45, specifically 33; for the city's shifting population, see Carp, *Rebels Rising*, 225.

31. Henry Bull, *Memoir of Rhode Island 1636–1783* (Newport, RI: Newport Historical Society, 1906), 3:137. Bull's history, first published serially in the local *Newport Mercury* during the 1850s and 1860s, is based on interviews conducted in the 1820s and 1830s with those who witnessed the events of the revolution in Newport.

32. For Newport's strategic importance, see Middlekauf, *Glorious Cause*, 436–437, and Andrew Jackson O'Shaughnessy, *The Men Who Lost America: British Leadership, the American Revolution, and the Fate of Empire* (New Haven, CT: Yale University Press, 2013), 96, 103. For the size of British warships in the eighteenth century, see Rif Winfield, *British Warships in the Age of Sail, 1714–1792* (St. Paul, MN: Seaforth Publishing, 2007), esp. chaps. 1–3.

33. For Prescott's command, see Neimeyer, "British Occupation of Newport," 33–34. For accounts of the 1778 Battle of Rhode Island, see Christian McBurney, *The Rhode Island Campaign: The First French and American Operation of the Revolutionary War* (Yardley, PA: Westholme, 2011); Charles Lippit, *The Battle of Rhode Island* (Newport, RI: Mercury, 1915); and Middlekauf, *Glorious Cause*, 436–438.

34. Michael Hattem, "'As Serves our Interest Best': Political Economy and the Logic of Popular Resistance in New York City, 1765–1776," *New York History* 98, no. 1 (2017): 40–70, specifically 46; Carp, *Rebels Rising*, 97. For more on the Livingston-DeLancey political rivalry and the politics of colonial New York, see Patricia Bonomi, *A Factious People: Politics and Society in Colonial New York* (New York: Columbia University Press, 1971), and Gary B. Nash, *The Urban Crucible: Northern Seaports and the Origins of the American Revolution* (Cambridge, MA: Harvard University Press, 1986), 300–305, 366–368.

35. Carp, *Rebels Rising*, 82–83.

36. Carp, 83–87.

37. Hattem, "As Serves our Interest Best," 66–67.

38. Ruma Chopra, *Unnatural Rebellion: Loyalists in New York City During the Revolution* (Charlottesville: University of Virginia Press, 2011), 70.

39. Carp, *Rebels Rising*, 97; Barnet Schecter, *The Battle for New York: The City at the Heart of the American Revolution* (New York: Walker, 2002), 61.

40. Schecter, *Battle for New York*, 65.

41. Judith Van Buskirk, *Generous Enemies: Patriots and Loyalists in Revolutionary New York* (Philadelphia: University of Pennsylvania Press, 2002), 13–19; Middlekauf, *Glorious Cause*, 334–335; Robert Middlekauf, *Washington's Revolution: The Making of America's First Leader* (New York: Alfred A. Knopf, 2015), 115–117.

42. Quoted in Schecter, *Battle for New York*, 88.

43. Schecter, 90.

44. Middlekauf, *Glorious Cause*, 347; Carp, *Rebels Rising*, 225; Schecter, *Battle for New York*, 102.

45. Quoted in Schecter, *Battle for New York*, 99.

46. Middlekauf, *Glorious Cause*, 347.

47. Middlekauf, 350–357.

48. For a description and analysis of this fire and the responsible parties, see Benjamin Carp, "The Night the Yankees Burned Broadway: The New York City Fire of 1776," *Early American Studies* 4, no. 2 (2006): 471–511.

49. Chopra, *Unnatural Rebellion*, 100–101, 211–222; Maya Jasanoff, *Liberty's Exiles: American Loyalists in the Revolutionary World* (New York: Alfred A. Knopf, 2011), 87–95.

50. For examples of state-sponsored violence in revolutionary America, see T. Cole Jones, "'The rage of tory-hunting': Loyalist Prisoners, Civil War, and the Violence of American Independence," *Journal of Military History* 81, no. 3 (2017): 719–746; Sullivan, *Disaffected*, 19–49; and Howard Pashman, *Building a Revolutionary State: The Legal Transformation of New York, 1776–1783* (Chicago: University of Chicago Press, 2018), 36–59.

51. Irvin, *Clothed in the Robes of Sovereignty*, 45; Nash, *Urban Crucible*, 378–382; Sullivan, *Disaffected*, 24–31.

52. Irvin, *Clothed in the Robes of Sovereignty*, 45–51.

53. Irvin, 105, 110, 140–141.

54. Irvin, 144–148; for more on revolutionary parades and processions, see David Waldstreicher, *In the Midst of Perpetual Fetes: The Making of American Nationalism, 1776–1820* (Chapel Hill: University of North Carolina Press, 1997), esp. 9–12.

55. Robert F. Oaks, "Philadelphians in Exile: The Problem of Loyalty During the American Revolution," *Pennsylvania Magazine of History and Biography* 96, no. 3 (1972): 298–325, specifically 302–307, and quote from James Lovell at 306; Irvin, *Clothed in the Robes of Sovereignty*, 149–150, 153; Sullivan, *Disaffected*, 76–83.

56. O'Shaughnessy, *Men Who Lost America*, 105–107; Middlekauf, *Glorious Cause*, 373–377.

57. O'Shaughnessy, *Men Who Lost America*, 108–111; Middlekauf, *Glorious Cause*, 391–399.

58. Carp, *Rebels Rising*, 225; O'Shaughnessy, *Men Who Lost America*, 109–111.

59. Sarah Logan Fisher, "'A Diary of Trifling Occurances': Philadelphia, 1776–1778," ed. Nicholas B. Wainwright, *Pennsylvania Magazine of History and Biography* 82, no. 4 (1958): 411–465, specifically 450.

60. Middlekauf, *Glorious Cause*, 396–401; Irvin, *Clothed in the Robes of Sovereignty*, 153–154.

61. O'Shaughnessy, *Men Who Lost America*, 110–111; Irvin, *Clothed in the Robes of Sovereignty*, 154.

62. Middlekauf, *Glorious Cause*, 388–391, 411–414; O'Shaughnessy, *Men Who Lost America*, 110–111, 113–118.

63. O'Shaughnessy, *Men Who Lost America*, 222; Middlekauf, *Glorious Cause*, 438.

64. O'Shaughnessy, *Men Who Lost America*, 193–197, 223–224; Brendan Simms, *Three Victories and a Defeat: The Rise and Fall of the First British Empire* (New York: Basic Books, 2008), 618; Stephen Conway, *The British Isles and the American War for Independence* (New York: Oxford University Press), 23–28.

65. Quoted in Jim Piecuch, *Three Peoples, One King: Loyalists, Indians, and Slaves in the Revolutionary South, 1775–1782* (Columbia: University of South Carolina Press, 2008), 127.

66. For the role of Native Americans during Burgoyne's expedition, see Middlekauf, *Glorious Cause*, 377; see also Alan Taylor, *American Revolutions: A Continental History* (New York: W. W. Norton, 2016), 179–181.

67. Middlekauf, *Glorious Cause*, 441–444; Piecuch, *Three Peoples*, 125–130.

68. Quoted in Piecuch, *Three Peoples*, 20.

69. Kenneth Coleman, *The American Revolution in Georgia, 1763–1789* (Athens: University of Georgia Press, 1958), 52–54.

70. Coleman, *American Revolution in Georgia*, 68–70.

71. Quoted in Piecuch, *Three Peoples*, 59.

72. Piecuch, 100–101; Coleman, *American Revolution in Georgia*, 80, 85–88, 87–88. For examples of loyalist persecution elsewhere, see Jones, "The rage of tory-hunting," and Thomas Ingersoll, *The Loyalist Problem in Revolutionary New England* (New York: Cambridge University Press, 2016), esp. chaps. 6–8.

73. Piecuch, *Three Peoples*, 85; Coleman, *American Revolution in Georgia*, 114.

74. For Georgia's travails with Native American groups during the early revolution, see Piecuch, *Three Peoples*, 108–120. For fear of early slave insurrections and raids against slave property, see Sylvia R. Frey, *Water from the Rock: Black Resistance in a Revolutionary Age* (Princeton, NJ: Princeton University Press, 1991), 64–66, 81–84.

75. Coleman, *American Revolution in Georgia*, 10, 96–97, 105, 107.

76. Piecuch, *Three Peoples*, 133–134, 137–138.

77. Piecuch, 144–145.

78. Carl Bridenbaugh, *Cities in Revolt: Urban Life in America, 1743–1776* (New York: Oxford University Press, 1955), 217; Piecuch, *Three Peoples*, 168–172; Coleman, *American Revolution in Georgia*, 127–129.

79. Piecuch, *Three Peoples*, 15–17; Carp, *Rebels Rising*, 170–171; Robert M. Weir, *Colonial South Carolina: A History* (Columbia: University of South Carolina Press, 1997), 321–323.

80. Piecuch, *Three Peoples*, 17–19; Carl Borick, *A Gallant Defense: The Siege of Charleston, 1780* (Columbia: University of South Carolina Press, 2003), 6–10; Middlekauf, *Glorious Cause*, 447–449.

81. Piecuch, *Three Peoples*, 68–72, 79–80; Weir, *Colonial South Carolina*, 332–333; Middlekauf, *Glorious Cause*, 447–448; Borick, *Gallant Defense*, 36–48.

82. For a detailed account of the siege of Charleston, see Borick, *Gallant Defense*; for the immediate aftermath, see Middlekauf, *Glorious Cause*, 449–456, Piecuch, *Three Peoples*, 178–180, and George McCowen Jr., *The British Occupation of Charleston, 1780–1782* (Columbia: University of South Carolina Press, 1972), 9–12.

83. Middlekauf, *Glorious Cause*, 455–463; Piecuch, *Three Peoples*, 193–198; O'Shaughnessy, *Men Who Lost America*, 256–272.

84. For the best profiles of Germain, Howe, and Clinton and their conduct of the war, see O'Shaughnessy, *Men Who Lost America*, 83–122, 165–246; for a more general study of British military culture during the war, see Frey, *British Soldier in America*.

Chapter 2

1. Ambrose Serle, *The American Journal of Ambrose Serle: Secretary to Lord Howe, 1776–1778*, ed. Edward H. Tatum (San Marino, CA: Huntington Library, 1940), 222–223, 225.

2. Serle, 225, 236, 264, 289.

3. For biographical details of both Howe brothers, as well as other commanders of British forces during the war, see Andrew Jackson O'Shaughnessy, *The Men Who Lost America: British Leadership, the American Revolution, and the Fate of Empire* (New Haven, CT: Yale University Press, 2013), esp. 83–122.

4. Serle, *American Journal*, 153.

5. For details on Clinton's wartime activities see O'Shaughnessy, *Men Who Lost America*, 207–246.

6. Serle, *American Journal*, 225; for Balfour's later activities see George McCowen Jr., *The British Occupation of Charleston, 1780–1782* (Columbia: University of South Carolina Press, 1972), 13.

7. Richard Frothingham, *History of the Siege of Boston, and of the Battles of Lexington, Concord, and Bunker Hill* (Boston: Charles Little and James Brown, 1851), 94–95.

8. William Howe, "A Proclamation," October 28, 1775, Massachusetts Historical Society, Boston, accessed March 18, 2015, http://www.masshist.org/revolution/doc-viewer.php?old = 1&mode = nav&item_id = 570; Frothingham, *History of the Siege of Boston*, 252–253.

9. Howe, "Proclamation."

10. Bernard Bailyn, *The Ordeal of Thomas Hutchinson* (New York: Belknap Press of Harvard University Press, 1974), 183.

11. Robert Ernst, "Andrew Elliot, Forgotten Loyalist of Occupied New York," *New York History* 57 (1976): 284–320, specifically 287–303.

12. General William Howe to Andrew Elliot, July 17, 1777, National Archives (hereafter NA), London, Sir Guy Carleton Papers, no. 620. Unless otherwise noted, all references to sources in the British National Archives used in this book were accessed on microfilm at the David Library of the American Revolution (Washington Crossing, PA), the Library of Congress (Washington, DC), or the South Carolina Department of Archives and History (Columbia, SC).

13. Ruma Chopra, *Unnatural Rebellion: Loyalists in New York City During the Revolution* (Charlottesville: University of Virginia Press, 2011), 148–149. A copy of Elliot's actual appointment can be found in "Orders and Regulations of the Superintendent General of the Police of the City of New York and its Dependencies Authorized by Major Genl. Daniel Jones," May 4, 1778, James Pattison Papers, Royal Artillery Institution, London (accessed on microfilm at the David Library of the American Revolution). Although Elliot was not officially appointed superintendent of police until May 1778, his appointment as superintendent of imports and exports in the summer of 1777 provided the basis for the offices of police in New York and Philadelphia.

14. Howe to Elliot, July 17, 1777, Carleton Papers, no. 620.

15. A list of full-time employees of the office of police can be found in *The British and American Register, with an Almanack for the Year 1782* (New York: Robertsons, Mills, and Hicks, 1781), 138.

16. Henry B. Dawson, "Correspondence with the Comptroller, Concerning the Records of the Department of Finance," in *Proceedings of the Board of Aldermen of the City of New York from April 3d 1862 to June 30th 1862* (New York: Edmund Jones and Co., 1862), 86:208–227, specifically 214–215; a list of vestrymen serving in 1781 can be found in *The British and American Register* (New York: Robertson, Mills, and Hicks, 1781), 138.

17. Andrew Elliot, Memorandum Book, c. 1783, pp. 42–44, box 7, folder 1, Andrew Elliot Papers, New York State Library, Albany.

18. "Rent Memorandum Book for The South, Dock, and West Wards," March 7, 1778, vol. 31, folder 44, Henry Clinton Papers, William L. Clements Library, University of Michigan, Ann Arbor; on the vestry's authority to collect those rents, see Dawson, "Correspondence with the Comptroller," 215. For more on British military culture's gendered dimensions, see

Emily Merrill, "Judging Empire: Masculinity and the Making of the British Imperial Army, 1754–1783" (PhD diss., University of Pennsylvania, 2015), and Sylvia Frey, *The British Soldier in America: A Social History of Military Life in the Revolutionary Period* (Austin: University of Texas Press, 1981), esp. chap. 3. For a study focusing on similar gender relations within the Continental Army, see Holly Mayer, *Belonging to the Army: Camp Followers and Community During the American Revolution* (Columbia, SC: University of South Carolina Press, 1999).

19. "Rent Memorandum Book," March 7, 1778, Clinton Papers.

20. "Rent Memorandum Book," March 9, 1778, Clinton Papers.

21. "An Account of Receipts and Disbursements of Cash belonging to the Publick Funds of the City of New York from the 15th April to 31 July 1783 Inclusive," John Smyth (New York City Public) Accounts, 1778–1783, p. 1, New-York Historical Society, New York, NY. A return of houses rented to the poor through August 25, 1783, can also be found in Smyth's accounts.

22. "Account of Receipts and Disbursements," 16; for an account of regulation of the weight and price of bread, see Dawson, "Correspondence with the Comptroller," 216.

23. "Account of Receipts and Disbursements," 17.

24. "Account of Receipts and Disbursements," 19.

25. "Final hand-over Accounts and Memorandum of Elliot as Superindendent General of Police in New York City, 1782–1783," box 3, folder 6, Elliot Papers.

26. "Quarterly Accounts of Pay Due to the Superindendent General of Police and officers, and disbursements [of] the police department in New York City, 1778–1783," box 3, folder 4, Elliot Papers.

27. "Quarterly Accounts of Pay Due," 18, 19.

28. "Orders and Regulations of the Superintendent General," July 24, 1778, Pattison Papers.

29. "Orders and Regulations of the Superintendent General," November 9, November 12, December 1, and December 7, 1778.

30. "Orders and Regulations of the Superintendent General," December 11, 1778.

31. "Orders and Regulations of the Superintendent General," December 11 and 16, 1778.

32. Orders to Various Officers and Civilians, August 2, August 4, and October 29, 1779, Correspondence of General Pattison as Commandant of New York, 1779–1780, Pattison Papers.

33. Order to the Police, August 2, 1779, Correspondence of General Pattison.

34. Order to Mr. Kerin, September 23, 1779, Correspondence of General Pattison.

35. For Elliot, see Howe to Elliot, July 17, 1777, Carleton Papers, no. 620; for Galloway, see Howe to Joseph Galloway, December 4, 1777, Carleton Papers, no. 782.

36. John Ferling, *The Loyalist Mind: Joseph Galloway and the American Revolution* (University Park, PA: Pennsylvania State University Press, 1991), 11–12, 28–29, 34, 37–40.

37. Howe to Elliot, July 17, 1777, Carleton Papers, no. 620.

38. Howe to Galloway, December 4, 1777, Carleton Papers, no. 782.

39. Andrew Elliot, memorandums titled "Exportation" and "Importation," c. October 1777, Carleton Papers, nos. 724, 725.

40. William Howe to Andrew Elliot, December 10, 1777, Carleton Papers, no. 794.

41. Joseph Galloway to William Howe, December 14, 1777, Carleton Papers, no. 805.

42. Andrew Elliot to William Howe, January 5, 1778, Carleton Papers, no. 842, 843.

43. William Howe to Andrew Elliot, January 22, 1778, Carleton Papers, no. 901.

44. Andrew Elliot to William Howe, February 18, 1778, Carleton Papers, no. 946; Joseph Galloway to William Howe, April 6, 1778, Carleton Papers, no. 1071.

45. Undated, unsigned memorandum, c. 1780, Alexander Leslie Letterbook, no page no., New York Public Library (accessed on microfilm at the South Carolina Department of Archives and History). Although the memorandum is unsigned, it was almost certainly authored by James Simpson, who at the time served as a political adviser to the army and worked in close consultation with Clinton in planning the occupation, and who refers to a plan he submitted to Sir Henry Clinton in a letter of July 16, 1780, Carleton Papers, no. 2915.

46. Undated, unsigned memorandum, c. 1780, Alexander Leslie Letterbook.

47. James Simpson, "Memorial of James Simpson, February 12, 1784," American Loyalist Claims, Series 1, NA (Audit Office Series 12, vol. 48, pp. 142–147), 142.

48. "Papers of the First Council of Safety of the Revolutionary Party in South Carolina, June–November 1775," *South Carolina Historical and Genealogical Magazine* 3, no. 3 (1920): 123–138, specifically 127.

49. For Simpson's scouting of South Carolina in 1779, see "James Simpson's Reports on the Carolina Loyalists, 1779–1780,"ed. Alan Brown, *Journal of Southern History* 21, no. 4 (1955): 513–519; the report itself is found in a letter from James Simpson to Sir Henry Clinton, August 20, 1779, MS 43/501, South Carolina Historical Society, Charleston. For Simpson's appointment as secretary to Clinton and his influence in occupied New York, see William Smith Jr., *Historical Memoirs from 26 August 1778 to 12 November 1783*, ed. William H. W. Sabine (New York: Arno Press, 1971), 155, 243–245.

50. Undated, unsigned memorandum, c. 1780, Alexander Leslie Letterbook.

51. Undated, unsigned memorandum, c. 1780, Alexander Leslie Letterbook.

52. McCowen, *British Occupation of Charleston*, 17–18.

53. Nisbet Balfour to Sir Henry Clinton, January 25, 1781, Alexander Leslie Letterbook.

54. For evidence of Wanton's position, see "Account of Pay due to Joseph Wanton Jun Esq. as Superintendent of Police at Rhode Island," October 25, 1779, box 156, Newport Historical Society, Newport, RI. The only other evidence relating to Newport's office of police are two receipts of payments from Wanton to Edward Thurston and John Howe, both dated December 21, 1779 (box 156, Newport Historical Society). The records of British-occupied Newport (along with municipal records from the colonial period) were carried off when the British evacuated the island, and sank when the British storeship carrying them went down in a storm during the voyage to New York. Although the records were eventually recovered and remain on deposit at the Newport Historical Society, water damage has rendered them almost entirely illegible.

55. See "Minute Book, Savannah Board of Police, 1779," ed. Lilla Halls, *Georgia Historical Quarterly* 45, no. 3 (1961): 245–257.

56. Patrick J. Furlong, "Civil-Military Conflict and the Restoration of the Royal Province of Georgia," *Journal of Southern History* 38, no. 3 (1972): 415–442, specifically 425.

57. Carlisle, Clinton, and Eden to Archibald Campbell, November 5, 1778, New York Public Library (accessed in facsimile at the Georgia Historical Society, Savannah).

58. Kenneth Coleman, "Restored Colonial Georgia, 1779–1782," *Georgia Historical Quarterly* 40, no. 1 (1956): 1–20, specifically 6.

59. Furlong, "Civil-Military Conflict," 422.

60. Furlong, "Civil-Military Conflict," 426.

61. Sir Archibald Campbell, *Journal of an Expedition against the Rebels of Georgia in North America*, ed. Colin Campbell (Darien, GA: Ashantilly Press, 1981), 43–44.

62. Wright to Germain, November 5, 1779, in *Collections of the Georgia Historical Society* (Savannah, GA: Morning News Office, 1873), 3:260; italics in the original.

63. "Journal of the Siege of Savannah," Georgia Provincial Congress Proceedings, 1775–79, MS 287, Georgia Historical Society, Savannah; copied from the *South Carolina and American General Gazette* of December 10, 1779. A similar account, verbatim in places but with a few variations and credited to a Captain Shaw, is enclosed in Wright to Germain, November 5, 1779 in *Collections of the Georgia Historical Society*, 3:262–268.

64. "Journal of the Siege of Savannah"; this same detail appears in Shaw's account.

65. "Journal of the Siege of Savannah"; the account published in the *South Carolina and American General Gazette* places both Wright and Lieutenant Governor John Graham alongside Colonel John Maitland at this battle; the account enclosed in Wright's missive to Germain omits this detail.

66. Wright to Germain, January 20, 1780, in *Collections of the Georgia Historical Society*, 3:272–273.

67. Furlong, "Civil-Military Conflict," 426–428.

68. Both Kenneth Coleman and Patrick Furlong have argued along these lines; see Coleman, "Restored Colonial Georgia," and Furlong, "Civil-Military Conflict."

69. "General Orders from 27th Septr 1777 to 21st February 1778 of the Army under the Command of General Sir William Howe," pp. 10–11, Pattison Papers.

70. For assizes before the revolution, see Carl Bridenbaugh, *Cities in Revolt: Urban Life in America, 1743–1776* (New York: Oxford University Press, 1955), 83–84.

71. On liquor, see *Newport Gazette*, March 6, 1777, 3. Fishing regulations are described in Henry Bull, *Memoir of Rhode Island 1636–1783* (Newport, RI: Newport Historical Society, 1906), 3:134–135. A hunting permit issued by General Robert Pigot in 1778 can be found in box 44 (Revolutionary Papers), folder 5, Newport Historical Society.

72. Miscellaneous Proceedings of the Board of Police, NA, Colonial Office (CO) Series 5, vol. 513, p. 19.

73. The fullest examination of British policy toward African Americans is Sylvia R. Frey, *Water from the Rock: Black Resistance in a Revolutionary Age* (Princeton, NJ: Princeton University Press, 1991). See also Gary Nash, *The Forgotten Fifth: African Americans in the Age of Revolution* (Cambridge, MA: Harvard University Press, 2006), and Cassandra Pybus, *Epic Journeys of Freedom: Runaway Slaves of the American Revolution and their Global Quest for Liberty* (Boston: Beacon Press, 2006).

74. "Orders relative to Refugee Negroes," June 7, 1779, Pattison Papers.

75. George Brinley to Francis Brinley, October 21, 1781, Malbone/Brinley Papers, Newport Historical Society.

76. Proceedings of the Board of Police, 1780–1781, NA, CO 5, vol. 520, pp. 2–3 (quote on p. 2).

77. Proceedings of the Board of Police, 1780–1781, p. 3.

78. James Wright to Lord George Germain, April 6, 1780, in *Collections of the Georgia Historical Society*, 3:284 (mitigating losses); Wright et al. to Germain, n.d., c. April 1779, Carleton Papers, no. 1962 (encouraging exiles to return).

79. Frey, *Water from the Rock*, 92, 100–101, 122–125; see also McCowen, *British Occupation of Charleston*, 101–103.

80. Proceedings of the Board of Police, 1780–1781, p. 8.

81. Proceedings of the Board of Police, 1780–1781, p. 2.

82. Proceedings of the Board of Police, 1780, NA, CO 5, vol. 519, p. 26.

83. Proceedings of the Board of Police, 1780, p. 35.

84. Proceedings of the Board of Police, 1780, pp. 7–8.

85. "Account of Receipts and Disbursements," 17–19.

86. Proceedings of the Board of Police, 1780, pp. 1 (poor relief); 6 (bridges and ferries); 4, 13 (street cleaning); 18 (burial grounds).

87. "Proceedings of the Board of Police, 1780–1781," p. 14.

88. Sir James Wright to "the Gentlemen of the Council," November 14, 1781, Sir James Wright Papers, Georgia Historical Society.

89. The destruction of "about 480 buildings," drawn from a now-lost account of the occupation, is recorded in Bull, *Memoir of Rhode Island*, 3:138. A British officer who had participated in the occupation testified in 1782 that at one point or another the British commander had "give[n] orders for the Cutting Down of almost every Tree on the Island for fuel" and that "many Houses were pulled down for the Reperation of others," particularly those belonging to absentees from the town. Henry Savage to George Rome, August 27, 1782, box 36, folder 4, George Rome Papers, Newport Historical Society.

90. "General Orders from 27th Septr 1777 to 21st February 1778," p. 155, Pattison Papers.

91. "Petition of Christopher Benson, 30 September 1778," vol. 42, folder 15, Clinton Papers.

92. Wright to Germain, May 20, 1780, in *Collections of the Georgia Historical Society*, 3:289. See also Furlong, "Civil Military Conflict."

93. "General Orders from 27th Septr 1777 to 21st February 1778," p. 155.

94. Correspondence of General Pattison, pp. 28–29, 127, 194.

95. Proceedings of the Board of Police, 1781, NA, CO 5, vol. 521, p. 39.

96. Correspondence of General Pattison, p. 98.

97. For perhaps the best study of city politics prior to the revolution, see Gary B. Nash, *The Urban Crucible: Northern Seaports and the Origins of the American Revolution* (Cambridge, MA: Harvard University Press, 1986).

98. Nash, *Urban Crucible*, 31–34, 282–291, 365–370; Emma Hart, "City Government and the State in Eighteenth-Century South Carolina," *Eighteenth Century Studies* 50, no. 2 (2017): 195–211, specifically 196–197; Jessica Roney, *Governed by a Spirit of Opposition: The Origins of American Political Practice in Colonial Philadelphia* (Baltimore: Johns Hopkins University Press, 2014), 98–103; Benjamin Carp, *Rebels Rising: Cities and the American Revolution* (New York: Oxford University Press, 2007), 77–83.

99. Chopra, *Unnatural Rebellion*, 110–111, 167–70.

100. Original Correspondence of the Secretary of State, South Carolina, NA, CO 5, vol. 176, folios 55, 84.

101. Furlong, "Civilian-Military Conflict," 426.

102. Chopra, *Unnatural Rebellion*, 225–226.

103. Correspondence with Civil Officers in America, NA, CO 5, vol. 176, folio 83.

104. Original Correspondence of the Secretary of State, New York, 1776–1778, NA, CO 5, vol. 1108, folio 63.

105. For this population estimate, see Carp, *Rebels Rising*, 225. The figure of five thousand represents the low point during the war; by 1783, returning residents and refugees had at least doubled the city's population.

106. Original Correspondence of the Secretary of State, New York, 1776–1778, folios 56–57.

107. Loyalty Oaths, Cornwallis Papers, NA, vol. 30/11/107, folios 3–32. For the wartime population estimate, see Carp, *Rebels Rising*, 225; for the prewar demographics, see Bridenbaugh, *Cities in Revolt*, 333.

Chapter 3

1. Daniel Stevens to John Wendell, February 20, 1782, in "Boyd-Stevens Letters," *Proceedings of the Massachusetts Historical Society* 48 (1915): 335–343, specifically 342; the event is also described in George McCowen Jr., *The British Occupation of Charleston, 1780–1782* (Columbia: University of South Carolina Press, 1972), 104, and Lauren Duval, "Mastering Charleston: Property and Patriarchy in British-Occupied Charleston, 1780–82," *William and Mary Quarterly* 75, no. 4 (2018): 589–622, specifically 616–619.

2. Stevens to Wendell, February 20, 1782, 343.

3. Stevens to Wendell, 342.

4. For more on the political and cultural implications of these events and additional examples, see Daniel O'Quinn, *Entertaining Crisis in the Atlantic Imperium, 1770–1790* (Baltimore: Johns Hopkins University Press, 2011), 1–38.

5. While the British Army facilitated the escape of several thousand of these people at the end of the war, many more who liberated themselves remained in North America or the Caribbean, and most were reenslaved in one form or another, as the institution of slavery became even more entrenched than ever in the early republican United States. For details, see Gary Nash, *The Forgotten Fifth: African Americans in the Age of Revolution* (Cambridge, MA: Harvard University Press, 2006), 39–50, and Silvia Frey, *Water from the Rock: Black Resistance in a Revolutionary Age* (Princeton, NJ: Princeton University Press, 1991), 173–179, 206–218.

6. Nash, *Forgotten Fifth*, 5–6.

7. Frey, *Water from the Rock*, 81–87, 118–120.

8. Boston King, "Memoirs of the Life of Boston King," in *Unchained Voices: An Anthology of Black Authors in the English-Speaking World of the Eighteenth Century*, ed. Vincent Carretta (Lexington: University Press of Kentucky, 1996), 351–368, specifically 352.

9. King, "Memoirs," 354–355.

10. King, "Memoirs," 355.

11. King, "Memoirs," 355–356.

12. The numbers here are uncertain, but contemporary and local estimates indicate that many more escaped slaves resided in occupied territories than were employed by the army on campaign. The number of free blacks serving in and traveling with General Charles Cornwallis's army in Virginia during the Yorktown Campaign, which had the largest ex-slave contingent of any British field army during the war, has been estimated at between 4,000 and 5,000 people at the time of Cornwallis's surrender in October 1781. At the time of British withdraw from the cities in 1782, the combined black populations of New York (at least 2,000), Charleston (10,000 to 12,000), and Savannah (5,000 to 6,000) numbered at least 17,000, and possibly as many as 22,000 people. Although these estimates include the enslaved people belonging to loyalists, who probably make up a majority of the number in Savannah and Charleston, if even a third were escapees the urban population still outnumbered the blacks traveling with the army. Estimates for Charleston, Savannah, and Cornwallis's army are from Frey, *Water from the Rock*, 106 (Savannah), 169 (Cornwallis), 177 (Charleston); the figure for New York is

from Andrew Elliot, Memorandum Book, c. 1783, p. 104, box 7, folder 1, Andrew Elliot Papers, New York State Library, Albany.

13. Nash, *Forgotten Fifth*, 1.

14. Frey, *Water from the Rock*, 163; see also Cassandra Pybus, *Epic Journeys of Freedom: Runaway Slaves of the American Revolution and Their Quest for Global Liberty* (Boston: Beacon, 2006), 69–70.

15. Correspondence of General Pattison as Commandant of New York, 1779–1780, p. 164. James Pattison Papers, Royal Artillery Institution, London (accessed on microfilm at the David Library of the Revolution).

16. Pybus, *Epic Journeys*, 30–35; see also Judith Van Buskirk, *Generous Enemies: Patriots and Loyalists in Revolutionary New York* (Philadelphia: University of Pennsylvania Press, 2002), 143–144.

17. Van Buskirk, *Generous Enemies*, 117–120.

18. The 2,775 figure comes from the "Book of Negroes" recorded on embarkation, in which ex-slaves recorded their names, origins, and occupations. It is probable that many more freed people also left with the British without having their names recorded. For more on this document, see the introduction to Graham Hodges, ed., *The Black Loyalist Directory: African Americans in Exile After the American Revolution* (New York: Garland, 1996). See also Nash, *Forgotten Fifth*, 47–48. For more on the fates of these people, see Pybus, *Epic Journeys*.

19. Proceedings of the Board of Police, 1780–1781, National Archives, London (hereafter NA), Colonial Office (CO) Series 5, vol. 520, p. 3.

20. Nash, *Forgotten Fifth*, 41–42.

21. "Memoranda for the Commandant of Charles Town," June 3, 1780, NA, Sir Guy Carleton Papers, no. 2800.

22. Van Buskirk, *Generous Enemies*, 147–149; see also Lauren Duval, "'she was very fond of soldiers': Laboring and Enslaved Women in the Occupied City," (seminar paper, McNeil Center for Early American Studies, University of Pennsylvania, Philadelphia, February 2, 2018), 13–19, cited with permission of the author.

23. "Certificate of a Negro Woman," March 8, 1778, MS no. Amer 1778 Wr28, John Carter Brown Library, Brown University.

24. Although no evidence of this exists for Jinnie, both sides relied on deserters and escaped slaves for intelligence on areas controlled by the other. See, for example, incidents during the invasion of Georgia cited in Frey, *Water from the Rock*, 84.

25. *Royal Georgia Gazette*, January 4, 1781, 4.

26. *Royal Georgia Gazette*, August 2, 1781, 4.

27. Proceedings of the Board of Police, 1780, NA, CO 5, vol. 519, p. 26.

28. Tench Coxe, Letterbook of Coxe, Furman, and Coxe, 1776–1779, p. 143, vol. 132, Coxe Family Papers, Historical Society of Pennsylvania, Philadelphia.

29. For more on the British Army's inconsistent practices regarding ex-slaves, see Frey, *Water from the Rock*, 123–127; see also Nash, *Forgotten Fifth*, 30–33.

30. King, "Memoirs," 353.

31. Nash, *Forgotten Fifth*, 37–38.

32. King, "Memoirs," 353.

33. Ezra Stiles, *The Literary Diary of Ezra Stiles, D.D., LL.D.*, ed. Franklin B. Dexter, vol. 2, *March 14, 1776–December 31, 1781* (New York: Charles Scribner's Sons, 1901), 105.

34. See, for example, some of the women discussed in Judith Van Buskirk, "They Didn't Join the Band: Disaffected Women in Revolutionary Philadelphia," *Pennsylvania History* 62, no. 3 (1995): 306–329.

35. Mary Gould Almy, "Journal of the Siege of Rhode Island," reproduced in *Weathering the Storm: Women of the American Revolution*, by Elizabeth Evans (New York: Charles Scribner's Sons, 1975), 245–270, specifically 260.

36. Mary Almy, Letters of Mary Gould Almy, box 1, folder 11, Newport Historical Society, Newport, RI. See also Almy, "Journal of the Siege of Rhode Island."

37. American Revolution Entry Books, 1773–1783, NA, War Office (WO) Series 36, vol. 2, December 17, 1776.

38. Fleet Greene, diary, July 15, 1777, Newport Historical Society.

39. "A List of Persons taken from the Town of Newport and put on Board the Lord Sandwich Prison Ship," c. October 1777, box 123, folder 21, Newport Historical Society.

40. Greene, diary, Newport Historical Society. These entries occur too frequently to cite them all. Over a monthlong period in the fall of 1777, for example, Greene recorded five instances of these vessels arriving or departing: on August 28, September 1, 7, and 28, and October 5.

41. American Revolution Entry Books, NA, WO 36, vol. 2, December 17, 1776.

42. American Rebellion Entry Books, NA, WO 36, vol. 2, October 22, 1777.

43. John Peebles, *John Peebles' American War: 1776–1782*, ed. Ira Gruber (Mechanicsburg, PA: Stackpole Books, 1998), 73, 81.

44. Peebles, *Peebles' American War*, 75.

45. Colonel Archibald Campbell to unknown recipient, January 9, 1779, Georgia Historical Society, Savannah.

46. *Newport Gazette*, April 17, 1777, 4.

47. For more on this phenomenon see O'Quinn, *Entertaining Crisis*, 166–169.

48. Hannah Lawrence Schieffelin, "Journal of Jacob and Hannah Schieffelin," box 1, Schieffelin Family Papers, New York Public Library.

49. Hannah Lawrence Schieffelin, "Notebook of Poems, 1774–1794," box 7, Schieffelin Family Papers.

50. Benjamin Irvin, *Clothed in the Robes of Sovereignty: The Continental Congress and the People out of Doors* (New York: Oxford University Press, 2011), 163–165.

51. E. Tauncey to Elizabeth Giles, March 7, 1782, Giles Family Papers, New-York Historical Society.

52. Hannah Lawrence Schieffelin, "Journal of a Lady's Courtship," box 1, Schieffelin Family Papers.

53. James N. Arnold, ed. *Vital Records of Rhode Island, 1636–1850*, 1st series (Providence, RI: Narragansett Historical Publishing, 1891–1912), 10:433–476.

54. Duval, "Laboring and Enslaved Women," 26.

55. William Rawle to Anna Rawle, n.d., c. 1778–1780, William Rawle Letterbook, p. 21, William L. Clements Library, University of Michigan, Ann Arbor.

56. William Rawle to Polly Rawle, February 26, 1781, William Rawle Letterbook, p. 21.

57. William Rawle to Anna Rawle, n.d., c. winter 1779–1780, William Rawle Letterbook, pp. 21–22.

58. A. Phillips to Elizabeth Shipton Giles, October 19, 1780, folder 15, Giles Family Papers, New-York Historical Society. For the courtship and marriage, see letters between the couple

in folders 1, 2, and 9, Giles Family Papers, New-York Historical Society. See also the Giles Family Papers, William L. Clements Library, esp. folders 1, 2, additional folder 1, and additional folder 2.

59. E. Tauncey to Elizabeth Giles, March 7, 1782, folder 15, Giles Family Papers, New-York Historical Society.

60. American Revolution Entry Books, NA, WO 36, vol. 1, January 3, 1776.

61. Stiles, *Literary Diary*, 2:97.

62. Trial of John Dillon and Robert Brown, January 7, 1778, NA, WO 71, vol. 85, pp. 203–212; quote at 203. Although from testimony it is clear that sexual assault occurred, the soldiers were convicted only of robbery and assault, likely because the rape was not "completed" as required for conviction in eighteenth-century British law.

63. Trial of Bartholomew McDonough, July 28–29, 1778, NA, WO 71, vol. 86, pp. 200–206; quote on 200.

64. Peebles, *Peebles' American War*, 74.

65. American Revolution Entry Books, NA, WO 36, vol. 2, December 24, 1776.

66. Trial of John Dunn and John Lusty, September 3, 1776, NA, WO 71, vol. 82, pp. 412–425.

67. For analysis of civilian rape trials, see Sharon Block, *Rape and Sexual Power in Early America* (Chapel Hill: University of North Carolina Press, 2006), 126–162.

68. Elizabeth Drinker, *Diary of Elizabeth Drinker*, ed. Elaine Crane (Boston: Northeastern University Press, 1994), 64, 66.

69. Drinker, *Diary*, 68.

70. Drinker, *Diary*, 68–70; quote at 69.

71. Memorial of Margaret Brush, January 20, 1779, Carleton Papers, no. 1696.

72. Recommendation of Mrs. Beasley, August 6, 1779, Carleton Papers, no. 2171.

73. Ruma Chopra, *Unnatural Rebellion: Loyalists in New York City During the Revolution* (Charlottesville: University of Virginia Press, 2011), 181–185.

74. H. Bancker to Everett Banker, May 9, 1783, Bancker Family Papers, New York Public Library.

75. Robert Ernst, "Andrew Elliot, Forgotten Loyalist of Occupied New York," *New York History* 57, no. 3 (1976): 284–320, specifically 310, 315.

76. Ernst, "Andrew Elliot," 319.

77. John Ferling, *The Loyalist Mind: Joseph Galloway and the American Revolution* (University Park: Pennsylvania State University Press, 1991), 63–34.

78. McCowen, *British Occupation of Charleston*, 16–17.

79. Jared Brown, *The Theatre in America During the Revolution* (New York: Cambridge University Press, 1995), 86.

80. Brown, *Theatre in America*, 88.

81. *Royal Gazette*, January 9, 1779; quoted in Brown, *Theatre in America*, 97.

82. Brown, *Theatre in America*, 90.

83. Brown, 98, 102–103.

84. Brown, 94, 107.

85. John Jackson, *With the British Army in Philadelphia: 1777–1778* (New York: Presidio, 1979), 200–206.

86. *Royal Georgia Gazette*, September 20, 1781, 2.

87. McCowen, *British Occupation of Charleston*, 116–117.

88. For a deeper analysis of this phenomenon, see the introduction to O'Quinn, *Entertaining Crisis*.

89. O'Quinn, *Entertaining Crisis*, 164–165.

90. O'Quinn, 179–183.

91. Brown, *Theatre in America*, 90.

92. O'Quinn, *Entertaining Crisis*, 182.

93. Peebles, *Peebles' American War*, 75.

94. *Newport Gazette*, January 30, 1777, 3; Newport Marine Society Minutes, 1775–1778, box 4, folder 3, Marine Society Papers, Newport Historical Society. "Prescut" refers to General Richard Prescott, one of the senior officers in Newport's garrison.

95. McCowen, *British Occupation of Charleston*, 123–124.

96. Examples of these entertainments permeate Serle's diary. See Ambrose Serle, *The American Journal of Ambrose Serle: Secretary to Lord Howe, 1776–1778*, ed. Edward H. Tatum (San Marino, CA: Huntington Library, 1940).

97. Peebles, *Peebles' American War*, 81.

98. Examples abound in the pages of the *Royal Gazette* (New York), the *Newport Gazette*, the *Royal Georgia Gazette*, the *Royal South Carolina Gazette*, and the *Pennsylvania Ledger*, among other newspapers.

99. Peebles, *Peebles' American War*, 75.

100. *Newport Gazette*, May 1, 1777, 5.

101. Edward B Welsh, "Joseph Wanton, Junior: An Eighteenth Century Newport Tragedy," *Newport History* 61, no. 1 (1988): 18–35, specifically 32.

102. Baroness Fredericke Riedesel, *Letters and Journals Relating to the War of the American Revolution*, trans. William L. Stone (New York: Arno Press, 1968), 172–173.

103. Van Buskirk, *Generous Enemies*, 155–156.

104. Irvin, *Clothed in the Robes of Sovereignty*, 154–156.

105. Peebles, *Peebles' American War*, 183; Irvin, *Clothed in the Robes of Sovereignty*, 154.

106. André's account appears in an article titled "Particulars of the Mischianza [*sic*] in America," *Gentleman's Magazine and Historical Chronicle* 48 (August 1778): 353–357. Howe's detractors used the Meschianza as an example of his mismanagement of the American war in a number of pamphlets and essays; for a few examples, see Josiah Tucker, *Dispassionate Thoughts on the American War* (London, 1780), and the anonymously authored "Detail and Conduct of the American War" (London, 1780), both of which are in the collections of the John Carter Brown Library.

107. For the former interpretation, see Irvin, *Clothed in the Robes of Sovereignty*, 153–158; for the latter argument, see O'Quinn, *Entertaining Crisis*, 148.

108. Loftus Cliffe to Unknown, September 23, 1776, folder 3, Loftus Cliffe Papers, William L. Clements Library.

109. Frederick MacKenzie, *Diary of Frederick MacKenzie*, ed. Allen French (Cambridge, MA: Harvard University Press, 1930), 1:127.

110. Stephan Popp, *A Hessian Soldier in the American Revolution: The Diary of Stephan Popp*, trans. Reinhart J. Pope (private printing, 1953), Newport Historical Society. For another version of Popp's diary, with slight variations, see Stephan Popp, "Popp's Journal, 1777–1783," trans. Joseph G. Rosengarden, *Pennsylvania Magazine of History and Biography* 26, no. 1 (1902): 25–41.

111. Johann Conrad Döhla, *A Hessian Diary of the American Revolution*, trans. Bruce Burgoyne (Norman: University of Oklahoma Press, 1990), 25, 28–29.

112. Trial of Nicholas Eggars, June 28, 1779, NA, WO 71, vol. 89, pp. 246–248; quote at 247.

113. Trial of John Stewart, January 20–29, 1779, NA, WO 71, vol. 82, pp. 233–241; quote at 236.

114. Trial of James Duncan, Thomas Buck, and James O'Brian, February 24, 1778, NA, WO 71, vol. 85, pp. 284–289.

115. American Revolution Entry Books, 1773–1783, NA, WO 36, vol. 1, July 9, 1774.

116. Trial of William Furman, September 4, 1778, NA, WO 71, vol. 87, pp. 283–284.

117. Trial of Duncan, Buck, and O'Brian, pp, 284–289; sentence at 286.

118. Alexander Leslie Letterbook, April 15, 1782, New York Public Library.

119. Trial of John Winters, September 9, 1776, NA, WO 71, vol. 82, pp. 426–428; quotes at 427.

120. American Revolution Entry Books, 1773–1783, NA, WO 36, vol. 1, July 25, 1774.

121. American Revolution Entry Books, 1773–1783, NA, WO 36, vol. 1, January 27, 1775.

122. American Revolution Entry Books, 1773–1783, NA, WO 36, vol. 2, December 11, 1777.

123. American Revolution Entry Books, 1773–1783, NA, WO 36, vol. 1, January 27, 1775.

124. Camp followers and the camp culture they created were not unique to the British Army during the Revolutionary War. For a deeper analysis of the experiences of camp communities on the Continental side, see Holly Mayer, *Belonging to the Army: Camp Followers and Community During the American Revolution* (Columbia: University of South Carolina Press, 2001).

125. MacKenzie, *Diary*, p. 7.

126. Trial of William Whitlow, October 26, 1779, NA, WO 71, vol. 90, pp. 397–405.

127. See, for example, an order found in an entry book from Staten Island during the summer of 1776, which states, "No Sutler or follower of the Army is upon any Account to retail spirituous Liquors (Wine Excepted) without a Licence from the Deputy Qr Mr Genl." American Revolution Entry Books, 1773–1783, NA, WO 36, vol. 5, July 10, 1776.

128. Trial of John Miller, February 3, 1778, NA, WO 71, vol. 85, pp. 240–241.

129. Trial of Anthony Allaire, March 28, 1781, NA, WO 71, vol. 93, pp. 287–311.

130. Trial of Luther Pennington, December 15, 1777, NA, WO 71, vol. 85, pp. 167–182.

131. Trial of David Patterson, September 6–7, 1780, NA, WO 71, vol. 92, pp. 319–327.

132. Trial of John Lindon, February 24, 1781, NA, WO 71, vol. 93, pp. 196–198.

133. Ferling, *The Loyalist Mind*, 44–45.

134. Bertram Lippincott III, "The Wanton Farm of Jamestown, RI," *Newport History* 58, no. 3 (1985), 73–78.

Chapter 4

1. For more on this interchange before the war, see T. H. Breen, *The Marketplace of Revolution: How Consumer Politics Shaped American Independence* (New York: Oxford University Press, 2005), and Thomas Doerflinger, *A Vigorous Spirit of Enterprise: Merchants and Economic Development in Revolutionary Philadelphia* (Chapel Hill: University of North Carolina Press, 2001).

2. Stephen Ayrault to Messrs. Welch, Wilkinson, and Martin, December 11, 1776, Stephen Ayrault Letterbook, 1767–1780, Newport Historical Society, Newport, RI.

3. Ayrault to Thomas Swanson, January 10, 1777, Ayrault Letterbook.

4. *Newport Gazette*, March 6, 1777, 4.

5. John Peebles, *John Peebles' American War: 1776–1782*, ed. Ira Gruber (Mechanicsburg, PA: Stackpole Books, 1998), 75.

6. *New York Gazette and Weekly Mercury*, November 25, 1776, 4.

7. *Pennsylvania Ledger*, December 6, 1777, 1.

8. *Pennsylvania Ledger*, December 10, 1777, 3.

9. *Royal Georgia Gazette*, January 25, 1781, 2.

10. *Royal South Carolina Gazette*, July 6, 1780.

11. James Simpson to Earl Charles Cornwallis, September 11, 1780, National Archives (hereafter NA), London, Cornwallis Papers, vol. 11/30/64, pp. 44–45; accessed on microfilm at the David Library of the American Revolution, Washington Crossing, PA.

12. Georgia Loyalists, "Dates & Facts respecting Georgia in the American Rebellion," c. 1782, Georgia Historical Society, Savannah.

13. Sir James Wright to Lord George Germain, January 25, 1781, in *Collections of the Georgia Historical Society* (Savannah, GA: Morning News Office, 1873), 3:333.

14. Such licenses are mentioned in Andrew Elliot to William Howe, January 5, 1778, NA, Sir Guy Carleton Papers, no. 842.

15. Andrew Elliot to Sir Henry Clinton, January 9, 1779, vol. 50, folder 35, Henry Clinton Papers, William L. Clements Library, University of Michigan, Ann Arbor.

16. Tench Coxe to Isaac Hartman, April 26, 1778, Letterbook of Coxe, Furman, and Coxe, 1776–1779, p. 288, Coxe Family Papers, Historical Society of Pennsylvania, Philadelphia.

17. Jacob E. Cooke, *Tench Coxe and the Early Republic* (Chapel Hill: University of North Carolina Press, 1978), 34.

18. Ayrault to Thomas Vardon, January 5, 1778, Ayrault Letterbook.

19. Samuel Carne to Unknown, October 12, 1780, Samuel Carne papers, 1780–1782, South Caroliniana Library, University of South Carolina, Columbia.

20. John Jackson, *With the British Army in Philadelphia, 1777–1778* (San Rafael, CA: Presidio Press, 1979), 147–148, 153. Jackson calculates that "about 200 merchants and sutlers arrived from New York" with the army and made up the majority of the 307 merchants active in the town during the occupation.

21. Sir James Wright to Lord George Germain, July 17, 1780, in *Collections of the Georgia Historical Society*, 3:308.

22. Jackson, *With the British Army in Philadelphia*, 150; Ruma Chopra, *Unnatural Rebellion: Loyalists in New York City During the Revolution* (Charlottesville: University of Virginia Press, 2011), 154–155.

23. Jackson, *With the British Army in Philadelphia*, 151–152.

24. Peebles, *Peebles' American War*, 184.

25. Unknown to Lord George Germain, March 31, 1779, vol. 9, Lord George Germain Papers, William L. Clements Library.

26. William Bull to Lord George Germain, February 16, 1781, NA, Secretary of State Papers, Colonial Office (CO) Series 5, vol. 176, folio 54.

27. William Burrows to Unknown, February 27, 1780, NA, Cornwallis Papers, vol. 30/11/105, "Intercepted Letters," p. 4.

28. Arthur Bowler, *Logistics and the Failure of the British Army in America, 1775–1783* (Princeton, NJ: Princeton University Press, 1975), 93–94.

29. Bowler, *Logistics*, 92–93.

30. Orders to Colonel Buskirk, July 22, 1779, Correspondence of General Pattison as Commandant of New York, 1779–1780, James Pattison Papers, Royal Artillery Institution, London; accessed on microfilm at the David Library of the American Revolution.

31. Gen. Daniel Jones, "Cattle taken out of the Lines," December 29, 1778, and "Orders against Hucksters in the Market," June 7, 1779, Pattison Papers.

32. *Newport Gazette*, June 12, 1777, 1 (fish); June 26, 1777, 1 (farm produce).

33. Carleton Papers, no. 1042.

34. Jackson, *With the British Army in Philadelphia*, 151.

35. Carleton Papers, no. 2593.

36. For some of the punishment inflicted on suspected female collaborators after Philadelphia's occupation, see Benjamin Irvin, *Clothed in the Robes of Sovereignty: The Continental Congress and the People out of Doors* (New York: Oxford University Press, 2011), 162–163.

37. Chopra, *Unnatural Rebellion*, 75–77.

38. Fleet Greene, diary, May 8, 1779, Newport Historical Society.

39. Alexander Leslie to Nathanael Greene, April 4, 1782, Alexander Leslie Letterbook, New York Public Library; accessed on microfilm at the South Carolina Department of Archives and History, Columbia, S.C.

40. William Howe, June 29, 1776, and December 18, 1777, Orderly Book, 1776–1778, William L. Clements Library.

41. Trial of Winifred McCowan, September 15, 1777, NA, War Office (WO) Series 71, vol. 81, pp. 393–400.

42. Loftus Cliffe to Unknown, September 21, 1776, folder 3, Loftus Cliffe Papers, William L. Clements Library.

43. "Report of the Board of Police to Gov. Wright," c. May 20, 1780, in *Collections of the Georgia Historical Society*, 3:292.

44. Alexander Wright affidavits, January 12 and 31, 1782, Georgia Historical Society.

45. For a full description of Tryon's plundering, see Paul Nelson, *William Tryon and the Course of Empire: A Life in British Imperial Service* (Chapel Hill: University of North Carolina Press, 1990), 148–166.

46. Bowler, *Logistics*, 98–99.

47. General Richard Prescott to Sir Henry Clinton, January 13, 1779, vol. 50, folder 32, Clinton Papers.

48. General Augustine Prevost to Sir Henry Clinton, April 16, 1779, Carleton Papers, no. 1925.

49. John Shy, *A People Numerous and Armed: Reflections on the Military Struggle for American Independence* (Ann Arbor: University of Michigan Press, 1993), 195–212; see also Silvia Frey, *Water from the Rock: Black Resistance in a Revolutionary Age* (Princeton, NJ: Princeton University Press, 1991), 168–171.

50. These prices are taken from Hugh Gaine's *New York Gazette and Weekly Mercury* (1776–1779) and James Rivington's somewhat less reliable *Royal Gazette* (1780–1782).

51. George Brinley to Francis Brinley, July 27, 1775, Malbone/Brinley Papers, Newport Historical Society.

52. Quoted in Deirdre Phelps, "Solomon Southwick (1731–1797): Patriotic Printer of Rhode Island" (unpublished manuscript, Newport Historical Society, 1983), 58.

53. Bowler, *Logistics*, 60–61.

54. Henry Savage to George Rome, August 27, 1782, box 36, folder 4, George Rome Papers, Newport Historical Society.

55. For one account see Henry Bull, *Memoir of Rhode Island, 1636–1783* (Newport, RI: Newport Historical Society, 1906), 3:138. Bull, whose history of colonial Newport was originally published the *Newport Mercury* between 1854 and 1861, draws his account of the occupation largely from an 1829 interview with Captain John Cahoon, who lived in Newport during the occupation, and other oral histories of the war from the early nineteenth century.

56. Bull, *Memoir of Rhode Island*, 3:135.

57. Baroness Fredericke Riedesel, *Letters and Journals Relating to the War of the American Revolution*, trans. William L. Stone (New York: Arno Press, 1968), 173.

58. Bowler, *Logistics*, 77–78.

59. Robert Pigot to Sir Henry Clinton, January 30, 1778, vol. 30, folder 37, Clinton Papers.

60. Ezra Stiles, *The Literary Diary of Ezra Stiles, D.D., LL.D.*, ed. Franklin B. Dexter, vol. 2 *March 14, 1776–December 31, 1781* (New York: Charles Scribner's Sons, 1901), 108. According to Stiles, the revolutionary government of Rhode Island only allowed those who had family in the Continental Army or Rhode Island militia to leave British lines.

61. Alexander Leslie to Sir Henry Clinton, December 1, 1781, vol. 185, folder 8, Clinton Papers.

62. Stiles, *Literary Diary*, 2:149. A copper, or farthing, was worth a quarter of a penny, so six coppers would have been equal to one and a half pence.

63. William Bull to Lord George Germain, February 16, 1781, NA, Secretary of State Papers, CO 5, vol. 176, folio 54–55.

64. William Eddis, *Letters from America, Historical and Descriptive, Comprising Occurrences from 1769 to 1777, Inclusive* (London: C. Dilly, 1792), 445.

65. Riedesel, *Letters and Journals*, 173.

66. Sir James Wright to Lord George Germain, June 14, 1781, in *Collections of the Georgia Historical Society*, 3:359.

67. Sir James Wright to Undersecretary Knox, February 23–March 5, 1782, in *Collections of the Georgia Historical Society*, 3:374.

68. Col. Nisbet Balfour to Sir Henry Clinton, October 2, 1781, Nisbet Balfour Letterbook, Society of the Cincinnati Library, Washington, D.C.

69. Alexander Leslie to Sit Henry Clinton, December 1, 1781, vol. 185, folder 8, Clinton Papers.

70. James Pattison to Alexander Leslie, August 1, 1779, Correspondence of General Pattison.

71. For details of the scope of the refugee crisis, see Chopra, *Unnatural Rebellion*, chap. 6.

72. "Instructions for the Inspector of Refugees," c. December 1781, Carleton Papers, no. 4020.

73. Petition of Miss Armstrong, Sarah Snoodon, and Miss Hill, March 9, 1780, Carleton Papers, no. 2626.

74. Petition of Rachel Myers, April 3, 1781, Carleton Papers, no. 3427.

75. Petition of Mary Tailer, September 4, 1781, Carleton Papers, no. 3766.

76. Chopra, *Unnatural Rebellion*, 136–139.

77. For a fuller account of the conditions of slave refugees in occupied areas, see Frey, *Water from the Rock*, chaps. 3 and 4.

78. James Simpson to Sir Henry Clinton, July 16, 1780, Carleton Papers, no. 2915.

79. Stiles, *Literary Diary*, 2:104.

80. Petition of Sarah Gay, April 4, 1781, NA, Cornwallis Papers, vol. 30/11/69, folder 32–33.

81. Genl. Pigot to Genl. Howe, September 30, 1777, vol. 24, folder 3, Clinton Papers.

82. Correspondence of General Pattison, p. 35.

83. Correspondence of General Pattison, p. 22.

84. Correspondence of General Pattison, p. 128.

85. "Rent Memorandum Book for The South, Dock, and West Wards," vol. 31, folder 44, Clinton Papers.

86. Correspondence of General Pattison, p. 62.

87. Samuel Freebody to John Freebody, January 25, 1779, Freebody Family Letters and Accounts, Newport Historical Society.

88. Thomas Brinley to Francis Brinley, July 7, 1775, Malbone/Brinley Papers.

89. George Brinley to Francis Brinley, July 27, 1775, Malbone/Brinley Papers.

90. Mary Garrish to Francis Brinley, September 6, 1775, Malbone/Brinley Papers.

91. Nathaniel Brinley to Francis Brinley, October 2, 1775, Malbone/Brinley Papers.

92. Thomas Brinley to Francis Brinley, July 7, 1775, Malbone/Brinley Papers.

93. George Brinley to Francis Brinley, March 24, 1777, Malbone/Brinley Papers.

94. George Brinley to Francis Brinley, July 11, 1777, Malbone/Brinley Papers.

95. George Brinley to Francis Brinley, May 24, 1778, Malbone/Brinley Papers.

96. George Brinley to Francis Brinley, October 20, 1778, Brinley Malbone Papers.

97. Nathaniel Brinley to Francis Brinley, April 24, 1779, Malbone/Brinley Papers.

98. George Brinley to Francis Brinley, October 21, 1781, Malbone/Brinley Papers.

99. George Brinley to Francis Brinley, August 24, 1783, Malbone/Brinley Papers.

100. Stephen Ayrault to John Adams and John Bours, January 2, 1777, Ayrault Letterbook.

101. John Adlum, Memoirs, vol. 2, pp. 102–104, 112–113, box 2, John Adlum Papers, William L. Clements Library.

102. Passes aggregated from Daybook, New York Commandant's Office, Pattison Papers.

103. Pass numbers 147 and 410, Daybook, New York Commandant's Office, pp. 40, 52.

104. Judith Van Buskirk, *Generous Enemies: Patriots and Loyalists in Revolutionary New York* (Philadelphia: University of Pennsylvania Press, 2002), 121.

105. Van Buskirk, *Generous Enemies*, 118–124. Although Congress, the Continental Army, and the governors of New York and New Jersey ostensibly objected to this trade, in practice their efforts to stop it were lukewarm, and at times revolutionary authorities even tacitly aided smugglers into and out of British-occupied New York City.

106. Andrew Elliot to Howe, January 5, 1778, Carleton Papers, no. 842.

107. Elliot to Sir Henry Clinton, January 9, 1779, vol. 50, folder 36, Clinton Papers.

108. Proceedings of the Board of Police, 1780, NA, CO 5, vol. 519, p. 26; see also McCowen, *British Occupation of Charleston*, 105.

109. Correspondence of General Pattison, pp. 1, 2, 6, 7.

110. Correspondence of General Pattison, p. 38.

111. Fleet Greene, Diary, July 31, 1777, Newport Historical Society.

112. Correspondence of General Pattison, p. 156.

113. Thomas Hazard, *Nailer Tom's Diary: Otherwise the Journal of Thomas B. Hazard of Kingston Rhode Island, 1778 to 1840*, ed. Caroline Hazard (Boston: Merrymount Press, 1930), 3.

114. Elizabeth Morris, letter, September 12, 1780, Loyalist Papers, Newport Historical Society.

115. Deposition of James Spicer, Master of the Flag Schooner Endeavor, August 26, 1781, Carleton Papers, no. 3571.

116. For works the importance of smuggling and interimperial commerce in the early British Empire, see Elena Schneider, *The Occupation of Havana: War, Trade, and Slavery in the Atlantic World* (Chapel Hill: University of North Carolina Press, 2018); Michael Jarvis, *In the Eye of All Trade: Bermuda, Bermudians, and the Maritime Atlantic World, 1680–1783* (Chapel Hill: University of North Carolina Press, 2012); Serena Zabin, *Dangerous Economies: Status and Commerce in Imperial New York* (Philadelphia: University of Pennsylvania Press, 2009); Ellen Hartigan-O'Connor, *The Ties That Buy: Women and Commerce in Revolutionary America* (Philadelphia: University of Pennsylvania Press, 2009); and Thomas Doerflinger, *A Vigorous Spirit of Enterprise: Merchants and Economic Development in Revolutionary Philadelphia* (Chapel Hill: University of North Carolina Press, 1986).

117. Trial of Timothy Downing, November 6, 1777, NA, WO 71, vol. 84, pp. 411–412.

118. Trial of Richard Brown and Elijah Davis, June 29–30, 1779, NA, WO 71, vol. 89, pp. 389–393.

119. Trial of Nicholas Van Dyke, Jacob Myers, and Caleb Clarke, October 11, 1777, NA, WO 71, vol. 84, pp. 352–353.

120. Correspondence of General Pattison, p. 44.

Chapter 5

1. David Ramsay, *The History of the Revolution in South Carolina, from a British Province to an Independent State* (Trenton, NJ: Isaac Collins, 1785), 2:263; Loyalty Oaths, National Archives, London (hereafter NA), Cornwallis Papers, vol. 30/11/107, pp. 3–32.

2. Jim Piecuch, *Three Peoples, One King: Loyalists, Indians, and Slaves in the Revolutionary South, 1775–1782* (Columbia: University of South Carolina Press, 2008), 176–179.

3. Silvia Frey, *Water from the Rock: Black Resistance in a Revolutionary Age* (Princeton, NJ: Princeton University Press, 1991), 122–123.

4. Donald Johnson, "The Failure of Restored British Rule in Revolutionary Charleston, South Carolina," *Journal of Imperial and Commonwealth History* 42, no. 1 (2014): 22–40, specifically 27; see also George McCowen Jr., *The British Occupation of Charleston, 1780–82* (Columbia: University of South Carolina Press, 1972), 87–88.

5. Lord George Germain to William Bull, April 4, 1781, Original Correspondence of the Secretary of State, NA, Colonial Office (CO) Series 5, vol. 176, folio 59.

6. "A Board of General and Field Officers convened at Head Quarters South-Carolina," April 15, 1782, Alexander Leslie Letterbook, New York Public Library (accessed on microfilm at the South Carolina State Department of Archives and History).

7. William Bull to Col. Nisbet Balfour, April 19, 1782, NA, CO 5, vol. 176, folio 104.

8. "List of Officers of the Board of Police with their Pay," c. June 2, 1782, Alexander Leslie Letterbook; the diminishing caseload can be observed in Proceedings of the Board of Police, 1782, NA, CO 5, vol. 526.

9. Proceedings of the Board of Police, 1782, p. 19.

10. Ezra Stiles, *The Literary Diary of Ezra Stiles, D.D., LL.D.*, ed. Franklin Dexter, vol. 2, *March 14, 1776–December 31, 1781* (New York: Charles Scribner's Sons, 1901), 131–134.

11. Stiles tended only to include people of middling and elite status in his analysis and excluded almost all women. The best modern population estimate for wartime Newport is in Benjamin Carp, *Rebels Rising: Cities and the American Revolution* (New York: Oxford University Press, 2007), 225.

12. Ambrose Serle, *The American Journal of Ambrose Serle: Secretary to Lord Howe, 1776–1778*, ed. Edward H. Tatum (San Marino, CA: Huntington Library, 1940), 172.

13. Hannah Lawrence Schieffelin, "Journal of Jacob and Hannah Schieffelin," box 1, folder 3, Schieffelin Family Papers, New York Public Library.

14. Hannah Lawrence Schieffelin, "Notebook of Poems, 1774–1794," box 7, Schieffelin Family Papers.

15. See Robert M. Calhoon, *The Loyalists in Revolutionary America, 1760–1781* (New York: Harcourt Brace Jovanovich, 1973), 175–187; Wingate quoted in same, at 179.

16. Janice Potter, *The Liberty We Seek: Loyalist Ideology in Colonial New York and Massachusetts* (Cambridge, MA: Harvard University Press, 1983), 16.

17. Bernard Bailyn, *The Ordeal of Thomas Hutchinson* (Cambridge, MA: Belknap Press of Harvard University Press, 1974), 204–205.

18. Robert Calhoon and Janice Potter, "The Character and Coherence of the Loyalist Press," in *The Loyalist Perception and Other Essays*, by Robert Calhoon, in collaboration with Timothy M. Barnes et al. (Columbia: University of South Carolina Press, 1989), 109–146, specifically 141. For an extensive literary analysis of antirevolutionary print culture in North America before 1776, see Phillip Gould, *Writing the Rebellion: Loyalists and the Literature of Politics in British North America* (New York: Oxford University Press, 2013); for the classic analysis of revolutionary print culture during this period, see Bernard Bailyn, *The Ideological Origins of the American Revolution* (Cambridge, MA: Harvard University Press, 1967).

19. Calhoon and Potter, "Loyalist Press," 112.

20. Leroy Hewlett, "James Rivington, Loyalist Printer, Publisher, and Bookseller of the American Revolution, 1724–1802: A Biographical Study" (PhD diss., University of Michigan, 1958), 121.

21. C. A., "For the Newport Gazette To the Printer," *Newport Gazette*, April 10, 1777, 1.

22. Calhoon and Potter, "Loyalist Press," 133–135.

23. For a complete recent account of the revolutionary press and its role in the war, see Robert Parkinson, *The Common Cause: Creating Race and Nation in the American Revolution* (Chapel Hill: University of North Carolina Press, 2017).

24. Serle, *American Journal*, 114, 185; Ruma Chopra, *Unnatural Rebellion: Loyalists in New York City During the Revolution* (Charlottesville: University of Virginia Press, 2011), 84–86.

25. Drusus, "To the Printers," *Royal Gazette* (South Carolina), June 10, 1780. Emphasis retained from original. My supposition of Drusus's identity is based on the timing of the writer's major essays to Simpson's time in Newport and the author's intricate knowledge of the workings and underpinnings of the board of police—if not Simpson himself, Drusus was certainly a prominent member of the occupation regime or a high-level loyalist ally of the British military.

26. Drusus, "For the Royal Gazette," *Royal Gazette* (South Carolina), May 2, 1781.

27. Larry Skillin, "From Proclamation to Dialogue: The American Press and the Emergence of an American Public Sphere, 1640–1725" (PhD diss., Ohio State University, 2009), 9.

28. Colin Wells, "Proclamations, Declarations, and Versifications: Textual Power and the Poetics of Resistance" (seminar paper, McNeil Center for Early American Studies, University of Pennsylvania, Philadelphia, April 15, 2016), 3–6, quotation at 3; cited with permission.

29. Sir William and Lord Richard Howe, "Declarations," July 14 and September 19, 1776, printed in *New York Gazette and Weekly Mercury*, October 7, 1776, 1. See also Chopra, *Unnatural Rebellion*, 54–55.

30. Hyde Parker and Archibald Campbell, "A Proclamation," January 4, 1779, NA, Sir Guy Carleton Papers, no. 9823.

31. Sir Henry Clinton, "A Proclamation," Original Correspondence of the Secretary of State, Georgia, NA, CO 5, vol. 665, folio 232.

32. Piecuch, *Three Peoples*, 178, 182–183.

33. For examples of skepticism and mocking of these proclamations, see Wells, "Proclamations, Declarations, and Versifications," 7–13.

34. Sir William Howe, "A Proclamation," March 20, 1777, printed in the *New York Gazette and Weekly Mercury* and *Newport Gazette* throughout March and April 1777.

35. James Wright, "A Proclamation," *Royal Georgia Gazette*, January 4, 1781, 2.

36. Andrew Elliot to Sir William Howe, February 18, 1778, Carleton Papers, no. 946.

37. "Form of an Oath administered to the Inhabitants of West Chester, King's, Queen's & Suffolk Counties," Original Correspondence of the Secretary of State, New York, NA, CO 5, vol. 1108, folio 23.

38. Miscellaneous Oaths of Allegiance, Original Correspondence of the Secretary of State, South Carolina, NA, CO 5, vol. 527, folio 1.

39. William Tryon to Lord George Germain, December 24, 1776, Original Correspondence of the Secretary of State, New York, NA, CO 5, vol. 1108, folio 20; for a complete list of initial signers, see also folios 69–98.

40. See, for example, the list printed in the *New York Gazette and Weekly Advertiser*, November 9, 1776, 3.

41. Chopra, *Unnatural Rebellion*, 183.

42. Chopra, 64–68 and 180–187. Chopra argues that, as circumstances worsened, loyalists transitioned from petitions, which "expressed staunch confidence in the British government," to memorials, "asking for necessities such as firewood, rations, and housing, display[ing] loyalist need" (181). While certainly different in intent, however, both petitions and memorials used much the same language in their attempts to achieve redress.

43. "Petition of Cornelius Luyster," October 11, 1779, Carleton Papers, no. 2368.

44. "Petition of Daniel and Henry Van Mater," February 24, 1779, Carleton Papers, no. 1769.

45. "Petition of William Williams," February 24, 1780, Carleton Papers, no. 2593.

46. "Memorial of Sarah Morris," April 1779, Carleton Papers, no. 1964.

47. "Memorial of Elizabeth Rogers," January 6, 1779, Carleton Papers, no. 2527.

48. "Memorial of Isaac Touro," March 13, 1780, Carleton Papers, no. 2637.

49. Although Touro did receive some support from the occupation regime and found employment ministering to a New York Jewish congregation, his income evidently proved not enough to sustain his family, as he eventually emigrated to Jamaica and died there on December 8, 1783. See Joseph Rosenbloom, *A Biographical Dictionary of Early American Jews: Colonial Times Through 1800* (Lexington: University of Kentucky Press, 1960), 169.

50. "Memorial of Ann Cook," October 12, 1779, Carleton Papers, no. 2369.

51. "Petition of Isabella Raymond," November 20, 1781, Carleton Papers, no. 3887.

52. "Memorial of Jane Cadmus," June 19, 1782, vol. 194, folder 27, Henry Clinton Papers, William L. Clements Library, University of Michigan, Ann Arbor.

53. Cadwallader Colden, Journal, pp. 196–197, 200–201, MS # HM 607, Huntington Library, San Marino, CA.

54. John Malbone, "Petition to Sir Henry Clinton," January 12, 1777, Malbone/Brinley Papers, Newport Historical Society, Newport, RI.

55. John Malbone, "Petition to Sir William Howe," March 7, 1778, Malbone/Brinley Papers.

56. John Malbone, "Petition to Sir Robert Pigot," n.d., c. 1778–1779, Malbone/Brinley Papers.

57. Stiles, *Literary Diary*, 131–132, 134.

58. John Trevett, "Journal of Events during the Revolution," box 44, folder 1, Newport Historical Society.

59. Trevett, "Journal," 255.

60. Elizabeth Drinker, *Diary of Elizabeth Drinker*, ed. Elaine Crane (Boston: Northeastern University Press, 1994), 69, 71; quote at 71.

61. Drinker, 74. For an account of the Quaker exiles, see Robert Oaks, "Philadelphians in Exile: The Problem of Loyalty During the American Revolution," *Pennsylvania Magazine of History and Biography* 96, no. 3 (1972): 298–319, 321–325.

62. Drinker, *Diary*, 74; see also Kenneth Radbill, "The Ordeal of Elizabeth Drinker," *Pennsylvania History* 47, no. 2 (1980): 147–172, specifically 165–166.

63. Henry Drinker and the other Quaker exiles in Virginia were released and returned to Philadelphia after the occupation ended, in large part due to the efforts of Elizabeth Drinker and other members of the city's Quaker community. See Oaks, "Philadelphians in Exile," 323–325.

64. Judith Van Buskirk, "They Didn't Join the Band: Disaffected Women in Revolutionary Philadelphia," *Pennsylvania History* 62, no. 3 (1995): 306–329, specifically 322–323.

65. Van Buskirk, "They Didn't Join the Band," 317 (ambivalence), 320 (seizure of property and death); see also Grace Growden Galloway, "The Diary of Grace Growden Galloway," ed. Raymond Werner, *Pennsylvania Magazine of History and Biography* 55, no. 1 (1931): 32–94, and 58, no. 2 (1934): 152–189.

66. The two Philadelphians hanged were Abraham Carlisle and John Roberts, whose crime was joining the city watch during the occupation. For details see Lois Masur, *Rites of Execution: Capital Punishment and the Transformation of American Culture, 1776–1865* (New York: Oxford University Press, 1991), 74.

67. Chopra, *Unnatural Rebellion*, 54–57.

68. William Smith, "Notes upon the enquiry whether it is expedient to declare any Part of the Province of New York at the King's Peace and to revive the Civil Government," May 25, 1780, William Smith Papers, New York Public Library. Emphasis in original.

69. Chopra, *Unnatural Rebellion*, 228n9.

70. For more on British officers' attitudes toward Americans during the war, see Stephen Conway, "To Subdue America: British Army Officers and the Conduct of the Revolutionary War," *William and Mary Quarterly* 43, no. 3 (1986): 381–407. For more on civil-military strife in occupied areas, see Stephen Conway, " 'The Great Mischief Complain'd of': Reflections on the Misconduct of British Soldiers in the Revolutionary War," *William and Mary Quarterly* 47, no. 3 (1990): 370–390.

71. Trial of John Cambel, NA, War Office series 71, vol. 84, pp. 159–177; quotes at 160, 163, 172, 175.

72. James Simpson to Sir Henry Clinton, September 3, 1780, vol. 121, folder 9, Clinton Papers.

73. Sir Henry Clinton to Nisbet Balfour, November 7, 1780, NA, Cornwallis Papers, vol. 30/11/4, f. 54.

74. McCowen, *British Occupation of Charleston*, 58–60.

75. Fleet Greene, letter to Captain John Calhoon, n.d., c. 1780–1790s, in Fleet Greene diary, box 44, folder 2, Newport Historical Society.

76. For a deeper analysis of Crèvecœur's text in its loyalist dimension, see Edward Larkin, "Loyalism," in *The Oxford Handbook of the American Revolution*, ed. Edward Gray and Jane Kamensky (New York: Oxford University Press, 2013), 300–302.

77. William Smith Jr., *Historical Memoirs from 26 August 1778 to 12 November 1783*, ed. William H. W. Sabine (New York: Arno Press, 1971), 128.

78. Smith, 145.

79. Smith, 147.

80. For more on Crèvecœur's persecutors, who included Isaac Ogden, scion of a powerful New York family, and David Matthews, former mayor of the city, see Smith, 126–127.

81. Shiela Skemp, *William Franklin: Son of a Patriot, Servant of a King* (New York: Oxford University Press, 1990), 238–239.

82. Smith, *Historical Memoirs*, 29; for more on the divisions between moderate and "hardline" loyalists, see also Chopra, *Unnatural Rebellion*, 108–135.

83. On Almy's postwar career in Newport, see Elizabeth Evans's interpretive note in Mary Gould Almy, "Journal of the Siege of Rhode Island," reproduced in *Weathering the Storm: Women of the American Revolution*, by Elizabeth Evans (New York: Charles Scribner's Sons, 1975), 245–270, specifically 269.

84. Jacob E. Cooke, *Tench Coxe and the Early Republic* (Chapel Hill: University of North Carolina Press, 1978), 35–36.

85. Tench Coxe to Richard Skinner and Benjamin Yates, December 20, 1777, and Tench Coxe to Edward Goold, May 7, 1778, Letterbook of Coxe, Furman, and Coxe, 1776–1779, pp. 127–130 and 306–307, Coxe Family Papers, Historical Society of Pennsylvania, Philadelphia.

86. Tench Coxe to John Cox, June 10, 1778, Tench Coxe Letterbook, May–December 1778. Coxe Family Papers.

87. In Philadelphia, approximately three thousand loyalists evacuated the city with the British Army out of a wartime population of at least twenty thousand—see Chopra, *Unnatural Rebellion*, 100. For Newport, numbers are less clear, but a letter of Rhode Island Governor William Greene dated November 14, 1779, estimates around 42 families left with the British, comprising perhaps 200 or 300 people out of a wartime population of between 2,300 and 5,530; see William Greene to Nathanael Greene, November 14, 1779, Greene Papers, Newport Historical Society. For the aggregated wartime population estimates see Carp, *Rebels Rising*, 225.

88. Details of the Hayne case appear in Ramsay, *History of the Revolution of South Carolina*, 2:278–285; see also Piecuch, *Three Peoples*, 274–275, and Robert Lambert, *South Carolina Loyalists in the American Revolution* (Columbia: University of South Carolina Press, 1987), 204–205.

89. John Colcock, "Case of Colonel Hayne," c. 1781, MS 43/83, South Carolina Historical Society, Charleston.

90. H. Bancker to E. Bancker, May 9, 1783, Bancker Family Papers, New York Public Library.

91. George Stanton to James DeLancey, May 20, 1783, James DeLancey Papers, New-York Historical Society, New York, NY.

92. Maya Jasanoff, *Liberty's Exiles: American Loyalists in the Revolutionary World* (New York: Alfred A. Knopf, 2011), 6.

93. For details on Elliot, see Robert Ernst, "Andrew Elliot, Forgotten Loyalist of New York City," *New York History* 57, no. 3 (1976): 284–320, specifically 318–319; for Smith, see Chopra, *Unnatural Rebellion*, 222.

94. Larkin, "Loyalism," 304–305.

95. Paul H. Smith, "The American Loyalists: Notes on their Organizational and Numerical Strength," *William and Mary Quarterly* 25, no. 2 (1968): 259–277, specifically 267.

Chapter 6

1. Henry Addison to Jonathan Boucher, June 4, 1780, Henry Addison Papers, William L. Clements Library, University of Michigan, Ann Arbor. Emphasis in the original.

2. Quote in Henry Addison to Jonathan Boucher, March 25, 1782, Addison Papers; for the Italian and Moravian schemes, see Addison to Boucher, November 22, 1782, Addison Papers.

3. Addison to Boucher, March 25, 1782, Addison Papers.

4. Addison to Sir Guy Carleton, October 7, 1783, Addison Papers.

5. Addison to Boucher, October 20, 1783, Addison Papers.

6. Addison to Boucher, November 14, 1784, Addison Papers.

7. Addison to Boucher, March 25, 1782, Addison Papers.

8. For an account of the negotiations as they related to loyalists, see Maya Jasanoff, *Liberty's Exiles: American Loyalists in the Revolutionary World* (New York: Alfred A. Knopf, 2011), 78–81; for a more detailed account of the negotiations more generally, see Richard B. Morris, *The Peacemakers: The Great Powers and American Independence* (New York: Harper and Row, 1965), esp. chaps. 12–15.

9. For the Boston exiles, see Andrew Jackson O'Shaughnessy, *The Men Who Lost America: British Leadership, the American Revolution, and the Fate of Empire* (New Haven, CT: Yale University Press, 2013), 86; for the Philadelphia exiles, see Ruma Chopra, *Unnatural Rebellion: Loyalists in New York City During the Revolution* (Charlottesville: University of Virginia Press, 2011), 100; for the wartime population estimates, see Benjamin Carp, *Rebels Rising: Cities and the American Revolution* (New York: Oxford University Press, 2007), 225.

10. Ira Gruber, *The Howe Brothers in the American Revolution* (Chapel Hill: University of North Carolina Press, 1974), 298.

11. Numbers for the evacuation of Newport are not as well documented as those of Boston and Philadelphia. Henry Bull's nineteenth-century *Memoir of Rhode Island*, based on the author's interviews with those who lived through the occupation, asserts that "of the Royalists, about 30 or 40 of the principal men with their families and effects, embarked in the fleet, and a large portion of the negro slaves, being offered their liberty, by doing, also embarked in the fleet"; Henry Bull, *Memoir of Rhode Island, 1636–1783* (Newport, RI: Newport Historical Society, 1906), 3:136. In a letter to his brother Nathanael, William Greene discloses the names of forty-six prominent individuals who left with their families; William Greene to Nathanael Greene, November 14, 1779, box 44, folder 9, Newport Historical Society, Newport,

RI. Typescript of original at the Redwood Library and Athenaeum, Newport, RI. Ezra Stiles records that a "Tory fleet" of approximately twenty armed ships and "a dozen or 15 sail of Nwpt vessels" joined the British fleet during the evacuation; Ezra Stiles, *The Literary Diary of Ezra Stiles, D.D., LL.D.*, ed. Franklin B. Dexter, vol. 2, *March 14, 1776–December 31, 1781* (New York: Charles Scribner's Sons, 1901), 386. My estimate has been reached by assuming from these sources that around forty elite families left, along with an equal number of non-elites, and perhaps one hundred enslaved people. With an average family size of five, eighty families would account for around four hundred people, with the additional one hundred slaves making up the difference. These could have easily been carried off on the civilian fleet that Stiles describes and may undercount the number of refugees, since many likely also sought passage on the British transports.

12. For an account of loyalists in the immediate aftermath of the British evacuation of Boston, see Thomas Ingersoll, *The Loyalist Problem in Revolutionary New England* (New York: Cambridge University Press, 2016), 190–197.

13. Chopra, *Unnatural Rebellion*, 100–101; Judith Van Buskirk, "They Didn't Join the Band: Disaffected Women in Revolutionary Philadelphia," *Pennsylvania History* 62 (1995): 306–329, specifically 320.

14. Stiles, *Literary Diary*, 2:390; Elaine Foreman Crane, *A Dependent People: Newport, Rhode Island in the Revolutionary Era* (New York: Fordham University Press, 1985), 160–163.

15. Nathaniel Philbrick, *Bunker Hill: A City, A Siege, A Revolution* (New York: Viking, 2013), 288–289.

16. Nathaniel Brinley to Francis Brinley, April 19, 1776. Malbone/Brinley Papers, Newport Historical Society, Newport, RI.

17. Nathaniel Brinley to Francis Brinley, August 31, 1776 (quoted), and April 24, 1779, Malbone/Brinley Papers.

18. Quoted in Jacob E. Cooke, *Tench Coxe and the Early Republic* (Chapel Hill: University of North Carolina Press, 1978), 41.

19. John Knowles, Certification of Tench Coxe's Subscription to the Oath of Allegiance and Fidelity, May 23, 1778, Coxe Family Papers, Historical Society of Pennsylvania, Philadelphia. See also Cooke, *Tench Coxe*, 41.

20. Tench Coxe to John Cox, June 10, 1778, Tench Coxe Letterbook, May–December 1778, Coxe Family Papers.

21. Tench Coxe to Unknown, n.d., Coxe, Furman, and Coxe Letterbook, 1776–1779, p. 141, Coxe Family Papers. The company's letterbook during this period is riddled with similar mutilations, which are not nearly so common in other sections.

22. Cooke, *Tench Coxe*, 42–43; quote on 42.

23. Anne M. Ousterhout, "Controlling the Opposition in Pennsylvania During the American Revolution," *Pennsylvania Magazine of History and Biography* 105, no. 1 (1981):3–34, specifically 23.

24. Benjamin Irvin, *Clothed in the Robes of Sovereignty: The Continental Congress and the People out of Doors* (New York: Oxford University Press, 2011), 161–163; quotes at 161.

25. See Elizabeth Evans's interpretive notes in Mary Gould Almy, "Journal of the Siege of Rhode Island," reproduced in *Weathering the Storm: Women of the American Revolution*, by Elizabeth Evans (New York: Charles Scribner's Sons, 1975), 245–270, specifically 249.

26. Evans, 269.

27. Quoted in Evans, 270.

28. Evans, 250; the letters were discovered in the late nineteenth century and published in the first volume of the *Newport Historical Magazine*, c. 1880–1881.

29. Bull, *Memoir of Rhode Island*, 138.

30. Bruce M. Bigelow, "Aaron Lopez: Colonial Merchant of Newport," *New England Quarterly* 4, no. 4 (1931): 757–776, specifically 773–775.

31. T. Cole Jones, " 'Displaying the Ensigns of Harmony': The French Army in Newport, Rhode Island, 1780–1781," *New England Quarterly* 85, no. 3 (2012): 430–467, specifically 457–465.

32. Newport Town Council, "Memorial of the town of Newport to the General Assembly of Rhode Island praying to be exempted from taxation," October 1781, Newport Town Council Records, Rhode Island Historical Society, Providence.

33. Stiles, *Literary Diary*, 2:132, 134.

34. John R. Bartlett, *Records of the State of Rhode Island and Providence Plantations* (Providence: A. C. Green and Brother, 1856–1865), 9:289.

35. George Brinley to Francis Brinley, October 21, 1781, Malbone/Brinley Papers.

36. Bartlett, *Records of the State of Rhode Island*, 9:658.

37. Brett Palfreyman, "Peace Process: The Reintegration of Loyalists in Post-Revolutionary America" (PhD diss., Binghamton University, 2014), 62–77; quotes at 66, 68.

38. William Rawle to Rebecca Shoemaker, January 1, 1782, William Rawle Letterbook, p. 147, William L. Clements Library, University of Michigan, Ann Arbor.

39. Rawle to Rebecca Shoemaker, March 8, 1782, and March 20, 1782, William Rawle Letterbook, pp. 150–152; Rawle to Polly and Anne Rawle, July 31, 1782, William Rawle Letterbook, pp. 164–165.

40. David Greene to Thomas Fraser, various dates 1778–1779, David Greene Letterbook, pp. 64–99, William L. Clements Library.

41. Greene to Thomas Fraser, June 29, 1781, David Greene Letterbook, p. 155.

42. Greene to John Rose, Esq., November 14, 1781, David Greene Letterbook, pp. 163–164.

43. Greene to John Rose, February 15, 1782, David Greene Letterbook, p. 172.

44. Greene to Messrs Lane, Son, and Fraser, February 12, 1782, and Greene to William Priddie, December 11, 1782, David Greene Letterbook, pp. 171, 204.

45. James Wright to Undersecretary Knox, February 16, 1782, in *Collections of the Georgia Historical Society* (Savannah, GA: Morning News Office, 1873), 371; Jim Piecuch, *Three Peoples, One King: Loyalists, Indians, and Slaves in the Revolutionary South, 1775–1782* (Columbia: University of South Carolina Press, 2008), 296; Jasanoff, *Liberty's Exiles*, 67–69.

46. For an account of the beginnings of loyalist resettlement in Nova Scotia, see Jasanoff, *Liberty's Exiles*, 157–175.

47. Silvia Frey, *Water from the Rock: Black Resistance in a Revolutionary Age* (Princeton, NJ: Princeton University Press, 1991), 182.

48. Frey, 182–183.

49. Jasanoff, *Liberty's Exiles*, 249–250.

50. David George, "An Account of the Life of Mr. David George, from Sierra Leone in Africa," in *Baptist Annual Register* 1 (1790–1793), ed. John Rippon, 473–484, specifically 477.

51. Piecuch, *Three Peoples*, 299–308.

52. Piecuch, 296–298.

53. Frey, *Water from the Rock*, 181.

54. Palfreyman, "Peace Process," 88–90.

55. Lord George Germain, "Propositions for the Employment of His Majesty's Forces in North America," c. February 1782, vol. 15, Lord George Germain Papers, William L. Clements Library.

56. Henry Strachey, "Lord Shelburne's Instructions to Me, October 20th, 1782," box 2, folder 62, Henry Strachey Papers, William L. Clements Library.

57. "Remarks relative to North America & the State of the Forts in the King's Possession, c. 1782," vol. 66, pp. 571–582, quotes at 576–578, William Petty, 1st Marquis of Lansdowne, 2nd Earl of Shelburne papers, William L. Clements Library.

58. Richard Oswald to Unknown [either Lord Shelburne or Lord Townsend], November 16, 1782, vol. 2, Oswald Papers, William L. Clements Library.

59. Chopra, *Unnatural Rebellion*, 198–199.

60. William Smith Jr., *Historical Memoirs from 26 August 1778 to 12 November 1783*, ed. William H. W. Sabine (New York: Arno Press, 1971), 542.

61. Chopra, *Unnatural Rebellion*, 200–201.

62. James Robertson to Andrew Elliot, April 14, 1783, in *The Twilight of British Rule in Revolutionary America: The New York Letter Book of General James Robertson*, ed. Milton M. Klein and Ronald L. Howard (Cooperstown, NY: New York Historical Association, 1983), 265.

63. For a deeper account of elite loyalist responses to the diplomatic peace process, see Chopra, *Unnatural Rebellion*, 200–214.

64. Donald F. Johnson, "The Failure of Restore British Rule in Revolutionary Charleston South Carolina," *Journal of Commonwealth and Imperial History* 42, no. 1 (2014): 22–40, specifically 35–36.

65. Laurens's quote and an account of this plan appear in Piecuch, *Three Peoples*, 290.

66. Piecuch, 288.

67. Frey, *Water from the Rock*, 177–178.

68. Gary B. Nash, *The Forgotten Fifth: African Americans in the Age of Revolution* (Cambridge, MA: Harvard University Press), 41–42; see also Frey, *Water from the Rock*, 178–179.

69. Frey, *Water from the Rock*, 177–179 (Moncrief quote on 178); see also George McCowen Jr., *The British Occupation of Charleston, 1780–82* (Columbia: University of South Carolina Press, 1972), 105–107, and Piecuch, *Three Peoples*, 288–291.

70. Alexander Leslie, "At a Board of General and Field Officers convened at Head Quarters South-Carolina 15th April 1782," April 15, 1782, Alexander Leslie Letterbook, New York Public Library; accessed on microfilm at the South Carolina Department of Archives and History, Columbia, SC.

71. Quoted in Piecuch, *Three Peoples*, 280.

72. John S. Pancake, *This Destructive War: The British Campaign in the Carolinas* (Tuscaloosa: University of Alabama Press, 1985), 238.

73. William Bull to Lord George Germain, November 11, 1781, National Archives (hereafter NA), London, Secretary of State Papers, Colonial Office (CO) Series 5, vol. 176, folio 77.

74. Alexander Garden, *Anecdotes of the Revolutionary War in America, with Sketches of Character of Persons Most Distinguished, in the Southern States, for Civil and Military Services* (Charleston, 1822), 371.

75. Piecuch, *Three Peoples*, 286–287; quote at 286.

76. Piecuch, 288.

77. Leslie, "At a Board of General and Field Officers"; for more on German desertion, see Rodney Atwood, *The Hessians: Mercenaries from Hessen-Kassel in the American Revolution* (New York: Cambridge University Press, 1980), 184–206.

78. Piecuch, *Three Peoples*, 318.

79. For details on the legacy of slave insurrections during the revolution on psyches of southern whites, see Frey, *Water from the Rock*, chaps. 7 and 8.

80. "Return of Refugees, and their Slaves arrived from Georgia and South Carolina," NA, Sir Guy Carleton Papers, no. 620.

81. Judith Van Buskirk, *Generous Enemies: Patriots and Loyalists in Revolutionary New York* (Philadelphia: University of Pennsylvania Press, 2002), 171–172.

82. Van Buskirk, *Generous Enemies*, 165.

83. For details of the preliminary treaty terms and final negotiations, see Morris, *Peacemakers*, 346–352.

84. Van Buskirk, *Generous Enemies*, 159–162.

85. George Stanton to James DeLancey, May 20, 1783, James DeLancey Papers, New-York Historical Society, New York, NY.

86. Palfreyman, "Peace Process," 70.

87. See Van Buskirk, *Generous Enemies*, 155–195 and Chopra, *Unnatural Rebellion*, 188–222.

88. Van Buskirk, *Generous Enemies*, 48.

89. Van Buskirk, 168.

90. Chopra, *Unnatural Rebellion*, 208; see also Jasanoff, *Liberty's Exiles*, 89–91, and Cassandra Pybus, *Epic Journeys of Freedom: Runaway Slaves of the American Revolution and Their Quest for Global Liberty* (Boston: Beacon, 2006), 64–67.

91. Boston King, "Memoirs of the Life of Boston King," in *Unchained Voices: An Anthology of Black Authors in the English-Speaking World of the Eighteenth Century*, ed. Vincent Carretta (Lexington: University Press of Kentucky, 1996), 355.

92. Van Buskirk, *Generous Enemies*, 172.

93. George Washington to Daniel Parker, April 28, 1783, in *Writings of Washington*, ed. John C. Fitzpatrick (Washington, DC: United States Government Publishing Office, 1938), 26:364–365.

94. Pybus, *Epic Journeys of Freedom*, 65–69.

95. Van Buskirk, *Generous Enemies*, 174.

96. "Trial of Jacob Duyree," NA, War Office (WO) Series 71, v. 97, p. 320–356; quote at 350; see also Van Buskirk, *Generous Enemies*, 174–175, and Chopra, *Unnatural Rebellion*, 214.

97. William Smith Jr., *Historical Memoirs*, 133n.

98. George Atkinson Ward, ed., *Journal and Letters of the Late Samuel Curwin, Judge of the Admiralty, Etc., An American Refugee in England, from 1775 to 1784* (New York: C. S. Francis, 1842), 493.

99. Van Buskirk, *Generous Enemies*, 191.

100. James Rivington to James DeLancey, December 20, 1783, DeLancey Papers, New-York Historical Society. For Rivington's fate, see Morton Pennypacker, *General Washington's Spies on Long Island and in New York* (Brooklyn, NY: Long Island Historical Society, 1939), 7. Pennypacker and later authors such as Alexander Rose have identified Rivington as a member

of the Culper Spy Ring for the Continental Army, which may explain his exemption from prosecution after the war. However, very little evidence exists to corroborate the printer's involvement, and it was certainly not a well-known idea until long after the war.

101. Biographical/Historical Information, finding aid to the Schieffelin Family Papers, New York Public Library, accessed January 2, 2020, http://archives.nypl.org/mss/2690; see also Van Buskirk, *Generous Enemies*, 194.

102. *Van Buskirk, Generous Enemies*, 194.

103. Palfreyman, "Peace Process," 169.

104. Robert Ernst, "Andrew Elliot, Forgotten Loyalist of Occupied New York," *New York History* 57, no. 3 (1976): 284–320, specifically 317–320.

105. John Ferling, *The Loyalist Mind: Joseph Galloway and the American Revolution* (University Park: Pennsylvania State University Press, 1991), 62–64.

106. Chopra, *Unnatural Rebellion*, 194; see also L. F. S. Upton, "Smith, William (1728–93)," in *Dictionary of Canadian Biography*, vol. 4 (Toronto: University of Toronto/Université Laval, 2003–), accessed April 23, 2018, http://www.biographi.ca/en/bio/smith_william_1728_93_4E.html.

107. George Brinley to Francis Brinley, August 24, 1783, Malbone/Brinley Papers.

108. Jasanoff, *Liberty's Exiles*, 6.

109. For the best estimate on the number of loyalists in revolutionary America, see Paul H. Smith, "The American Loyalists: Notes on Their Organizational and Numerical Strength," *William and Mary Quarterly* 25, no. 2 (1968): 259–277, specifically 267.

Epilogue

1. For biographical details on Ramsay, see Arthur Schaffer, *To Be an American: David Ramsay and the Making of the American Consciousness* (Columbia: University of South Carolina Press, 1991).

2. David Ramsay, *The History of the Revolution of South Carolina, from a British Province to an Independent State* (Trenton, NJ: Isaac Collins, 1785), 2:117, 263.

3. David Ramsay, *The History of the American Revolution* (London: John Stockdale, 1793), 2:161.

4. Ramsay, *History of the American Revolution*, 2:145.

5. Ramsay, *History of the Revolution of South Carolina*, 2:265.

6. Ramsay, *History of the American Revolution*, 2:165.

7. Ramsay, *History of the American Revolution*, 1:263.

8. Ramsay, *History of the American Revolution*, 2:288.

9. Ramsay, *History of the American Revolution*, 2:172.

10. Ramsay, *History of the Revolution of South Carolina*, 2:298.

11. For more on this, see David Waldstreicher, *In the Midst of Perpetual Fetes: The Making of American Nationalism, 1776–1820* (Chapel Hill: University of North Carolina Press, 1997), and Benjamin Irvin, *Clothed in the Robes of Sovereignty: The Continental Congress and the People out of Doors* (New York: Oxford University Press, 2011).

12. For material and other incarnations of this new American nationalism, see Kariann Yakota, *Unbecoming British: How America Became a Post-Colonial Nation* (New York: Oxford University Press, 2011).

13. See Alfred Young, *The Shoemaker and the Tea Party: Memory and the American Revolution* (Boston: Beacon Press, 1999), esp. 12–13.

14. For more on this, see the introduction to Lester Cohen, *The Revolutionary Histories: Contemporary Narratives of the American Revolution* (Ithaca, NY: Cornell University Press, 1980), and Arthur Shaffer, *The Politics of History: Writing the History of the American Revolution, 1783–1815* (New York: Precedent Publishing, 1975), chap. 1.

15. For biographical details on Ramsay, see Arthur Schaffer, *To Be an American: David Ramsay and the Making of the American Consciousness* (Columbia: University of South Carolina Press, 1991), esp. 54–58.

16. Mercy Otis Warren, *History of the Rise, Progress, and Termination of the American Revolution, Interspersed with Biographical, Political, and Moral Observations* (Boston: Manning and Loring, 1805), 1:338–339; for biographical details on Warren, see Rosemarie Zagarri, *A Woman's Dilemma: Mercy Otis Warren and the American Revolution*, 2nd ed. (Boston: John Wiley and Sons, 2015).

17. Ramsay, *History of the American Revolution*, 2:184.

18. Jedidiah Morse, *Annals of the American Revolution: or a Record of the Causes and Events Which Produced, and Terminated in the Establishment and Independence of the American Republic* (Hartford, CT, 1824), 260.

19. Alexander Garden, *Anecdotes of the Revolutionary War in America, with Sketches of Character of Persons most Distinguished, in the Southern States, for Civil and Military Services* (Charleston, SC: A. E. Miller, 1822), 258.

20. Samuel Wilson, *A History of the American Revolution: Intended as a Reading Book for Schools* (Stonington, CT: W. Storer, 1826), 127.

21. Charles [Carlo] Botta, *History of the War of the Independence of the United States*, trans. George Alexander Otis (Cooperstown, NY: H. and E. Phinney, 1845 [first published 1810]), 1:435.

22. Warren, *History of the Rise, Progress, and Termination*, 1:194.

23. Perhaps the most evocative account of Prescott's capture in the postwar decades is found in Catherine Read Williams, *Revolutionary Heroes: Containing the Life of Brigadier Gen. William Barton, and also, of Captain Stephen Olney* (Providence, RI, 1839), 51–60.

24. Wilson, *History of the American Revolution*, 318.

25. See, for example, Garden, *Anecdotes*, 262–265, and Botta, *History of the War*, 187, 295.

26. See, for one example of this criticism, Ramsay, *History of the American Revolution*, 2:288.

27. Ramsay, *History of the American Revolution*, 2:282.

28. Garden, *Anecdotes*, 246.

29. Botta, *History of the War*, 2:177–178 (quotes at 177); Garden, *Anecdotes*, 277.

30. Warren, *History of the Rise, Progress, and Termination*, 1:339.

31. Ramsay, *History of the American Revolution*, 2:102.

32. Botta, *History of the War*, 2:255.

33. Warren, *History of the Rise, Progress, and Termination*, 2:203.

34. *The Thrilling and Romantic Story of Sarah Smith and the Hessian* (Philadelphia, 1845), Huntington Library, San Marino, CA.

35. Garden, *Anecdotes*, 237.

36. Botta, *History of the War*, 145

37. Warren, *History of the Rise, Progress, and Termination*, 1:341.

38. This argument tracks with the work of Robert Parkinson on treatment of race in newspapers and print media during the war itself, which sought to demonize Native Americans and blacks for siding with the British. See Robert G. Parkinson, *The Common Cause:*

Creating Race and Nation in the American Revolution (Chapel Hill: University of North Carolina Press, 2016), esp. chap. 9.

39. Garden, *Anecdotes*, 227.

40. Ramsay, *History of the American Revolution*, 2:172–173.

41. Garden, *Anecdotes*, 243.

42. Botta, *History of the War*, 2:261.

43. Garden, *Anecdotes*, 267.

44. Ramsay, *History of the Revolution of South Carolina*, 2:263.

45. For the New York law, see Howard Pashman, *Building a Revolutionary State: The Legal Transformation of New York, 1776–1783* (Chicago: University of Chicago Press, 2018), 86–87; for South Carolina, see Rebecca Brannon, *From Revolution to Reunion: The Reintegration of the South Carolina Loyalists* (Columbia: University of South Carolina Press, 2016), 55–59; for selective reintegration, see Brannon, *From Revolution to Reunion*, 67–99, and Brett Palfreyman, "Peace Process: The Reintegration of Loyalists in Post-Revolutionary America," (PhD diss., Binghamton University, 2014).

46. Warren, *History of the Rise, Progress, and Termination*, 2:194.

47. Ramsay, *History of the Revolution of South Carolina*, 2:271.

48. Ramsay, *History of the Revolution of South Carolina*, 2:278–285; see also Botta, *History of the War*, 377, and Garden, *Anecdotes*, 250.

49. Garden, *Anecdotes*, 371.

50. Botta, *History of the War*, 1:431.

51. Garden, *Anecdotes*, 244–245.

52. Garden, 258.

53. Ramsay, *History of the American Revolution*, 2:114, 145.

54. Warren, *History of the Rise, Progress, and Termination*, 2:90.

55. For recent analyses of this overoptimism, see Andrew Jackson O'Shaughnessy, *The Men Who Lost America: British Leadership, the American Revolution, and the Fate of Empire* (New Haven, CT: Yale University Press, 2013), 98–99, 187–191; Aaron Sullivan, *The Disaffected: Britain's Occupation of Philadelphia During the American Revolution* (Philadelphia: University of Pennsylvania Press, 2019), 47–49; Jim Piecuch, *Three Peoples, One King: Loyalists, Indians, and Slaves in the Revolutionary South, 1775–1782* (Columbia: University of South Carolina Press, 2008), 125–132.

56. Wilson, *History of the American Revolution*, 280.

57. For more on this see Shaffer, *Politics of History*, 36.

58. Ramsay, *History of the American Revolution*, 1:313.

59. Warren, *History of the Rise, Progress, and Termination*, 1:341.

60. Garden, *Anecdotes*, 224n.

61. This is not to say that these authors did not name loyalists in general, but simply that they did not name individual loyalists complicit in occupation regimes.

62. For the editorials during the 1788 congressional election, see *Federal Gazette*, November 22, 1788, 2. For the charges of loyalism that came up throughout Coxe's political career, see Jacob E. Cooke, *Tench Coxe and the Early Republic* (Chapel Hill: University of North Carolina Press, 1978), 44–45.

Adams, John, 1, 38, 166
Adams, Samuel, 19
Addison, Henry, 163–66, 174–75, 189
Adlum, John, 133
Africans and African Americans: attempts at reenslavement of ex-slaves, 69, 73–74, 86–88, 187–88; enslaved population in revolutionary Georgia and South Carolina, 13–14, 46–48, 50, 79; postwar migrations of, 160, 175–77, 186–88, 223n18; seeking freedom with the British army, 8, 44–47, 51, 63–64, 69–75, 80–88, 110, 128, 180–84, 186, 194–95, 222n12. *See also* slavery
alcohol: as a commodity in occupied ports, 72, 114–15, 131, 134; use and abuse of by British soldiers, 91, 95–96, 107, 109–10
Allan, Sally, 3
allegiance: attempts by British to identify and coerce, 5, 13, 16, 43, 47, 51, 53, 57–60, 62, 68–71, 73–75, 78–79, 143, 145–49, 157–58, 191–92; attempts by revolutionaries to identify and coerce, 28, 39, 45–46, 68, 141, 167; changes wrought by military rule, 4–5, 10, 12–13, 15, 111, 158–61, 168; flexibility of among civilian populations, 6–8, 65–66, 87, 96, 127, 138–42, 150–56, 158–59, 162–63, 168, 194–95, 200–202; scholarship on, 8–9. *See also* loyalists; oaths of allegiance
Almy, Benjamin, 89, 153, 170
Almy, Mary, 89, 153, 158, 161, 167, 170–71, 189
American Civil War, 8
André, John, 99, 102–3
Antigua, 174–75. *See also* West Indies
assizes, 72. *See also* prices; shortages
Ayrault, Stephen, 114–16, 132, 172

Balfour, Nisbet, 57
Bancker, Evert, Jr., 159, 186, 188

Black Dragoons, 183
Bonaparte, Napoleon, 8
Boston, Massachusetts: British evacuation, 111, 166–68; civil administration under occupation, 59–60; colonial economy and society, 12–14; drunkenness in, 47–48; pre-revolutionary British occupation, 18–20; revolutionary siege of, 20–25, 122, 124, 131–32
Botta, Carlo, 193, 196, 198–200, 202–4
Brandywine, Battle of, 40
Brinley family, 73, 122, 131–32, 167–68, 172, 189
British Army: campaigns in North America, 11, 18, 21–22, 30–31, 34–35, 40–41, 46–47, 50–51, 83, 175, 183–84; collaboration with loyalists and former officials, 56–57, 60, 66–67, 69–70, 144–45, 162–63, 171–72, 195, 205; crimes accused of in postwar histories, 192–96, 198–200, 203; discipline in, 25, 53, 135; interactions with occupied populations, 54, 90–91, 95–96, 98–106, 110–11, 126, 129, 132, 150–54, 158, 160–61, 166, 175–77; logistics of, 21, 117–22, 124–25, 130, 180–81; policies regarding slavery and enslaved people, 69, 80–83, 83–86, 88, 128, 160, 181–82, 187–89; relationships with civilian women, 3, 5, 80–83, 88–94, 98–106, 142–43, 173; recruitment of loyalist soldiers, 44, 47–48, 51, 58–59, 72, 109–10, 139–40, 172, 182–83; treatment of prisoners, 24, 90–91, 94, 133–34, 178, 197; violence against civilians, 5, 24, 81, 94–96, 109–11, 113, 120–21, 150, 198–99. *See also* courts-martial; military culture; military families; police; Royal Navy
Bristol, Rhode Island, 26–27
Brooklyn, New York, 34, 63, 75, 135
Brown, William, 59

Bull, William, Jr., 48, 77–78, 117, 126, 140, 182, 204

Bunker Hill, Battle of, 20, 23–25,

Burgoyne, John, 21, 40–41, 43–44, 103

Camden, Battle of, 51, 156, 197

Campbell, Archibald, 44, 46–47, 70–71, 91, 145, 176, 198

Campbell, William, 48

camp followers. *See* military families

Carey, Henry, *Chrononhotonthologos* (1734 play), 98

Carleton, Guy, 165, 175, 179, 186, 197

Caribbean. *See* West Indies

Charleston, South Carolina: British campaigns against, 11, 44, 47–48, 50–52, 146; British evacuation of, 175, 180–84; civil administration under occupation, 54, 56–58, 67–70, 72–79, 85–86, 88, 98, 139–41, 144–47, 159, 165, 180, 188; colonial economy of, 12–14; enslaved people and ex-slaves under occupation, 81–88, 128; life under occupation, 81–84, 101, 108, 110, 115–17, 120, 125–26, 156, 159, 191–92, 196–97, 199–204; revolutionary occupation of, 35, 48–50

Cherokee Indians, 44–45, 48–50, 177–78

civil government: calls for restoration of in occupied territories, 55, 140, 77–79, 180–81; overthrow of in 1774–76, 11, 20–21, 35–37, 53; restoration of in occupied Georgia, 47–48, 57–58, 70–72. *See also* police

Cliffe, Loftus, 106, 120

Clinton, Henry, 2, 21, 29, 31, 40–41, 43–44, 48, 50–54, 57, 68, 70, 86, 97, 99–100, 140, 146–47, 151, 156, 197, 201

Colden, Cadwallader, Jr., 151, 157, 186

committees and councils of safety, 16–18, 20–21, 25–26, 29, 39, 44–45, 48, 59, 68, 201

confiscation of property: by British forces, 21–22, 45–46, 51, 75–76, 115, 135–36, 154–55, 158, 196; by revolutionary forces, 25, 28–29, 33, 45, 171, 178, 181, 184–85, 201

Connecticut, 12, 84, 120–21, 134, 150, 174–75, 198

Continental Army, 15, 31, 33–35, 38–41, 43, 45, 50–51, 70–72, 89, 91, 118, 121, 153–56, 170, 177, 180–82, 186, 188, 191, 201–2

Continental Congress, 11, 32–33, 37–41, 46, 56, 65–66, 71, 154, 164, 178–79, 184, 191

contractors, 5, 62–63

Cornwallis, Charles, 2nd Earl, 48, 51, 122, 140, 172, 197, 201

courts-martial, 64, 95, 107–8, 120, 136, 155–56

Coxe, Tench, 10, 88, 116, 158–61, 167–69, 191, 204–5

Cooke, Nicholas, 27, 87

Creek Indians, 44–46, 177–78

Crèvecœur, John Hector St. John, 157–58, 188

Cumberland, Richard, *The West Indian* (1771 play), 98–99

currency: revolutionary paper money, 132–33, 171; specie, 74–75, 112, 115, 133–34; wartime inflation, 22, 72–73. *See also* prices; shortages

dances and balls, 53, 80–82, 101–3, 116

deforestation, 35, 124–25, 221n89

DeLancy, James, 160, 185–86

Delaware, 11, 40, 164

desertion, 27–28, 43, 93, 98, 106–8, 183, 192, 200

d'Estaing, Jean Baptiste Charles Henri Hector, comte, 71

dinner parties, 32, 56, 80, 82, 101–3, 116, 154, 158

disaffected, 9, 148, 209n14. *See also* allegiance, loyalists

disease: effects on manpower in the British army, 43, 122; in occupied Charleston, 128, 192; smallpox, 3–4, 33, 71, 84, 88; venereal, 2–3

Drinker, Elizabeth, 10, 95–96, 153–55

Döhla, Johann, 106

Drusus (pseudonym), 144

Dudley, Charles and Catherine, 28–29

dueling, 81, 109–10

Dunmore, John Murray, 4th Earl, 44, 187

East Florida, 43, 45–47, 143, 175–77, 180, 182

Ethiopian Ball, 81–83

Elliot, Andrew, 10, 54–57, 60–68, 76, 78, 97, 115, 134, 146, 160, 180, 189

English Civil War, 7, 37

exile: as punishment in occupied territories, 64, 119, 156, 197; of loyalists by revolutionary regimes, 6, 16, 18, 29, 45, 55, 68, 96–97, 127–28, 132, 149, 151, 157, 162–63, 167–68, 173–75, 204; of Philadelphia Quakers, 39–40, 154; postwar, 160, 175–78, 180–82, 185–90. *See also* refugees export trade, 14, 60–61, 65–67, 112, 115–16, 134. *See also* import trade; smuggling

family networks, 18, 28, 31, 46, 89–91, 97, 116, 127–28, 131–32, 134–35, 142, 151, 153–54, 162, 164, 166–74, 176–77, 185–86
Fielding, Henry, *The Mock Doctor* (1732 play), 99
flags of truce, 90, 134–36
foraging, 21, 35, 41, 149, 180–81, 196
fortifications, 21, 24, 31, 34–35, 40–41, 43, 47, 50, 71–72, 84–85, 129, 140, 179, 182
France: alliance with United States, 11, 41–44, 157, 199; French Revolution, 7–8; military activities in North America, 31, 71–73, 89, 114, 167, 171–72, 174; negotiations with Britain for peace, 15, 162, 165–66, 177–180, 184; route for return of exiles, 174. *See also* Treaty of Paris
Franklin, Benjamin, 65–66, 166
Franklin, Elizabeth, 56
Franklin, William, 77–78, 157, 166, 180, 192

Gage, Thomas, 11, 20–23, 59, 107, 144, 197
Gaine, Hugh, 63, 144
Galloway, Grace, 153–55, 167
Galloway, Joseph, 10, 55–57, 65–68, 97–98, 111, 116, 154, 167, 184, 189, 204
gambling, 5, 81, 100–101, 109
Garden, Alexander, 182, 193, 196–200, 202–4
Gentleman's Magazine, 103
George, David, 176–77, 182
George III, King, 43–44, 56, 179; birthday celebrations for, 45; destruction of equestrian statue of in New York City, 33, 38
Georgia: enslaved people in, 83, 87–88, 177; restored British rule in, 43–44, 47, 55, 58, 70–72, 78, 114–15, 117, 120–21, 145, 197, 203; revolutionary state of, 17, 37, 45–48, 177–78, 182
German mercenaries, 4, 29, 39, 41, 51, 93, 99, 102, 106, 108, 120–21, 124, 130, 151, 183, 198–99
Germain, George, Lord, 43–44, 53, 71–72, 78–79, 117, 140, 155, 165, 178, 180, 182
Giles, Aquila, 93–94
Greene, David, 174–75
Greene, Fleet, 90–91, 157
Greene, Nathanael, 181–82, 201

Grenada, 71, 88. *See also* West Indies
Gordon, Thomas Knox, 77–78

Halifax, Nova Scotia, Canada, 19, 29, 34, 43, 45, 165
Hamilton, Alexander, 172–73, 185, 189
Hancock, John, 19, 25, 38
Havana, Cuba, 8
Hayman, James and Thomas, 74–75
Hayne, Isaac, 159, 201–2, 236n88
Hessians. *See* German mercenaries
Hewes, George Robert Twelves, 194
Home, John, *Douglas* (1756 play), 99–100
Howard, Martin, Jr., 25, 28, 77–78
Howe, Richard, 1st Earl, 29, 34, 55, 102–3, 141, 145–46, 166
Howe, William, 21, 34–35, 40–43, 53–54, 56–57, 59, 61, 65–67, 76, 99–100, 102–3, 119–20, 145–46, 166, 203
Hudson River Forts, 40–41, 127
Hutchinson, Foster, 59
Hutchinson, Thomas, 19

import trade, 56, 60–61, 65, 112–17, 124, 158–59. *See also* export trade, smuggling
Inglis, Charles, 144, 155
Innes, Alexander, 69, 204
Integer (pseudonym), 144
Ireland, 66, 117, 130

Jamaica: destination for loyalist refugees, 176, 234n49; trade with North America, 115, 134–135. *See also* West Indies
Jay, John, 166, 172–73, 189
Jones, Daniel, 57, 64

King, Boston, 10, 83–85, 88, 160, 186–87

Lancaster, Pennsylvania, 40
Leake, Sally, 3, 91
Leigh, Egerton, 204
Leslie, Alexander, 101, 125, 180–83
Lexington and Concord, Battles of, 1, 16, 20–21, 23, 25, 45
Lisle, George, 176
Livingston and DeLancey rivalry in colonial New York, 31–32, 77
Livingston, William, 164
Long Island, New York, 11, 33–35, 93–95, 106, 108, 124–26, 131, 134, 136, 145, 159, 196
Lopez, Aaron, 171–72

Louis XVI, King, 8

loyalists: British efforts to support, 16, 43, 51, 72, 166, 184; collaboration with British authorities, 2, 10, 18, 20, 55–59, 65–70, 73–74, 115–16, 163–64; creation of a vocabulary of loyalism, 13, 138–40, 145–51; dissatisfaction with occupation regimes, 77–78, 155–58, 180; enslaved people and ex-slaves, 83–88, 128, 160, 175–77, 181–83, 186–88; erosion of support for British empire, 113, 138–41, 152–53, 158–61, 163–65, 172–175; ideology of, 142–45; loyalist press, 63, 143–44; loyalist women in occupation society, 89, 93–94, 142, 153–55, 170–71; postwar diaspora, 166, 177–78, 189–90; refugees in occupied territories, 21, 26, 35, 43, 53–54, 59–60, 119–20, 125–28, 135, 149–52, 166, 175, 179–80, 184; reintegration into postrevolutionary society, 163–65, 168–70, 172–75, 185–86, 188–89, 194–95, 199–205; revolutionary efforts to suppress, 18, 25–26, 28–29, 32–33, 35, 37–39, 45–46, 48, 50, 132, 167–68, 182–84, 201; scholarship on, 6, 9–10, 160–61; service in British military, 44, 47–48, 51, 77, 85, 96, 108–9, 120, 139, 160–61, 183; treatment by first generation of revolutionary historians, 192, 194, 197, 199–205. See also allegiance; oaths of allegiance; refugees

lumber, 12, 15, 28, 35, 44, 59, 64, 75, 112–13, 115, 123–26, 130, 151–52, 154. See also deforestation; shortages

MacKenzie, Frederick, 106, 109

Malbone, John, 151–52, 160

marines, 21, 34, 51. See also British Army

markets, 115, 118–19, 124–25, 133–34. See also export trade, import trade, smuggling

marriages, 5, 28, 84, 89, 92–94, 97, 100–102, 116, 142–43, 174, 189. See also British Army: relationships with civilian women

Maryland: British-occupied territories in, 11; revolutionary state of, 39, 94, 115, 163–65

Meschianza, 102–5, 170, 226n106

memorials. See petitions

militia: loyalist, 44–45, 47–48, 50, 126, 139–40, 177, 183, 187, 192, 201; revolutionary, 18–21, 23, 26–27, 29, 34, 37–38, 45–47, 50–51, 68, 121, 143, 159, 177, 182, 191, 197, 201

military culture, 3, 5, 80–81, 92, 97–100, 102–3, 106–7, 109–10, 142. See also British Army

military families, 2–3, 5, 20, 62, 81, 108–9, 113, 120, 128–30, 154

Moncrief, James, 47, 101, 182

Montresor, John, 35

Morse, Jedidiah, 193, 196, 204

Narragansett Bay, 25–26, 90, 124, 135

Native Americans, 9, 14, 41, 44, 46, 48, 157, 176–77, 199. See also Cherokee Indians; Creek Indians

neutrality, 2, 4, 9, 23, 26, 37, 51, 141, 174. See also allegiance; disaffected; loyalists

New Jersey: British foraging and plundering in, 35, 41, 119–21, 196, 198; loyalist refugees from, 109, 126, 149–50, 204; refuge for New York loyalists during 1770s, 61, 66; travel and commerce with British-occupied New York, 118, 133–35

Newport, Rhode Island: British conquest, 11, 29–31; British evacuation, 11, 50–51, 83, 110–11, 158–59, 166–67, 170, 173, 177, 190; civil administration under occupation, 44, 57, 66, 70, 72–73, 75, 119–21, 143, 197; life under occupation, 2–4, 87, 89–94, 99–102, 106, 109, 111, 114–16, 122, 124–25, 128–32, 135, 141, 151–53, 156–57; French occupation, 171; prerevolutionary economy and society, 12, 14, 26, 150; postoccupation society, 171–72, 178; revolutionary occupation, 25–29; strategic importance, 11, 31, 41, 43

newspapers, 10, 63, 74, 87–88, 91–92, 98, 101, 114–15, 123, 143–45, 147–49, 184, 187,

New York: British campaigns in, 11, 34–35, 40–43, 103, 145; revolutionary state of, 33, 61, 119–21, 127, 149, 151, 157, 173, 185–86, 201

New York City: British campaigns in and around, 11, 34–35, 106, 120–21, 145, 196, 202; British evacuation, 165, 172–73, 175, 179–80, 184–86, 197; civil administration under occupation, 10, 54–58, 60–68, 73, 75–79, 129–32, 134–36, 141, 145–48, 158; colonial economy and society, 12–14; enslaved and ex-slaves under occupation, 73, 83–86, 132, 182, 184, 186–88; life under occupation, 92–94, 97–100, 102, 106–8, 110–11, 114–19, 122–26, 133–34, 142–44, 159–60; recruitment of loyalists in, 44; refugees in, 96, 126–28,

149–52, 155, 157–58, 163–65, 172–73, 197, 204; prerevolutionary politics, 31–33; postrevolutionary society, 188–89; revolutionary occupation, 32–34; strategic importance, 11, 29, 31, 35, 43, 140, 165, 178

New York Gazette and Weekly Mercury, 63, 123. *See also* Hugh Gaine

North Carolina, 39, 77; British campaigns in, 12, 51, 122, 197; illicit trade with occupied Charleston, 135–36

North, Frederick, 2nd Earl of Guilford, 173, 178

Nova Scotia, Canada, 19, 179, 184; loyalist resettlement in, 84, 160, 175–77, 181–82, 186, 189

oaths of allegiance: to Great Britain, 47, 53, 71, 78–79, 87, 138–39, 147–49, 154–57, 160, 191–92, 195, 200; Quakers' refusal to sign, 4, 39; to revolutionary Pennsylvania, 168

Oliver, Peter, 20, 23, 59

Oswald, Richard, 179

Pagett, George, 74–75

Parker, Hyde, 71, 145

parole, 51, 94, 133–34, 156, 159, 174, 201

Pattison, James, 64–65, 129

Peebles, John, 91, 95, 100–101, 103, 114, 117

Pennsylvania: British-occupied territories outside of Philadelphia, 11; revolutionary state of, 37–40, 56, 65–66, 154, 157, 164, 168–69, 173, 204

Percy, Hugh, 2nd Duke of Northumberland, 10, 101

petitions, 76–77, 96, 126–27, 139, 148–52, 234n42

Philadelphia, Pennsylvania: British campaign against, 11, 40–43, 203; British evacuation, 43, 67, 83, 111, 158–59, 166, 190; civil administration under occupation, 56–57, 65–67, 72, 75–76, 97–98, 120, 154, 167; colonial economy and society, 12–14, 77; enslaved and ex-slaves under occupation, 83, 88; life under occupation, 56, 92, 94–99, 101–05, 107–8, 114–17, 119, 122, 191, 198; postoccupation society, 153–55, 166–70, 173–74, 177–78, 189, 204–5; recruitment of loyalists in, 44; revolutionary occupation, 37–39, 53

Plater, George, 164

plundering, 46, 113, 115, 120–21, 127, 136, 192, 195–99, 202–3

police, 60; in Charleston, 54, 56, 67–69, 72–78, 85, 88, 97–98, 101, 140–41, 144, 159, 180, 191, 204; in Newport, 70, 111; in New York, 56, 60–67, 76–77, 118, 159; in Philadelphia, 56, 65–67, 97–98, 154, 167; in Savannah, 70. *See also* civil government

poor relief, 55, 58, 61–63, 68, 75, 122, 127, 188, 195

Powell, Robert, 69

Prescott, Richard, 31, 101, 121, 197

Prevost, Augustine, 47, 71, 197

prices, 15, 114, 146; for food, 63, 72, 119, 122–23, 125–28, 130, 133; for fuel, 123–25; inflation of, 118, 122–23, 127–28, 132. *See also* currency; shortages

prison ships, 3–4, 90, 157, 178, 200

prisoners of war, 3–4, 9, 24, 51, 90–91, 93–94, 96, 119, 125, 128, 133–34, 136, 143, 149, 157, 167–68, 174–75, 178, 197–98. *See also* parole; police; prison ships; provost jails

privateering, 11, 84–85, 97, 115–16, 124, 134, 175

proclamations, 59, 63, 71, 138, 144–49, 168, 182

profiteering, 133

prostitution, 3, 91, 106

Providence, Rhode Island, 26, 135

provisioning, 26–27, 33, 35, 44, 67, 113–16, 118–22, 125–28, 130–31, 146, 181. *See also* prices; shortages

provincial congresses, 16–17, 45, 61

provost jails, 91, 192, 200

public works, 31, 58, 60–61, 74–75, 79

Quakers: community in occupied Newport, 2, 4, 26; exile from revolutionary Philadelphia, 39–40; women navigating occupation, 92–93, 95–96, 154

quartering of troops, 20, 31, 35, 40, 53, 62, 76, 91, 95–96, 109, 123, 128–30, 138, 153–54

Quebec, Canada, 40, 154

Ramsay, David, 191–93, 196–201, 203–5

rape, 5, 81, 94–96, 110, 196. *See also* British army: violence against civilians

Rawle, William, 93, 173–74, 184, 191

refugees, 11: attempts to return to the revolutionary United States, 162–65, 176, 183–84; enslaved and ex-slaves, 74, 86–88, 128, 175–76, 181–82, 184; destitution of, 77, 96, 112–

refugees (*continued*)
13, 119–20, 125–28, 130, 148–52;
disillusionment with British rule, 158–59;
influx into New York City, 35, 61–64, 111–
13, 126–27, 158–59, 165; military service of,
43, 45, 77, 120, 192; postwar diaspora, 167,
175–78, 184, 188; suspicion of by elite loyalists, 139, 155; treatment by British authorities, 125–28, 148–52, 178–80; treatment by
first generation of revolutionary historians, 192, 197. *See also* exile; loyalists; militia
Riedesel, Fredericke, Baroness, 102, 124–26
Rivington, James, 63, 123, 143, 188, 241n100
Rhode Island, revolutionary state of, 25–27,
29, 73, 87, 90, 132, 135, 156, 170–73, 197
Robertson, James, 133, 180
Rochambeau, Jean-Baptiste Donatien de
Vimeur, comte de, 171
Rockingham, Charles Watson-Wentworth,
2nd Marquess, 165
Rowe, Nicholas, *Jane Shore* (1714 play), 99
Royal Gazette (New York newspaper), 63, 123.
See also James Rivington
Royal Gazette (South Carolina newspaper),
143
Royal Navy, 3, 11, 19, 26–28, 33, 45, 51, 60, 64,
67, 76, 107–8, 110, 112, 150, 156, 165, 187
Rush, Benjamin, 2
Russian Revolution, 7
Rutledge, John, 182–83

Saint Augustine, East Florida, 143, 156
Saint Christopher, 134. *See also* West Indies
Saint Eustatius, 134, 174. *See also* West Indies
Saint Lucia, 182. *See also* West Indies
Saratoga, Battle of, 41, 44, 51, 103, 143
Savannah, Georgia: British conquest, 11,
46–47; British evacuation, 140–41, 165,
175–78, 182–84; colonial economy and
society, 12–14, 211n23; Franco-American
siege, 47–48, 71–72; enslaved and ex-slaves
under occupation, 47, 73–74, 83, 87–88,
128, 176–77; life under occupation, 91, 99,
114–15, 120–22, 126, 129; restored civil government under occupation, 47–48, 57–58,
70, 72, 75–76, 146, 198; revolutionary occupation, 17, 35, 44–46, 53
Schieffelin, Hannah Lawrence, 92–93, 142,
188–89
Schieffelin, Jacob, 92–93, 142

Serle, Ambrose, 55–57, 101, 141, 144
Sierra Leone, 160, 177, 189
Simpson, James, 10, 54–57, 67–69, 73, 78, 97–
98, 101, 115, 128, 140, 144, 156, 204, 233n25
Shakespeare, William, *Henry IV Part I* and
Othello, 99
Shy, John, 9
Shelburne, William Petty, 2nd Earl, 165, 178–
80, 184
Shipton, Elizabeth, 93–94
Shoemaker, Rebecca, 184
Shoemaker, Samuel, 189, 191
shortages, 44, 58, 135, 163: of food and fuel, 6,
59, 113, 118, 122–26, 138; of housing, 113, 123,
128–30. *See also* currency; lumber; prices;
provisioning; quartering of soldiers
slavery: British policies on, 58, 69, 73–75, 85–
86, 128; perceived threats to institution of,
82–83, 183, 193, 198–99. *See also* Africans
and African Americans
smallpox. *See* disease
Smith, William, Jr., 10, 32, 155, 157–58, 160,
179–80, 185, 188–89
smuggling, 6, 26, 67, 88, 131–137, 146, 158, 176,
182
social clubs, 100–101
soldiers' wives. *See* military families
Sons of Liberty, 19–20, 26, 32
South Carolina: British campaigns outside of
Charleston, 12, 43, 47, 51, 67–68, 70, 84, 120,
145, 147, 159, 197; revolutionary state of, 37,
48, 50, 68, 143–44, 180–83, 191, 201
Southern Strategy, 11, 43–45, 48
Spain, 8, 44, 115, 176–77, 184
Staten Island, New York, 11, 34–35, 39, 108,
136, 145–46,
Stiles, Ezra, 89, 94, 128–29, 141, 152, 167, 172
Strachey, Henry, 178–79

Tauncey, Elizabeth, 92, 94
Tarleton, Banastre, 197
Tillinghast, William, 2–4
Timothy, Ann, 74
theater, 5, 80, 82, 98–102
Theatre Royal (New York City), 98–100
Tonyn, Patrick, 45
tories. *See* loyalists
Touro, Isaac, 150, 234n49
Treaty of Paris, 15, 162, 165–66, 177–80, 184,
190

Trinity Church (New York City), 35, 92, 155
Tryon, William, 32, 55, 57, 79, 102, 121, 144, 147–48, 158, 192, 198

Valley Forge, 40–41, 154
vengeance, 9, 18, 158, 196, 201, 203
Virginia: British campaigns in, 12, 44, 122, 222n12; Quaker exiles in, 39, 154; revolutionary state of, 115, 187

Wallace, James, 26–28
Walton, Cornelia, 185–86
Walton, William, 185, 189
Wanton, Joseph, Jr., 70, 111, 172, 219n54
Wanton, Sarah, 101–2
Wanton, William, 26
Wanton, William, Jr., 29
Warren, Mercy Otis, 193, 196–99, 201, 203–4
Washington, Harry, 187

Washington, George, 32–34, 38, 40–41, 133, 154
Washington, Martha, 37, 154, 164–65, 170–71, 187–88
West Indies, 12, 14, 19, 26, 43–44, 47, 66–67, 71, 74, 88, 112, 114–16, 134, 158, 169, 173–75, 182
Wilkes, John, 48
William Henry, Prince (future King William IV), 102
Wilson, Samuel, 193, 196, 203–4
World War II-era military occupations, 8
Wright, Alexander, 69, 121
Wright, James, 1st Baronet, 10, 44–45, 47, 58, 71–72, 75–76, 78, 126, 175, 189

York, Pennsylvania, 40–41
Yorktown, Battle of, 15, 82, 122, 140, 159, 161, 163–67, 171–75, 177, 180, 222n12
Young, Alfred, 194

ACKNOWLEDGMENTS

This book is the product of nearly ten years of research, writing, and editing and owes intellectual, emotional, and financial debts to countless people and organizations. The first of those is Timothy Breen. Tim helped conceive this project, read and critiqued countless drafts, provided insights and reading recommendations, and was an unfailingly supportive advocate for the work from beginning to end. His invaluable advice, criticism, and mentorship improved the book throughout every stage of the process. By example and instruction, he taught me what it is to be a historian, a writer, and a scholar, for which I will be forever in his debt. (Apologies, Tim, for all the excess modifiers in this paragraph and this section as a whole).

I wrote the bulk of this text in three places: at Northwestern University, at the McNeil Center for Early American Studies at the University of Pennsylvania during a yearlong fellowship, and at North Dakota State University. At Northwestern, Scott Sowerby and Caitlin Fitz helped to conceptualize this study at its early stages, read and commented thoughtfully on each chapter, and provided steadfast support throughout the research and writing process, for all of which they deserve thanks. Melissa Macauley and Mike Sherry also deserve credit for helping to sharpen the arguments in at least two chapters, and they both have my gratitude. Sara Maza, Dylan Penningroth, and Alexandra Owen all shaped my historical thought process through their seminars, even if they did not directly influence the work. My fellow travelers at Northwestern and in the greater Chicago community provided both insight at various stages of the project and invaluable emotional support over my six years there. Andrew Baer, Kevin Baker, Ashley Bavery, Jonathyne Briggs, Kyle Burke, Charlotte Cahill, Myisha Eatmon, Emma Goldsmith, Beth Healy, Mariah Hepworth, Alistair Hobson, Jamie Holeman, Jason Johnson, Matthew June, Matthew Kahn, Charles Keenan, Amanda Kleintop, Celeste MacNamara, Rebecca Marchial, Julia Miglets, Wen-Qing Ngoei, Brian O'Camb, Sally Olson, Keith Rathbone, Lucy

Reeder, Megahn and Strother Roberts, Aram Sarkasian, Aleksandra Sherman, Emelie Takayama-Michel, Rachel Taylor, Peter Thilly, and Marlous Van Waijenburg all deserve thanks for intellectual contributions and for providing a supportive and lively atmosphere. This book may have been written without the pub trivia competitions, pickup football games, karaoke sessions, and board-game nights that marked my life in the Windy City, but it would have been much less fun. During my time in Chicago, I was fortunate enough to have as roommates the incomparable Alexandra Lindgren-Gibson and Leigh Soares, first-rate scholars and supportive friends who have my thanks. Sara Jackto and Robert Winkeler helped me escape my work when I needed to and supported me through life's trials and tribulations. Ian Saxine went above and beyond by reading drafts, sharing research strategies, and generally providing good humor and support throughout my time in Chicago and afterward.

The McNeil Center for Early American Studies is an intellectual incubator like none other, for which I will be eternally grateful. Its director, Dan Richter, deserves sincere thanks for the role he plays in both assembling the Center's community and supporting those working in it. Dan was also kind enough to read the entire manuscript at multiple stages and to make insightful comments and ask probing questions throughout. The fellows and speakers who came through Philadelphia during my time there inspired me as I wrote the text. Comments from my brown-bag session at the Center helped spur my revisions, and attendees of a full McNeil Center Seminar read and commented on a version of Chapter 5, which made it exponentially stronger. The entire McNeil community has my sincere thanks, but special mention goes to Noelani Arista, Michael Blaakman, Wayne Bodle, Sara Damiano, Andrew Fagal, Paul Gilje, Claire Gherini, C. Dallett Hemphill, Brenna Holland, Philippa Koch, Peter Kotowski, Cathy Matson, Roderick McDonald, Emily Merrill, Mairin Odle, Sarah Rodriguez, Sean Trainor, and Michael Zuckerman for their contributions to this project and their hospitality during my time in Philadelphia.

My colleagues at North Dakota State University are the kind that everyone wishes for. Deans Kent Sandstrom and David Bertolini gave me access to financial support to do additional research for this project, as did Vice Presidents for Research and Creative Activities Kelly Rusch and Jane Shuh. In the Department of History, Philosophy, and Religious Studies, departmental chairs John Cox and Mark Harvey supported me from the time of my appointment to the present with both time and resources to finish this book. For transforming Fargo from a job posting to a true home, I owe my colleagues and friends in the NDSU community a debt I will never be able to repay. To Anastassiya Andrianova, Lisa Arnold, Ashley Baggett, Tracy Barrett, Tommy Bell, Bradley and Neely Benton, Sarah Boonstoppel, Sean Burt, Dennis Cooley, Katy Cox, John Creese, Pam Emmanuelson, Eric Espinoza, Kristen Fellows, Tony Flood, Jake Friedman, Alison Graham-Bertolini, Alex Hsu, Tom Isern, Meghan Kirkwood, Julia Kowalski, Kjersten Nelson, Marcela Perrett, Linda Quigley, Angela Smith, Amy and Mark Taggart, Verena Thiele, Chrys Vogiatzis, Christina Weber-Knopp, Chris Whitsel, and Heath Wing, thank you. Anne Blankenship, who started the same year I did, deserves special mention here both for her stalwart support of my work and for modeling how to balance writing, teaching, and life outside of academe with grace and aplomb.

In addition to the support from my professional and intellectual homes, I received insightful criticism and comments on this project from a number of scholars I encountered at libraries, conferences, and other venues throughout the research and writing process, all of whom deserve thanks for their generosity. Daniel Richter and Johann Neem read the entire manuscript as judges for the Society for Historians of the Early American Republic's manuscript prize. Winning that prize opened up new opportunities, not the least of which was introducing me to my editor at the University of Pennsylvania Press, the indefatigable Robert Lockhart. Bob, Dan, and Johann provided excellent feedback and helped me begin the process of turning that raw text into a publishable book manuscript. As editors of the Press's Early American Studies series, Bob and Dan have read multiple drafts of this manuscript, and their suggestions and criticisms have improved it greatly. In the final stages of writing, Bob and the editorial team at the University of Pennsylvania Press have provided excellent support in the revision and publication process for this book.

Patrick Griffin read almost the entire manuscript at one point or another and has consistently given valuable criticism. Benjamin Carp helped me to think through the project at a very early stage, read early versions several chapters, and has been a constant supporter of the work. T. Cole Jones read chapters and provided advice as both a military historian and a first-rate analytical thinker. Ruma Chopra intervened as I began to write, with helpful criticism and advice on the chapter structure and research process. The participants of the 2016 Omohundro Institute Scholars' Workshop—Megan Cherry, Neal Dugre, Mairin Odle, Melissa

Pawlitowski, and Bryan Rindfleish—gave invaluable comments and critiques at that forum, as did the Institute's editorial and academic staff. Of the latter, I am particularly grateful to Karin Wulf, Brett Rushforth, and Joshua Piker for pushing me to consider fresh angles and new questions. Fred Anderson, Lauren Duval, Elija Gould, Eric Hinderaker, Howard Pashman, Jim Piecuch, and Robert Venables all read various parts of the work and gave excellent feedback, from which this book has benefited greatly.

The attendees of various meetings of the Omohundro Institute of Early American History and Culture, the Organization of American Historians, the Society for Historians of the Early American Republic, and many other conference venues have provided valuable criticism of aspects of this work over the last seven years. I take this opportunity to thank all who have read, listened to, and commented on my work over this period. Articles based on this research have appeared in the *Journal of Imperial and Commonwealth History*, the *Journal of American History*, and the edited volume *Experiencing Empire* (University of Virginia Press, 2017). I owe a great deal to the editors and anonymous readers of each of these publications. The aspects of these works that are reproduced here are used with permission.

I received financial support from a number of libraries and archives during the research phase of this project, without which the book would not have been possible. I received fellowships from, and experienced unfailing hospitality at, the William L. Clements Library (twice), the David Library of the American Revolution, the John Carter Brown Library, the Society of the Cincinnati, the Newport Historical Society, the Huntington Library, and the Fred W. Smith National Library for the Study of George Washington at Mount Vernon. All of these institutions have my sincere thanks. The David Library and its staff, especially Meg McSweeney, deserve special mention for sheltering me during Hurricane Sandy. It is a special place and will be missed when its collection moves to Philadelphia. Brian Dunnigan of the Clements Library deserves thanks for devoting two full days to guiding me through the Clements's expansive collection of Revolutionary War maps, as does Bert Lippincott of the Newport Historical Society for sharing with me a small part of his encyclopedic knowledge of early Rhode Island. In addition to financial support from the above-mentioned archives and libraries, this book owes a debt of gratitude to librarians and archivists at the Library of Congress, the Massachusetts Historical Society, the New York State Library, the New York Public Library, the New-York Historical Society, the Historical Society of Pennsylvania, the South Caroliniana Library, the South Carolina Historical

Society, the South Carolina Department of Archives and History, and the Georgia Historical Society. The staffs of these institutions were unfailingly helpful and courteous, and this work would have been far poorer without them.

My family provided unwavering love and support throughout the writing process. My mother, Susan Buckingham, has for a long time been my biggest cheerleader, reading countless drafts and supporting me in myriad ways—both emotional and financial—over years of research and writing. For her decades of love and devotion, I owe her more than I can say here. My father and stepmother, Syd Johnson and Gale Auguste, also loved and supported me through the long years of research and writing. While neither lived to see the final product, I hope that, wherever they are, they are able to read and enjoy it, and that they take pride in their part in it.

Final thanks must go to my dear wife, Sara, who came onto the scene late in the project but without whom I could not have finished this book. My life has never been the same since I met her in October 2017, and I cannot imagine how I would have gotten through the final stages of this work without her confidence, love, and support. To Sara, I love you beyond what I ever thought possible, and my love grows more and more every day.

All mistakes herein are my own, and all credit belongs to others.